New Towns:
Why—And for Whom?

edited by
Harvey S. Perloff
Neil C. Sandberg

New Towns:
Why—And for Whom?

PRAEGER SPECIAL STUDIES IN U.S. ECONOMIC, SOCIAL, AND POLITICAL ISSUES

Praeger Publishers   New York   Washington   London

Library of Congress Cataloging in Publication Data

New Towns Symposium, Los Angeles, 1972.
    New towns: why—and for whom?

    (Praeger special studies in U.S. economic,
social, and political issues)
    Sponsored by the American Jewish Committee
and the UCLA School of Architecture and Urban
Planning.
    Bibliography: p.
    1. Cities and towns—Planning—United
States—Congresses. I. Perloff, Harvey S., ed.
II. Sandberg, Neil C., ed. III. American
Jewish Committee. IV. California. University.
University at Los Angeles. School of Architecture
and Urban Planning. V. Title.
HT167.N45   1972   309.2'62   73-1094

PRAEGER PUBLISHERS
111 Fourth Avenue, New York, N.Y. 10003, U.S.A.
5, Cromwell Place, London S.W.7, England

Published in the United States of America in 1973
by Praeger Publishers, Inc.

In recent years the federal government has declared—through housing acts in 1968 and 1970 (the former under a Democratic administration, the latter under a Republican one)—that it is part of national policy to encourage the development of new communities, through subsidies if necessary. This legislation clearly reflects dissatisfaction with present-day large-city living, and the hope that better forms of urban life could be developed along new-town lines.

If national resources are to be directed at the construction of new towns, then such issues as the purposes and form of such development, who is to gain and who is to pay, and what patterns of living are to be encouraged in these new towns should certainly be matters of major national concern. The present volume adresses itself to these issues. It brings together studies by long-time students of new-town development, as well as social commentators, in the hope of throwing light on the dangers and possibilities of the future as the nation embarks on the development of new communities.

In order to promote a dialogue on the central issues, the School of Architecture and Urban Planning at the University of California at Los Angeles, with the support of the American Jewish Committee (which has been particularly interested in the human aspects of new town development and has sponsored a series of related conferences), invited a number of knowledgeable individuals to prepare papers and to expose their ideas at a conference held at the university during June 1972, with participants from a variety of countries, disciplines, and practical backgrounds. The commentaries on the papers were often pointed and critical, but helpful, and on the basis of these (as well as suggestions from the editors), most of the papers were substantially revised. The present volume is the product of these revisions, with a number of the commentaries included. It encompasses three major themes: (1) what we can learn from the experience of other countries, (2) what human considerations should come into play in the development of new towns in the United States, particularly with regard to life styles, social mixing, and governance, and (3) what possible forms new communities may take.

Strong disagreements emerge on almost every major issue, yet some significant overriding concepts are introduced that deserve serious consideration in molding our national approach to new-town development in the future. The key point is that the new-towns concept has evolved substantially from its original formulation by

Ebenezer Howard at the end of the nineteenth century, through the experience with new-town development over half a century, and through the introduction of new ideas about alternative forms of urban development. The first three studies—those by Robinson, Shachar, and Lichfield—focus directly on what is to be learned through the rather substantial experience of several countries; much of the third section and all of the fourth section (which consists of the commentaries by Thompson, and Alonso Wheaton) concern themselves with alternative forms of urban development as related to the new-towns concept.

What emerges is a rather dramatic refitting of a basically simple original concept (geared to the situation and thinking at the end of the nineteenth century) to meet the evolving needs of a large and complex late-twentieth-century United States.

In a period of new-found environmental awareness, it is easy to understand the appeal of Ebenezer Howard's ecologically oriented "garden city," introduced in a book published in 1898 with a wonderful nineteenth-century title, Tomorrow: A Peaceful Path to Reform (later revised as Garden Cities of Tomorrow). To urbanites subjected to the noise, crowding, grime, irritations, and dangers of a giant city, the image of a carefully planned, small "balanced" urban community in a garden setting, where it is possible to be close to nature as well as to work and friends, has from the very beginning been a very attractive one.

The United States early experimented with the Garden City idea, first through privately constructed Radburn, New Jersey in the 1920s, then through three small new communities (the best known of which is Greenbelt, Maryland) built by the New Deal government in the 1930s to help promote the new-town idea.*

It was not until after the trauma and terror of World War II, and in, not surprisingly, Great Britain, the home of Ebenezer Howard, that the new-towns concept became a central feature of a national urban development policy. In the first instance the aim was to "decant" population from London; other objectives—such as providing stimulus to depressed areas—were later added. Urban development was to proceed, at least in part, according to a conscious national strategy aimed at achieving a more satisfying urban life. This was a novel and important turning point in urban history.

Actually, the Soviet Union had developed a large national new-town building program even earlier than Britain, but it was so much a part of the national plan for economic development and resources

---

*Norris, Tennessee, a planned community in the Tennessee Valley Authority area, can be considered a fourth New Deal new town.

exploitation that the significant city-building aspects tended to be overlooked. Thus it was the British example that was to have the major impact elsewhere, particularly in (1) Scandinavia, where the Garden City idea was as congenial to the national culture as it was in Great Britain, and was seen as an outlet for the love of nature and pleasant living; (2) Israel, where a flood of immigrants had to be settled, and security and developmental needs had to be met; (3) Canada, which saw new towns as an attractive form for handling the development of its natural resources frontier.

In recent decades literally hundreds of new towns have been built, nearly all of them importantly influenced in one way or another by the Garden City ideas. In the process, however, many changes in the original ideas have been made to accommodate the various objectives and national styles that characterize the different national programs and, equally important, to overcome some of the serious difficulties with the original new-town concept that increasingly emerged over time. It is interesting to note the full scope of the substantial evolution that has taken place. Let us look at just the bare outlines of this evolution.

The Concept: The New Town as envisaged by
Ebenezer Howard and his Disciples

Central Purpose:
> To avoid the further congestion of large urban centers and to provide opportunities for life close to nature and to all town activities.

Characteristics:
- Built according to a predetermined plan of development.
- Small in size, so that people can know each other and reach work and services easily.
- Independent—free from any constraints of existing populations, and particularly of the central city.
- Self-contained and self-sufficient: a minimum of in-and-out commuting, and adequate jobs for all resident workers.
- Balanced: not only in regard to economic diversity (as above) but with population heterogeneity—with respect to age, occupation, income and class, and ethnicity.
- A plan and design to accomodate all these features, with closeness to nature (a garden setting) and pleasant living and working conditions.

The Outcome: Evolution of the New-Town Concept over
Three-Quarters of a Century:

1898 ff.	Howard's initial proposal, with disciples spreading the gospel	
1920s-1930s	Radburn and "greenbelt" towns in United States	Attempt to build-in all the Garden City features (but weak on "social balance," with families at both ends of the income scale missing).
Postwar Period 1940s-1950s	British Mark I towns; Israeli major new-towns program; government-supported Scandinavian and Canadian new-towns programs initiated	Most Garden City features present, except social balance. However, purposes greatly broadened to include exploitation of resources frontier, assistance to depressed regions, and organization of metropolitan growth on a planned basis.
	Privately built new towns in United States	Essentially typical suburbs, a short distance from built-up section of the metropolis.
1960s-present	British Mark II and III towns; Scandinavian Israeli, and Canadian new-town programs expanded	Towns much larger (up to 250,000 population); encouragement of migration among towns on a regional basis; many built as extensions of existing villages and towns.
	A few new towns built in underdeveloped world	Large cities to serve as capitals and to open up undeveloped sections of the country.

United States subsidized new-towns program Proposals for new cities with populations as high as 1 million	Objectives: to encourage new style of community building—planned and largely self-sufficient, preserving the natural environment, offering housing opportunities for poor and minorities; also to help revitalize the inner city.

What we see is the power of the central idea of new towns, which extends over three-quarters of a century and still retains its appeal. It is joined, at the same time, with a far-reaching departure from specifics that have been found either to not fit national needs and objectives or to be internally inconsistent. (These shortcomings and their impacts are spelled out in detail in the first three chapters of this book.) We also find that two of the central objectives of new towns (as conceived by their proponents) have never been realized. These are the notions that new towns should provide an environment for technical and social innovation to enhance the quality of urban life, and should make possible "social balance"—a heterogenous population (in terms of age, social class, and race) comparable to that of the nation as a whole. These failures are particularly troublesome when viewed from the present-day U.S. standpoint. For if we look at new towns in the context of present-day America—affluent and powerful, but socially troubled, and with a man-made and natural environment under great pressure—these are the very features that, if achievable, would make new towns worthy of high-priority support. If the Europeans and Israelis, with much more willingness to use the power of government for national urban purposes, have had so little success with these two features, can the United States hope to achieve them? Most of the studies in the third and fourth parts of this volume address themselves to this critical issue. The message that comes across, at least as I read it, is twofold:

1. In the United States today, new towns deserve public support only if they can genuinely meet the needs for innovation with regard to patterns of living and life style, class and racial integration, relation to the natural environment, and modes of governance. A so-called new town that is simply a typical white middle-class suburb but just a few miles further out hardly deserves governmental support.

2. The probabilities of achieving new-town development with social purpose will be greater if we stand ready to stretch the new-towns concept beyond where it has already been stretched, so that it includes (1) inner-city development (new-towns-intown), (2) the planned expansion of existing cities both to decentralize population and to help declining areas (new-on-old towns), (3) the creation of a true Experimental City, and (4) the guidance of development through general policies and general standards rather than through predetermined master plans (the Alonso version).

These ideas are at a high level of abstraction. None of them have been tested for feasibility; nor do any of them touch on operational issues, such as financing. They are, at this stage, simply ideas that deserve further discussion and feasibility-testing. But new ideas are particularly important now. The carrying-out of the old ideas and the old patterns will surely not meet our greatest urban needs. It may be as Rabinovitz and Smookler suggest, that we are incapable today of carrying out such complex and far-reaching goals. The government may simply not be up to it, particularly given the present-day bureaucratic tendencies and the limited social perceptions of so many people (highlighted in Gans' study and in Kaplan's survey in Texas) and what they demand of government today.

Most of the authors, however, think that at least we ought to try to achieve something better than in the past. Each has his or her own ideas of how this could be done. It seems to me that such ideas deserve attention. As Margaret Mead says, "If new towns would give us an opportunity to develop social forms and architectural styles which would make life more human again, then they could make a great contribution."

A NOTE FROM
THE AMERICAN JEWISH COMMITTEE

The American Jewish Committee was pleased to sponsor the Conference on Human Factors in New Town Development. As a human relations organization, the AJC throughout its 66 years of experience has sought to create opportunities for dialogue on the critical social problems of the day.

In drawing on the most advanced research at universities as well as the experience of leading practitioners, the AJC is looking for new ways in which diverse groups can live together harmoniously in society. The AJC believes that, through providing possibilities for integrative socioeconomic and interracial experiences, new towns can provide not only urgently needed additional housing but also another important alternative in the effort to deal with the crucial problems of urbanization.

It is hoped that this volume represents a useful contribution to a public discussion on this subject among all segments of the population, including developers, builders, planners, investors, social scientists, legislators, and the general community.

CONTENTS

LIST OF TABLES AND FIGURES

PART

I

**LESSONS
FROM THE EXPERIENCE
OF OTHER COUNTRIES**

SMALL, INDEPENDENT, SELF-CONTAINED AND BALANCED NEW TOWNS: MYTH OR REALITY?

Ira M. Robinson

Certain related concepts have always been associated with the idea of new towns since its inception. It has always been assumed that they should be relatively small in size, and self-contained with respect to living and working arrangements. Also, new towns should be newly created on undeveloped land, be independent of any major metropolitan center, and provide all the requirements of day-to-day living. Finally new towns (so the concept goes) are to be balanced communities, not only in terms of employment and population and the provision of industrial, commercial, recreational, and residential areas, but also with regard to age, income, and class composition. These concepts appear so often in connection with the term "new town" that they have been almost inseparable. According to one typical definition, for example, the expression "new town" means "a town deliberately planned and built, and a 'self-contained' town: a town which provides in addition to houses, employment, shopping, education, recreation, culture— everything which marks the independent satisfying town."[1]

These concepts have been used in connection with proposals for new towns in the United States—even when the proposals are for new towns on the edge of existing cities or in the central city (new-towns-intown).[2]

My purpose in this study is to examine each of these concepts in light of the actual experience of new towns in several different parts of the world, primarily Great Britain, Israel, Canada, and Scandinavia. For each of these concepts, I shall explain the origin, philosophy, and purpose behind it—as seen by the originators. Much of this discussion deals with the ideas of Ebenezer Howard, considered the father of the new-towns idea (he called them "garden cities").[3] Howard and his disciples (notably Raymond Unwin, Thomas Adams, C. B. Purdom, and F. J. Osborn) were responsible for developing the principles underlying the British new-towns program, principles that profoundly affected the planning and building of new towns every-where. These principles were, in the main, formally adopted by the British New Towns (Reith) Committee, which was set up in 1945 to develop the guidelines and procedures for the postwar new-towns program.[4]

I shall also examine the extent to which actual events have corresponded with the original concept in the new towns studied, including a description of the changes and adaptations, if any, that have occurred in applying the concept. My concern here, as implied in my title, is with discovering whether and to what extent each of the concepts is a myth or reality. (I should state here and now that I found most of them, in one degree or another, myths!) Finally I shall draw some lessons from this analysis that may have applicability to any new-towns program in the United States. I am not concerned here with the pros and cons of a U.S. new-towns program; rather I am taking the need for such a program as given, and am saying essentially that here are some insights from the experiences of other countries that may be relevant and applicable to such towns when and if they are built. The new towns I have studied were built to serve a variety of purposes, and I am assuming that a similarly varied group of new towns will be part of the U.S. program. In particular I assume that the decentralization of our congested metropolitan areas will be the principal spur for the development of new towns here in the United States, and that, in line with the recommendations of an increasing number of persons, such new towns will be linked with the problems of race and poverty in our central cities. Thus the experiences of those new towns built elsewhere to help decongest large urban centers will be especially relevant here.

PURPOSES AND TYPES OF NEW TOWNS

New towns have been built, are being built, and are proposed to be built all over the world. They are intended to serve various functions, which may be summarized in the following five categories:

1. To serve as capital cities,
2. to fulfill strategic or military needs,
3. to exploit natural resources or to develop the potentialities of the land,
4. to relieve congestion in existing large urban centers and/or to organize more rationally existing and future metropolitan growth,
5. to cope with population growth, movements of population, or special features of a population, and
6. to be part of a national planning and development policy.

4

The new towns investigated in this study fit several but not all of these categories. Many of the Israeli towns—those built to provide for the settlement of Jewish populations in areas facing security problems, particularly along the borders with Lebanon, Jordan, and Syria—fall into Category 2. All of the Canadian new towns studied were created in order to exploit some natural resource (Category 3). The original eight London new towns, as well as several of the recently developed British new towns (Warrington, Peterborough, Northampton, and Milton Keynes), plus the Scandinavian new towns (Vallingby, Farsta, Skarholmen and Tapiola), all fall into Category 4.* Several of the British new towns (Aycliffe, Washington, Peterlee, Corby, Telford, Glenrothres, and Cwmbran) and most of the Israeli new towns were built to cope with some special population problem; e.g., either to deal with a declining population or economic activity, or to attract new immigrants to an undeveloped region (Category 5).

As may be expected, a number of the new towns were developed in order to serve dual purposes; e.g., Skelmersdale and Runcorn were built not only to ease the congestion in Liverpool but also to create new economic centers in that part of Britain. Finally it should be noted that all of Israel's new towns, regardless of their specific purposes, were built as part of a national planning and development policy.

POPULATION SIZE

Most of the new towns built in the countries surveyed were planned to be comparatively small to medium in size. Except for two recently designated "town expansions," none of the British new towns have over 90,000 persons, nearly half of Israel's new towns are under 40,000 in population, and the Canadian new towns are even smaller. This planning principle stems from the proposals of Ebenezer Howard and other nineteenth-century Utopian philosophers, who argued for the advantages of a small town as an antidote to overcrowding and other adverse conditions that were then prevalent in the large industrial and commercial cities of Britain. They objected to the growth of the big city at the expense of the countryside, the crowding and the noisy slums, the increasingly long journey to work, and the rootlessness and social problems of the migrants from rural areas.

---

*Scandinavian planners often refer to their metropolitan-area new towns as city or town "sectors."

Howard's original formulation called for a limitation on both the numbers and the areas of a garden city. He recommended 32,000 inhabitants in the initial garden city and its rural surrounding belt, and 58,000 in a later town to be central to an associated group of towns. Moreover these population figures represented maximum levels of growth. Once having reached its ultimate population, the garden city should grow no more, and further growth should take place in additional garden cities.

Nearly 50 years later the Reith Committee suggested an "optimum normal population range" from 30,000 to 50,000, with related districts in the builtup area of the new town totaling from 60,000 to 80,000.[5] As can be seen in Table 1.1, most of the original (Mark I) British new towns were indeed planned for a population target within this range.

Typically the new towns under review suffered at one time, or currently suffer, from the well-known economic disadvantages associated with communities of small size. These disadvantages include, among others:

1. A tendency not to be industrially diversified, to be dominated by one or two major industries and thus to experience economic instability. For example:

   the Canadian new towns are typically based on a single resource-based industry, and tend to have a boom-or-bust character;[6]

   • manufacturing industry in Israeli new towns is dominated by the textile industry, which accounts for 34.2 percent of all employees; unfortunately textiles show the least rise in productivity and the least prospects for future growth.[7]

2. A reluctance on the part of some firms to establish themselves in small or medium-sized communities that have not yet gained any status or prestige, where manpower is limited, where there is a lack of ancillary services, and where they feel cut off from the world of information, ideas, and business.[8]

3. A high risk of instability, and limited adaptability. A declining firm can be a local disaster, and new firms are less likely to develop because of the sparseness of linkages. Moreover a dismissed worker has fewer changes for reemployment, and young people have fewer career opportunities. For example:

   • one of the serious problems afflicting Israeli new towns is that there are few opportunities for advancement, a major reason for the high population turnover and the large out-migration, especially of young persons.[9]

4. Small communities tend to have a larger-than-average-sized industrial plant, thus becoming one-company towns with absentee ownership and all the attendant problems associated with them. For example:

● Canadian new towns are the purest examples of this phenomenon, as one of their distinguishing characteristics is that they are "company towns," some in name, and most of them in spirit;
● the same situation exists in the Israeli new towns, where, in 1964, 8.7 percent of the businesses had 100 or more employees, as against 2.7 percent for the nation as a whole. This phenomenon is due partly to efforts on the part of the state (which provides public loans to new industries) to assist primarily big enterprises, which soon make a noticeable difference in the labor market. Moreover big industries owned by state or public companies or by powerful overseas investors, having greater technical, organizational, and financial resources behind them, find it much easier to hold their own in the development regions and new towns.

5. Small communities cannot provide industrial agglomeration economies for self-sustaining growth.

6. Small communities cannot provide a wide variety of public services or facilities. If they do, though, the costs are extremely high. For example:

the British new towns during their early stages suffered from a shortage of essential services, facilities, and amenities, due to financial restrictions;[10]
● the Israeli new towns are characterized by a lack of essential urban facilities and services, especially cultural institutions—a major cause of their inability to attract and/or hold workers of high socioeconomic status;
● the Canadian resource-based new towns face just the opposite situation—they are characterized by an abundant supply of modern shopping centers, churches, schools, libraries, etc. of of a size and in number far beyond those found in ordinary communities of the same population size. The "problem" is that these are all provided by "the company," with the result that it tends to produce an attitude of "let-the-company-do-it" and the absence of the usual duties, responsibilities, and freedom of citizenship present in normal community.

Because of these disadvantages in the size of their new towns, current thinking among planners in Britain, Israel, Canada, and Scandinavia is to increase the size of existing new towns, and to plan for larger ones when and if such towns are built in the future.

Many of the British new towns have proved so successful that they have grown at a much faster rate than originally anticipated. As a result the initial population targets of most of the "older" new towns have been substantially increased to provide for second-generation growth. (Compare columns 3 and 5 in Table 1.1.) In a few cases—e.g., Basildon, Crawley, and East Kilbride—the revised target population is 100,000 or over. Moreover, plans for the

TABLE 1.1

British New Towns: Location and Population, Existing and Proposed, 1962 and 1971

New Town	Date of Designation	Location	Population Processed[a]	Dec. 31, 1962 Actual	Population Processed[a]	Dec. 31, 1971 Actual
LONDON RING						
Basildon	Jan. 4, 1949	30 miles east of London	86,000 106,000	58,000	103,600 134,000	85,000
Bracknell	June 17, 1949	28 miles west of London	undecided 50,000-60,000	22,390	55,000-60,000 60,000	35,000
Crawley	Jan. 9, 1947	30 miles south of London	62,000 70,000	56,300	b 84,300	67,700
Harlow	Mar. 25, 1947	23 miles north of London	undecided 80,000	60,640	not finally decided	79,000
Hatfield	May 20, 1948	20 miles NW of London	26,000 29,000	21,600	25,000 29,500	26,800
Hemel Hempstead	Feb. 4, 1947	29 miles west of London	65,000 80,000	58,700	65,000 80,000	70,500
Stevenage	Nov. 11. 1946	30 miles north of London	60,000 80,000	49,500	80,000 100,000-105,000	70,000
Welwyn G.C.	May 20, 1948	22 miles north of London	42,000 50,000	31,000	42,000 50,000	44,200
Total for London Ring				364,130		478,200
OTHERS IN ENGLAND						
Aycliffe	Apr. 19, 1947	12 miles south of Durham	15,000 20,000	13,700	40,000 45,000	23,850
Corby	Apr. 1, 1950	80 miles north of of London	55,000 75,000	39,500	undecided 83,000	50,000
Milton Keynes	Jan. 12, 1967	55 miles north of London	—	—	83,000 200,000	47,000
Northampton[c]	Feb. 14, 1968	60 miles north of London	—	—	250,000 230,000	134,930
Peterborough[c]	Aug. 1967	65 miles north of London	—	—	187,000 187,000	88,700
Peterlee	Mar 10, 1948	10 miles east of Durham	25,000 30,000	14,400	28,000 30,000	25,400
Redditch	Apr. 10, 1964	15 miles south of Birmingham	—	—	70,000 90,000	38,000
Runcorn	Apr. 10, 1964	14 miles south of Liverpool	—	—	70,000-75,000 90,000	40,000
Skelmersdale	Oct. 9, 1961	13 miles north Liverpool	—	—	73,300 80,000	30,200
Telford[d]	Dec. 12, 1968	23 miles NW of Birmingham	—	—	225,000 250,000	82,000

New Town	Date of Designation	Location	Population, Proposed[a]	Dec. 31, 1962 Actual	Population, Proposed[a]	Dec. 31, 1971 Actual
Warrington[c]	Apr. 26, 1968	15 miles east of Liverpool	—	—	191,000 202,000	129,600
Washington	July 24, 1964	6 miles SE of Newcastle	—		65,000 80,000	29,450
Total for others in England				99,600		719,130
SCOTLAND AND WALES						
Cumbernauld	Dec. 9, 1955	15 miles NE of Glasgow	undecided 70,000	8,350	70,000 90,000-100,000	34,000
Cwmbran	Nov. 4, 1949	18 miles NE of Cardiff	45,000 55,000	32,000	undecided 55,000	42,000
East Kilbride	May 6, 1947	9 miles south of Glasgow	undecided 70,000	34,500	82,500 90,000-100,000	65,500
Glenrothes	June 30, 1948	20 miles north of Edinburgh	32,000 50,000-55,000	14,140	55,000 75,000	30,000
Irvine	Nov. 9, 1966	24 miles S.W. of Glasgow	—	—	95,000 120,000	45,000
Livingston	Apr. 17, 1962	15 miles west of Edinburgh	—	—	70,000 100,000	16,400
Mid-Wales (new town)	Dec. 18, 1967	78 miles north of Cardiff	—	—	11,000 13,000	6,100
Total for Scotland and Wales				88,990		239,000
Total for Great Britain				520,229		1,436,330

[a]Two figures are given in the proposed population columns. The upper figure is the population size targeted (as of 1962 and 1971) for when the new town is proposed to stop "importing" people and jobs. The lower figure is the new towns planned ultimate population to be reached (as of 1962 and 1961) by natural increase.

[b]Planned migration has already stopped.

[c]Town expansion under New Towns Act.

[d]Includes and supercedes previously designated new town of Dawley.

Sources: Information on location is from The New Towns, Ministry of Housing and Local Government (1963).

Data on date of designation, and 1971 population figures, are from Town and Country Planning (January 1972), p. 40.

Data on 1962 population are from F. J. Osborne and Arnold Whittick, The New Towns: The Answer to Megalopolis (1963 edition), p. 342.

recently built or designated new towns (the Mark II and Mark III towns) call for target populations of up to 250,000.

Harold Wilson, then prime minister, commented on the reasons for these larger target populations:

> . . . not just because by concentrating our efforts on bigger schemes we can achieve a faster and more economical rate of building—though this is important. Town dwellers today are demanding an ever wider range of urban facilities, and many of these can be provided economically only in larger towns. At the same time, increased mobility has made it possible to think in terms of larger towns without the loss of the sense of community provided in the first generation new towns.[11]

New-town planners are also basing their revised size-goals on regional planning and development objectives. In Britain a concept is emerging that has already received governmental approval; the planning of entire city-regions. Each city-region is to provide for many hundreds of thousands of people, with the new town (or several new towns) as the focus of the region, all planned by the same agency.

In Israel similar proposals have been put forward to deal with the problems of Israeli new towns (among such problems being that of small size). The Lichfield Report has proposed for consideration and study three alternative regional-physical growth strategies (in addition to the current official Distribution of Population Plan and a continuation of existing trends) to concentrate and consolidate future new-town growth in selected towns in order to provide the inhabitants with the advantages of a large scale of settlements.[12] In general all three alternatives aim, by planning for more concentrated urban centers, to offer the opportunity for rapid "takeoff."

One solution to the problems faced by small, resource-based development towns, such as those typical in Canada, is to plan such towns in connection with an economic and resources development program for the region in which they are to be located.[13] Increased mobility and the availability of modern means of transportation now make it possible to build a centralized "combine town" to serve a large resource region—in contrast to previous, and to a large extent current, practices, in which resource developers build in proximity to their operations very small separate "townsites" (often just camps), each with minimal housing, recreational, commercial and other facilities to serve their workers.

A combine town can offer a number of important economic, social, and political advantages, including the ability to provide better utilities, stores, schools, hospitals, and other amenitites of modern urban living. Also, by bringing together workers (and their families) from several different enterprises, a larger market is created that can be a positive factor in attracting local, market-oriented industrial and commercial activities—thus helping to provide greater economic stability. A number of new towns planned to serve as combine service centers have already been built in Canada, including several existing villages that are being expanded.

The Scandinavian countries are also altering their approaches to the planning of new towns, emphasizing the regional aspects of new-town development. The current Stockholm satellite towns are serving as regional service centers for an expanding population; in Finland the garden city of Tapiola (population 20,000) is seen as the first of a series of regional new-town centers along the Finnish coast, serving populations of 100,000 or more.

INDEPENDENT AND NEWLY CREATED TOWNS

In the early days of planning for the first-generation British new towns, there were conflicts over the strategy of locating each of them in relationship to its mother city from which population was to be decanted. Initially, reflecting the views of Howard and others, there was a strong desire for independence from the mother city. There were, after all, no reasons for thinking that this would not be possible, if the workers walked to work and if the new towns were to be basically self-contained. Since industries were tending to move away from areas of high rents and taxation, it was assumed that the new towns could be established wherever cheap land and low tax rates could be obtained. However there were others who feared that such towns might fail; hence they saw as an important ingredient of success some degree of proximity to the larger cities, especially to London. Thus, as indicated in Table 1.1, all eight of the first London new towns were located within 20-35 miles of London.

Current thinking in Britain seems to favor larger developments farther out, with the concept of independence now representing the notion of counter-magnets to central city attractions. New towns are now in development as much as 70 miles or more from London (e.g., Peterborough and Northampton), and, as noted earlier, they are much larger, to ensure success.

The original concept of building new towns free from any of the constraints of existing populations or developments has been modified over the years in Great Britain. Indeed, even several of the first-generation (Mark I) new towns were actually based on small existing villages or towns.

11

The idea of taking existing towns and villages and expanding them received added impetus under the Town Development Act of 1952. This act permits a central city and an outlying small jurisdiction to enter into an agreement whereby the outlying jurisdiction (the receiving area) may accept people and industry from the central city (the exporting area) in order to help the larger center and at the same time strengthen the base of the smaller jurisdiction. Each jurisdiction contributes to the cost, with government grants and subsidies also being available. By the middle of 1971, sixty-eight town expansions, representing 162,795 dwellings, were being carried out in England; there were almost as many in Scotland, mostly on a very small scale.[14]

A new policy since 1960 lays greater stress on large-scale expansion of medium-sized towns throughout southeastern England (such as Warrington, Peterborough, and Northampton) to contain the growth of Greater London. This policy proposes to link development to an existing town of a reasonable size, mainly to take advantage of existing facilities in the early stages of development. It also aims to have a ready supply of jobs and manpower, an existing strong administrative machinery, and a population structure that includes from the beginning young recent school graduates needed in office employment; at the same time the modernization of the structure of the existing town can proceed side by side with new development.[15]

As implied above, the concept of independence of new towns is related to the idea of self-containment and self-sufficiency, an issue to be examined next.

SELF-CONTAINMENT AND SELF-SUFFICIENCY

From the writings of Howard and his disciples, it can be inferred that the goal of self-containment had three interrelated aims: (1) a minimum of in-and-out commuting, (2) a level of employment to match the level of job demands from the economically active resident population, and (3) a cross section of economic activities so that the new town is not dominated by a single industry or occupation; this would minimize economic instability.

As pointed out by a recent critic of this concept, the problem has been that, from the start, "self-containment" has had a dual meaning.[16] One meaning of the term simply refers to the facilities that exist in a town: a self-contained new town that has a complete range of urban facilities—sufficient employment, shopping, health, education, etc. But in general usage this definition has been fused with a second meaning—that of a social purpose. Under this meaning a self-contained new town is seen as one in which the residents can live full lives, satisfying all their daily needs within its boundaries; the town provides the environment for the life of a complete community— it is "an experiment in social living."[17]

The distinction is important because the two meanings have been merged even though objective conditions require their separation. One needs to ask whether, in regard to employment, the idea of the self-contained and self-sufficient new town is valid or attainable, especially given today's economic and technological developments.

When new towns are founded independently outside urban regions to capitalize on a natural resource or to encourage the economic development of undeveloped regions (as in the case of the Canadian and most of the Israeli new towns), there are usually enough jobs for their inhabitants. Since these towns are explicitly established for purposes of industrial development, and since they are typically located in geographically isolated areas, the planners provide a direct link between the number of jobs and the number of resident workers.

It is a different story in the case of those new towns built to help decongest the populations of large urban centers and direct metropolitan growth. Here the issue of balance between employment and population has been approached differently, judging from the British and Scandinavian experiences.

Great Britain

Not unexpectedly, achievement of a balance between employment and the working population has been one of the basic principles of the British new-towns program. The objective of self-containment and self-sufficiency (and, as we shall see later, of "balance" as well) was an established policy handed on for implementation to the development corporations that were to build the towns. Consequently each corporation paid particular attention to the two basic elements of "working and living"—that is, employment and housing—trying to keep these in balance at each stage of town growth, as well as when a town reached its ultimate size.

One way of measuring the extent of self-sufficiency in a community (in terms of employment) is by its job index—the number of jobs per 100 economically active residents, with the ideal index being 100. A commuting or dormitory town would typically have a low index, while an industrial town and the central city of a metropolitan area, typically would have a high index, often greater than 100.

But the balance of jobs and resident workers, as reflected in the job index, does not tell the full story regarding self-sufficiency. The potential of balance can be realized only if the two factors—jobs and working people—are interrelated; that is, if the people who live in the town are those who work in it. If the two factors are not interrelated, there will be cross movement, with residents traveling out to work elsewhere, while jobs in the town are filled by people who live outside.

I have calculated a self-sufficiency index for the eight London new towns, based on the number of in-and-out commuters per 100 residents working in the new town in which they live (see Table 1.2). The lower this index, the greater the degree of self-sufficiency. For all eight London new towns, the index in 1966 was 76; that is, for every 100 persons who live and work in the same new town, 76 additional persons either live in the new town and work outside, or live outside and commute to the new town for work. Among the eight towns, the index ranges from a low of 49 in Stevenage and Harlow to 242 in Hatfield.*

Between 1961 and 1966 some changes occurred in the degree of self-sufficiency. Welwyn Garden City and Hemel Hempstead became more self-sufficient; in the case of three others, the degree of self-sufficiency remained about the same; only in Hatfield, Bracknell, and Stevenage did it decline. Welwyn Garden City's increase in self-sufficiency is understood in light of the slowdown in industrial growth that occurred there in this period. It is significant in view of the employment boom these towns experienced that self-sufficiency in Hemel Hempstead, Harlow, Crawley, and Basildon either increased or remained the same; it means that most of the new jobs were taken up by residents. Indeed in the 1961-66 period the proportion of new-town residents commuting outside for work fell from an average of 29 percent to an average of 27 percent.

Contrary to what might have been expected, Ogilvy found that the new towns' in- and out-commuters did not primarily come from or go to London. Instead the work ties were mainly with communities within a radius of about 10-11 miles, with the size of the town influencing the proportion of commuters. The most significant change that occurred between 1961 and 1966 was that workers were coming from areas much farther away, as well as from adjacent districts. In short, the new towns had become important employment centers in their own right for workers in surrounding areas.

It would appear, therefore, that increased mobility was a major factor contributing to the shattering of the self-containment concept in the case of the London new towns. As transportation and

---

*Hatfield is an exception to the general pattern of the London new towns; its prime function is to cater to the neighboring aircraft industry, which is outside the new town area.

TABLE 1.2

Job Indexes and Commuting-to-Work Patterns, London Ring New Towns, 1961 and 1966

Town	1961			1966		
	Job Index[a]	Percent Employed New-Town Residents Working in New Town	Self-Sufficiency Index[b]	Job Index[a]	Percent Employed New-Town Residents Working in New Town	Self-Sufficiency Index[b]
Crawley	101.3	76.5	63	111.5	80.3	63
Hemel Hempstead	79.9	66.1	72	84.4	68.1	71
Welwyn G.C.	124.6	77.1	92	121.5	76.6	89
Hatfield	59.4	38.5	215	60.0	36.2	242
Basildon	82.2	59.9	104	107.1	68.2	104
Bracknell	115.3	74.5	88	126.0	75.8	98
Harlow	86.0	74.9	49	97.1	79.3	49
Stevenage	109.2	85.9	44	111.5	84.9	49
Total, London Ring new towns	94.1	70.7	75	102.8	73.5	76

$$^{a}\text{Job index} = \frac{\text{number of new jobs in new town}}{\text{number of employed residents in new town}} \times 100$$

$$^{b}\text{Self-sufficiency index} = \frac{\text{total number of in- and out-commuters}}{\text{total number of employed residents of new town who work in new town}} \times 100$$

Sources: Job-index data and taken directly from A. A. Ogilvy, "Employment Expansion and the Development of New Town Hinterlands, 1961-1966," Town Planning Review, XLII, 2 (April 1971), Table 3. Employment percentages and self-sufficiency indexes are calculated from the data in tables in Ogilvy's article.

communications improved, so did closer relations between new towns and those nearby. Many new towns, in fact, became centers of growth for their surrounding regions.

But regardless of evidence to the contrary, the words "self-contained" are still used; they even appear in reports by the new-towns corporations planning the latest round of new towns (the so-called Mark III towns), although these towns, designed for the motor age, must cater to high levels of car ownership and usage, in contrast to the Mark I new towns where the principal means of transport was expected to be the bicycle. An examination of the districts in which the Mark III towns will be located, and the number of jobs available in surrounding towns, suggests that most of these towns will have even larger interchanges of population than do the Mark I towns around London.

Scandinavia

The situation in Scandinavia is unlike that in Britain. The plans for new towns and city sectors developed in connection with the capital cities of Scandinavia are not based on the need for self-sufficiency with respect to employment.* Instead the aim has been to provide as many jobs as possible without trying to seek a balance between employment and the working population.

In no instance is there a balance in numbers between jobs and the working residents. In Tapiola it is estimated that only around 25-30 percent of the employed residents actually work in the town; the other residents commute to Helsinki and other nearby places for work.

Similarly, in the Vallingby district of Stockholm, 20 percent of the 25,000 working people there in 1960 worked in the district, 50 percent worked in the center of Stockholm, and 30 percent worked elsewhere. By 1966, however, local jobs had risen from 9,000 to 13,000 so that commuting was less, but still considerable.

Each of the urban-regional plans stresses the importance of freedom of choice offered to their citizens, a principle embodied in choices of place of work, shopping, recreation, and housing. This

---

*An interesting exception to this is the proposed policy of the Oslo (Norway) planners who, in order to minimize the amount of work commuting, are endeavoring to encourage a balance of jobs and population for the metropolitan area as a whole and for large areas within the region.

principle suggests, on the one hand, that the new towns be as balanced as possible to give maximum satisfaction to the needs of local inhabitants, but on the other hand it presumes that they cannot be treated as completely independent units. Of course such freedom of choice can be implemented only where transportation and communication permit easy travel throughout the entire region. It is for this reason that the planners have stressed the importance of efficient, comfortable means of transportation, especially public rail transportation, and have set maximum acceptable traveling times, which range from a 45-minute radius from the center of Copenhagen to a 30-minute radius from Stockholm and Helsinki.

BALANCE

Balance has been part of the ideology of planned new communities for some time in the past. The idea of a balanced community has meant, as we have seen, diversity of industry and dwellings, and balanced physical development. But it has also come to include the notion of population heterogeneity with respect to age, occupation, income, ethnicity, and class. Once again we must turn to the British for the origin and development of this concept.

The concern for balance goes back to the early British industrialists who created "new model" towns and villages in the nineteenth century in order to improve conditions of labor and living for their workers. The presence of a socially mixed community containing persons of diverse social classes was an important element in their schemes.[18] A similar idea was held by Ebenezer Howard, who recommended the presence of "all true workers of whatever grade" in his proposed garden cities.[19]

So widespread was the British planners' acceptance of the balance concept in the 1930s and 1940s that the word was actually included in the terms of reference given to Britain's Reith Committee, set up to develop the principles and procedures for the later new-towns program. While the committee expressed some doubts about the meaning of the term, it eventually came to the conclusion that the main problem was "one of class distinction. . . . [If] the community is to be truly balanced, so long as social classes exist, all must be represented in it. A contribution is needed from every type and class of person, the community will be the poorer if all are not there."[20]

The idea of social balance for the British new towns was largely a reaction and response to the one-class—that is, working class—character of the housing estates that had been built throughout Britain between the two world wars. To the members of the Reith Committee as well as to those public officials in the 1945 Labour government who were responsible for planning the new towns, contact between the classes in every area of life was seen as one basis for the general reform of British society. More specifically it was felt that exposure to a mixed environment would enlargen people's horizons and thereby benefit society as a whole.

In light of the substantial influence of these views on new towns in Britain and elsewhere, it is important to ask how successful the countries under review have been in attracting balanced populations and in meeting the problems that have ensued. Needless to say these questions are especially important for the planning and development of American new towns, if, as I assume, one of the major aims of such new towns is to attract low-income blacks and other minorities from the ghettos and central cities.

Israeli New Towns

In the 25 years since the founding of Israel some 30 new towns have been established there, with the number of towns and their population growth following the rise and fall in immigration.

The mass influx of immigrants made the quick beginning on the new towns possible and, in a decisive way, gave them their character— so much so that in everyday talk the communities are often called "immigrant towns." This influx, however, also established the towns' ethnic characteristics. Before the establishment of the state, 85 percent of all immigrants had been European in origin. In the following period, European immigration lost its lead and in 1955 reached an all-time low of only 5.4 percent. (Since then it has risen and dropped, swinging with the policies of the Soviet Union and other Eastern European countries regarding the granting of emigrant visas to Jews.) In short, the new towns absorbed a larger percentage of Afro-Asians than of European-American immigrants, with the distribution of ethnic groups in the new towns in 1961 showing 24 percent and 47 percent for those of European-American and Afro-Asian origin respectively, and with 29 percent being Israeli-born. In 1967 only 17 percent of the Israeli population was of European-American origin; 49 percent was of Afro-Asian origin, and 34 percent was Israeli-born.

The large number of children in Afro-Asian families, their strong clan ties, their low cultural-educational level, their deep (Sephardic) religiousness—indeed, their whole way of life—have contributed to the problems of the new towns. These include the low educational level of the population and labor force, the difficulties of developing leadership, and the high turnover of population—all of which lead to a cumulative downward effect.

British New Towns

The experiences of British new towns, especially those in the London region, have been very different from Israel's with respect to the balancing of occupational/income and racial/ethnic characteristics of the population. The meaning of a socially balanced community has been conceived, in general, to be one that conforms to the class characteristics of England and Wales as a whole, with most development corporations using the national figures as a standard of comparison when publishing statistics on their own class distribution.

The British new towns have been reasonably successful in recruiting socially balanced populations, if these are defined in terms of some national or regional average.[21] In particular they have managed to avoid the one-class (predominately working class) image of the prewar housing estates. However, while they have been successful in attracting the professional and executive middle classes, they have been unsuccessful in bringing in substantial numbers of unskilled and semiskilled workers.

Several factors help to explain this situation. First, the industrial selection policy influencing the nature of industry that moves to new towns has led to the recruitment of a population with large proportions of skilled workers, as well as professional and intermediate employees. Second, the success of the new towns in later years in attracting service and distributive industries has contributed to the presence of a high proportion of middle-range and professional employees. A final factor has been the policy of development corporations to allow for private, unsubsidized dwellings to be built, which has given an added impetus to attracting middle-class and professional families.

Indeed, it is this very policy that came under attack in Great Britain in the mid-1960s on the grounds that the new towns have not been serving the populations with the greatest housing need. While it is always assumed that the new towns, especially those around London, would help to relieve the surplus populations living in overcrowded and ill-housed conditions in London, the procedures used for selecting the populations did not help achieve the objective of social balance.

The explanation for this lies partly in the scheme used to recruit populations. The Greater London area was divided into sectors to which each new town was linked. Firms would apply to the new towns serving their sector, and, if accepted, would bring with them as many workers as wished to move. These workers and their families would be housed by the development corporation, irrespective of housing need. Further recruitment would be linked through the Industrial Selection Scheme to the housing lists of the local authorities, which entered into agreements with new towns for the reception of their overspill populations. Selection of a worker from these lists could occur only if an appropriate vacancy arose in a new town and if a worker with the required skill applied for it. If suitable labor could not be obtained by this means, then recruitment anywhere in Greater London, or in the country as a whole, was possible. The main criterion was that workers by suitable for the jobs available in the new town, and would live and work there.

Another factor in this situation pertains to the type of industry that moved out of London. This has been predominately the mobile manufacturing industry, about half of which is engineering. Most of these firms have come from the fringe areas of London County and the inner suburbs, and the majority of employees moving with their firms have also come from these or neighboring boroughs. By contrast, the inner areas of London contain many immobile industries, or firms unsuited or unwilling to move out. Thus the population of these inner areas has had relatively less chance of moving to the new towns.

This policy has had deleterious effects on the persons left in the inner parts of London and on housing conditions in those areas. With pressures on accommodation in the central areas growing, owing to such factors as slum clearance and the higher rents that follow conversion and rehabilitation, some families have been forced to seek cheaper accommodations farther out. Frequently this has led to further subdivision and to multiple occupation of dwellings. As a consequence, areas hitherto not plagued by "housing stress" have soon come to lie in the path of this outward movement.

This familiar process of population movement has resulted in housing deterioration and further retrograde effects. For example, as mobile families have moved out of London to suburban or fringe areas or to new towns, those less mobile have been left behind and have become more "visible." They include workers whose jobs tie them to London, families who could cannot afford municipal housing, or are not eligible for it, and immigrants from abroad or other parts of the country.

As a result, there has been a concentration of people with severe housing needs out of all proportion to the resources available to meet them, presenting local authorities with serious problems. In short, while social policy in the shape of overspill planning (that is, the achievement of social balance in new towns) has helped to solve the housing problems of one section of the community, the unintended consequence of this policy has been to aggravate the problems of another section of the community.[22]

This situation, when coupled with the further program of planned overspill up to 1981, has led some persons and groups to call for a reevaluation of the policies for recruiting populations to the new towns. The Milner Holland Committee noted that "many of these families will not wish to leave London or will be tied to London by their work and excluded from new and expanded towns for this reason, or by their inability to secure the more skilled jobs available in those towns."[23] Hence, if the policy of "self-containment" remained in force, populations would be selected on the basis of jobs made available by firms that move out to the new towns, resulting in the selection of families not necessarily in acute need of rehousing.

According to its proponents, a new policy involving a more effective use of planned overspill in new towns, which would relieve the pressing housing needs of the major cities, would have several advantages:

• it would provide many of those with the most pressing housing needs in London and other major cities with the chance of moving out;

• it would enhance the possibility of providing more varied and interesting housing designs for the working class;

• it would enable sizable numbers of black and Asian workers and their families, now living in ghettos in London, to obtain decent housing and other amenities of urban life.

The new towns had never attracted many black or Asian people; rather they tended to recruit higher proportions of skilled workers than are found in these populations. Some observers feel that there are reasons for believing that minority workers may be well received, and that the new towns could serve as "anti-ghettos."[24] Since the populations of these towns are quite young and without deep local roots and long traditions, they may be less resistant to this kind of change than older, more settled communities. A random sample of the relatively few black and Asian residents living in new towns in 1965 indicated that they were very happy about their new life, and encountered little resistance or animosity from the white families there.

In the late 1960s, government policy in regard to overspill did change, and now the new towns must contribute to the relief of housing stress in London and the other major conurbations. It is recognized, of course, that this new policy brings with it risks and a set of new problems, and only time will tell how it works. These problems include the following three:

1. Those recruited are unlikely to have the skills necessary for the jobs available. The Milton Keynes planners, in their interim report on the plan for their new city, recognized this problem when they stated that "there is likely to be a conflict between the skills required by industries and the skills available among one of the kinds of migrants Milton Keynes is seeking—those in the worst housing need in London."[25] Accordingly the planners recommended immediate

development of training programs so that these persons could develop the skills required.

2. If jobs are not available for this group of persons, they would have to commute back to London or the other exporting areas from which they came. This, of course, would increase the amount of commuting and disturb those who still hold to the notion of self-containment and self-sufficiency of new towns. But, as the proponents of the new policy argued, and as our earlier discussion demonstrated, there is already plenty of work-travel movement in and out of new towns, making the concept of self-containment and self-sufficiency partly a myth. In view of the need to relieve the housing needs of the large cities, there is no reason why future new-town populations should not depend partially upon employment in the exporting areas. Besides, such workers may be successful in finding employment in the industries of the surrounding region, which are often stimulated by the development of a new town. In short, as proponents of the new policy have argued, it would be more reasonable to recognize explicitly what now happens anyway in the new towns; namely, that they provide dwellings but not jobs for a proportion of their population.

3. Heavy housing subsidies and other special forms of assistance will be needed to attract skilled workers and make their transition to the new towns easier, financially and otherwise. However, as pointed out by the Milton Keynes planners and Heraud, such subsidies should not "frighten away middle class tenants."

The British new towns have also been quite unbalanced in terms of age of population, especially in their early days. Most of them have tended to attract young couples with children, with relatively few middle-aged and older people. The Milton Keynes planners acknowledge that if these missing age groups are to be attracted, special means must be used. As well as providing special housing subsidies, the recruitment policy should not be tied to the existing skills of potential residents. These persons must be allowed to move to the new city, even if jobs are not readily available, with dwellings provided especially for them, outside the industrial selection system.

The Milton Keynes planners were also concerned about the need to attain balance in the provision of homes, jobs, and services at all stages in the new city's growth. Imbalances can cause harrowing difficulties, as was the case with many of the early British new towns and with some Canadian resource-based new towns as well. This requires that expansion of employment and social services keep pace with population growth. It means that roads, sewers, power, gas, and water all should be installed in phase, and not delayed relative to investment in homes and factories. It also means that schools, colleges, health centers, and hospital and recreation facilities must be provided without a time-lag relative to need.

LESSONS

Based on this investigation of the experience of new and expanded towns in several countries, one can draw lessons for possible application to a new-towns program in the United States. I draw these lessons with full recognition that there are important differences between the countries studied and the United States as to legislation, geography, history, philosophy (e.g., the role of the private versus the public sectors), etc. However I think these issues are independent of the special circumstances of each country, and therefore may prove applicable to American conditions. I have grouped them in the form of questions corresponding to the key new-towns concepts investigated in this study.

What Population Size?

1. There is no ideal or optimum population size for all cities, since the "best" size for any city is dependent on such variables as composition of population and economic activities, geographic setting, accessibility and relationship to other towns and cities in the surrounding region, technological developments (especially with respect to transportation and communications), etc. Instead, new towns should be planned to have an adaptive ability, a flexibility to accommodate most scales of activity within a rapidly changing urban/technological society.

2. While in general there is no single optimum population size of cities, the experience of the countries surveyed does provide two important lessons regarding size range. First, the population sizes for which most of the independent nonmetropolitan new towns surveyed were planned and built (50,000-80,000), following the original Howard concept, were too small; as a result they suffered from the familiar economic, social, financial, and political problems associated with small communities. Second, based on the recent plans of the new-towns programs in the countries surveyed, plus other experiences,[26] there is sufficient evidence to suggest that cities in the size range 125,000-300,000 offer most of the advantages of large size (e.g. agglomeration economies) and none of the disadvantages of the very large metropolis.

3. The advantages of a single large city can be realized by small and medium-sized new communities if planned on a regional basis—that is, as part of a cluster of new towns, including expanded towns and existing towns and cities. With good regional transportation and communication systems making possible interindustry links between small and medium-sized cities within a region, and between

23

these cities and the mother city, key elements of agglomeration can be achieved without requiring actual physical agglomeration. This points up the critical importance of regional infrastructure policy in the planning and building of new towns. It also indicates the need for greater emphasis on the appropriate functions, locations, and sizes of new towns, and on the relationships between new and existing cities within a regional context—an issue now concerning British, Israeli, Canadian, and Scandinavian new-towns planners.

Independent or Metropolitan Cities?

1. Except for new towns built to serve a special purpose—such as to exploit a material resource or meet a particular population problem—the construction of relatively independent new cities beyond the commuting range of any existing metropolitan area is an extraordinarily difficult undertaking. In Great Britain, where the public authorities responsible for new-town development exercise great financial and administrative powers (greater than any currently contemplated in the United States), after over 25 years of effort the new population in the new towns constitutes only 6.9 percent of the growth of total population since the inception of the New Towns Act in 1946. Moreover, British planners have virtually abandoned the original concept of building relatively independent, nonmetropolitan new towns; instead they now favor peripheral or satellite cities adjoining middle-sized metropolitan areas beyond commuting range of London or the big Midlands industrial centers, and the expansion of fair-sized existing cities into larger new towns.

Similarly, in Sweden, Denmark, and Finland, most of the new cities are either peripheral or satellite to the capital cities of Stockholm, Copenhagen, and Helsinki. These peripheral or satellite cities are built around or along public mass-transit lines connecting the new center to the capital city.

2. A policy of selecting strategically located existing towns for expansion, rather than substituting completely new towns, has several advantages:

• a better range of services, amenities, and jobs are usually available in established towns, since they serve a much larger area than the town itself;

• it is often cheaper to expand an existing town, although this depends on the amount of unused capacity that exists;

• it is possible to attract quickly the varied types of people desired (e.g., minorities, old as well as young, etc.), since it is not necessary to wait for the building of the necessary community facilities.

3. The "expanding towns" concept, if used in conjunction with new-towns development on a regional basis, has real implications for revitalizing our metropolitan areas. It provides an opportunity to draw an ever-closer relationship between old- and new-town growth, between central city and suburban growth, between rebuilding, expanding, and new developments, and between urban and rural population distribution—all within the framework of a single developmental process. Such adaptations would provide a greater opportunity to think in terms of general upgrading of the quality of life of an urbanizing region as a whole rather than of a single town, city, or neighborhood. It would also provide the potential for revitalizing the growth possibilities of small units of government, or portions of them, now deteriorating for lack of financial or technical assistance.

4. The exporting area-receiving area arrangements of Britain would appear to lend themselves to the ghetto problems of American central cities. This would entail selecting existing towns in a metropolitan area to house a certain number of ghetto residents, in exchange for which the exporting area and/or the state or federal government would provide grants for the cost of the additional housing, utilities, amenities, etc.

Self-Containment and Self-Sufficiency?

1. The establishment of independent new towns that are self-contained or self-sufficient in terms of employment is (again with the exception of special-purpose cities) a most difficult if not impossible achievement. The British experience is most enlightening here, as self-containment has been an explicit objective of the new-towns program since its inception. Yet, despite the extraordinary controls and powers the public authorities exercise over the amount and rate of industrial growth and the provision of housing, the eight London new towns have experienced a large amount of commuting for work, both in and out of the new towns. It would appear that the journey to work offers many advantages and must be accepted as the necessary price paid for greater industrial stability, superior employment possibilities, and a higher standard of living. For employers it means, among other advantages, a welcome mobility of labor as well as a flexible labor market. For workers the journey to work opens up the prospect of additional, varied, and better jobs, and it facilitates adjustment to changing circumstances, such as factory relocation, flexibility for home ownership, and necessary opportunities for secondary wage-earning jobs.

2. New towns should be viewed in their regional context and, in most instances, as centers for future regional growth. Work-travel

movements can be expected to occur primarily in connection with the towns and cities in the surrounding hinterlands of the new towns, and secondarily with the mother city from where most of the new-town residents will probably come. Thus regional settlement concepts should replace the traditional isolated, bounded-area concept, along the lines of current thinking in the countries surveyed in this study. The concept of self-containment should be applied, as it were, on a regional basis.

3. While the journey to work is a fact of life that must be recognized, it is still true that minimizing such a journey is a desirable objective—especially for those in the population who are less mobile or who prefer to live close to their work. For reasons discussed earlier, realization of this objective requires, in the first place, larger communities than the traditional concept of population size calls for, in order to develop a large mix of diversified industries to satisfy the employment skills of a varied labor force. Second, to realize this objective it is also necessary to control both industrial and population growth, especially the rate and timing of both, so that they are in reasonable balance over time. The closer this relationship is to a ratio of 1:1 (100:100) the greater the chance for minimizing the number and proportion of in-and-out commuters, and the greater the degree of self-sufficiency.

How to Achieve Population Balance?

1. As suggested by Downs, Weissbourd, and others, and as the British experience clearly demonstrates, a new-towns program in the United States should be planned in relationship to the problems of our central cities. Any new towns built to organize metropolitan growth on a more orderly basis—whether they be either independent and self-contained communities or satellites—should aim to attract, in part, low-income and minority groups now living in the worst housing and other adverse conditions in the ghettos. Otherwise new towns will become another escape hatch for middle-class whites. Indeed the problems of our central cities may even become exacerbated unless the pressures on housing and public services are relieved through a new-towns program. While new towns should be viewed as a significant mechanism for dealing with the problems of our central cities, it is also essential that extensive efforts be made concurrently to improve the attractiveness and economic viability of the central cores of our growing urban regions.

2. If we want our new towns to be truly balanced in terms of population composition, special efforts must be made to attract un-skilled and semiskilled workers, blacks and other minorities, and

middle-aged and older people—persons who under normal circumstances would not be attracted or permitted to move to new communities. It will also require that recruitment policies not be tied to the existing skills of the potential residents. In addition, efforts should be made to attract industries—and not just the so-called clean industries— that can use their skills. At the same time, job-training programs should be instituted to develop the skills required by the more advanced types of industries.

While such efforts are under way, these residents should be assisted to commute to their old jobs in the mother city, or to jobs in the surrounding region. Although self-sufficiency is a desirable longterm objective, it should not be slavishly adhered to in view of other more worthwhile objectives—e.g., providing decent housing and other urban facilities and amenities to persons now living in poor housing and deteriorated neighborhoods in the major large cities.

3. To attract and hold all of the types of persons we want in our new towns—middle-class professionals and executives, as well as low-income people, minority groups, and older people—it is important that there be a sufficient number and variety of urban services, facilities, and amenities available, and right from the beginning of development.

There is a need to have jobs, services, amenities, and housing keep pace with each other, and not get out of phase.

NOTES

1. Foreword by Dame Evelyn Sharp to Jean-Viet, New Towns: A Selected Annotated Bibliography (New York: UNESCO, 1960). [In French and English.]

2. See, for example, President Johnson's message on "The Crisis of the Cities" to the 90th Congress, as reported in Public Papers of the Presidents of the United States: Lyndon B. Johnson, Book I, January 1 to June 30, 1968. (Washington, D.C., 1970), p. 262.

3. Ebenezer Howard's ideas were originally published in his book Tomorrow: A Peaceful Path to Reform, in 1898, later revised as Garden Cities of Tomorrow, in 1902, and subsequently reissued on several occasions to the present day.

4. Interim Report of the New Towns Committee, Ministry of Town and Country Planning (London: March 1946); and Final Report of the New Towns Committee (London: July 1946).

5. Final Report of the New Towns Committee.

6. Ira M. Robinson, New Industrial Towns on Canada's Resource Frontier (Chicago: University of Chicago, 1962), Program of Education and Research in Planning, Research Paper No. 4, Ch. VI.

7. Erika Speigel, New Towns in Israel (New York: Praeger Publishers, 1967), p. 55.

8. Pierre Merlin, New Towns: Regional Planning and Development, (London: Methuen and Company, 1971), Ch. 2.

9. Nathaniel Lichfield, Israel's New Towns: A Development Strategy, Vol. I (Jerusalem: State of Israel Ministry of Housing, August 1971), pp. 4.7.2, 7.3.5, and 7.3.8; and Alexander Berler, New Towns in Israel (Jerusalem: Israel Universities Press, 1970), pp. 164-85.

10. Lesley E. White, "The Social Factors Involved in the Planning and Development of New Towns," in U.N. Department of Economic and Social Affairs, Planning of Metropolitan Areas and New Towns (New York: United Nations, 1967), pp. 194-200.

11. Harold Wilson, "The Prime Minister at Stevenage: Extracts from an Important Speech," Town and Country Planning, XXXVI, 1 (January-February 1968), 31.

12. Lichfield, op. cit., Ch. 9.

13. Robinson, op. cit., Ch. VIII.

14. Hazel Evans, "Britain's New Towns: Facts and Figures," Town and Country Planning, XL, 1 (January 1972), 47-53.

15. South East Joint Planning Team, Strategic Plan for the South East (London, 1970); and South East Economic Planning Council, A Strategy for the South East (London, 1967).

16. A. A. Ogilvy, "The Self-Contained New Town, Employment and Population," Town Planning Review, XXXIX, 1 (April 1968), 38-54; and "Employment Expansion and the Development of New Town Hinterlands, 1961-1966," Town Planning Review, XLII, 2 (April 1971), 113-29.

17. A. C. Duff, general manager for Stevenage for ten years, wrote a book entitled Britain's New Towns: An Experiment in Living (1961). Also, the Barlow Commission described the first two garden cities, Letchworth and Welwyn Garden City, as "complete towns and also as experiments in social living"; See Royal Commission on the Distribution of the Industrial Population, Report (1940).

18. Harold Orlans, Stevenage, a Sociological Study of a New Town (London: Routledge and Kegan Paul, 1952).

19. Ebenezer Howard, Garden Cities of Tomorrow (rev. ed., London: Faber and Faber, 1965), p. 51.

20. Final Report of the New Towns Committee, p. 10.

21. B. J. Heraud, "Social Class and the New Town," Urban Studies, V, 1 (February 1968), 33-58.

22. B. J. Heraud, "The New Towns and London's Housing Problem," Urban Studies, Vol. III, No. 1 (1966), p. 12.

23. Cited in Ibid., p. 16.

24. John Barr, "New Towns as Anti-Ghettoes," New Society (April 1, 1965) pp. 4-6.

25. Llewelyn-Davies, Weeks, Forestier-Walker, and Bor, Milton Keynes Plan: Interim Report to the Milton Keynes Development Corporation (December 1968), p. 107.

26. See, for example Britton Harris, "Urban Centralization and Planned Development," in Roy Turner, ed., India's Urban Future (1962); and Stanford Research Institute, et al., "Costs of Urban Infrastructure for Industry as Related to City Size: India Case Study," Ekistics, XXVIII, 168 (November 1969). 316-20.

2

**THE ROLE OF NEW TOWNS
IN NATIONAL AND
REGIONAL DEVELOPMENT:
A COMPARATIVE STUDY**
Arie S. Shachar

The aim of this study is to evaluate the existing and potential roles of new towns around the world within the context of national (or regional) urban development policy. It begins by applying one performance criterion for the past achievements of new towns—namely, the relative share of new towns within the general urbanization process of a country. The empirical examination provides the factual framework for the second part of the study, which attempts to identify the major economic, spatial, and social roles of new towns, according to the level and type of economic and social development of various countries, and the groups of population that may benefit from new-town development.

It is difficult to evaluate past experience with new-town development, because an explicit formulation of the goals and objectives to be achieved by building new towns is rarely made. Even where a formulation of goals exists, it has not been relevant in some situations, since the actions taken were motivated by latent goals not specified formally in the planning process. Another problem is the absence of a regular and systematic monitoring system that follows up the achievements and the failures of new towns. This results in a scarcity of reliable information concerning some of the basic aspects of new towns, such as costs of development, level of satisfaction of the population, and impact of social processes. Moreover the exceptional interest in the form and design of new towns has not been matched by a parallel evaluation of the economic, social, and organizational aspects of new-town development.

The carrying out of a comparative study is also hampered by the many existing definitions of a new town. For the purpose of this study, it should be emphasized that the concept of a new town is not limited by its form or location within an urban area or outside of it. The new town could be located far away from an existing urban area, very close to it, or even within an existing metropolitan area. In order to be defined as a new town the urban settlement has to meet the following requirements:

- a predetermined comprehensive plan for building and development;
- an extensive economic base, with a broad range of employment opportunities within the town;
- a variety of housing types and prices to enable a wide range of income classes and life style preferences;
- an internal transportation system, as well as one that provides convenient access to other communities within the region;
- full provision of community facilities, public services and amenities;
- an effective local government or a development agency (public or private) that has control over the staging and development of the new town.[1]

The purpose of this definition is to exclude from the discussion a large number of new communities that are actually oversized suburban expansions or subdivisions. It also enables us to identify those countries in which new towns are of significant importance in national urbanization and development processes. This examination will be carried out by comparing the population living in the new towns with the general growth of urban population in the country.

Great Britain provides the most distinct example of a new-towns national policy. An examination of the 27 new towns in Britain at the end of 1971 eight in the London Ring, two in Wales, five in Scotland, and twelve in other districts) indicated a total of 1,436,330 people as workers and residents, with 718,800 as new residents.[2] The newcomers constituted 1.2 percent of the entire population and 6.9 percent of the increase in population since the designation of new towns under the New Towns Act of 1946. The annual increase of the new towns' population in 1971 was 20,842 persons, less than 7 percent of the total population increase in that year.

When planned migration ceases, the proposed total population of all British new towns will reach on their completion, 2.4 million, with an ultimate population, allowing for natural increase, reaching close to 2.8 million people. Thus, despite a national commitment extending over 25 years, and the investment of nearly £1 billion by the end of 1971, the achievement has been one of only marginal importance, constituting considerable change neither in the urban way of life nor in the pattern of settlement of Britain. However it should be emphasized that the major contribution of the British new towns should not be measured only by the size of resident population but by the innovative impact thay have on the theory and practice of town planning all over the world, by establishing high standards for quality of life in urban areas, and by proving the feasibility of a new-towns policy on a national scale.

Another country with a national policy of establishing new towns is Israel, which established its first new towns in 1949. This represented a major national policy commitment. The relative share of the new towns in the country's urbanization process is a measure of the degree of their importance in the urban fabric of Israel. The total population living in 34 new towns by the end of 1970 amounted to 530,000 people, constituting about 17.5 percent of the total population, or 21.1 percent of the total urban population. The new towns absorbed about 30 percent of the total population increase of Israel between the years 1948 and 1970. Their relative importance within the overall Israeli population has grown constantly since the initial stages of the new-towns policy: 1950, 6.2 percent; 1955, 10.1 percent; 1960, 14.1 percent; 1965, 17.3 percent.[3] The increase in the relative share of new towns within the total Israeli population, however, has slowed down in recent years; according to the national planning goals for 1983, the new-town population should then constitute 22 percent of the total. These figures show that even in such a special case as Israel, a major part of the general growth is absorbed by the existing towns—despite comprehensive national planning that sets growth goals for every settlement in the country, a highly centralized system of resource allocation, the substantial influence on the migration movements of the population by means of subsidies in housing, a policy of settling peripheral areas, and the high relative importance placed on new towns within the country's overall urbanization policy.

Several countries in Western Europe also include the building of new towns within the framework of their urban and regional planning. Among them it is particularly instructive to examine the relative importance of new towns in Holland and Sweden. As in Israel, new towns in Holland were designed to open up new areas and populate them by setting up urban and rural settlements. The new towns built in this context are Emmeloord in the Northeast Polder, Dronten in East Flevoland, and Lelystad in South Flevoland.[4] The towns Emmeloord and Dronten have already reached the final stages of their development, whereas Lelystad is still in the initial stages of building. The population in these three towns in 1972 reached approximately 29,000 persons, which constituted 0.8 percent of the total Dutch population, or 0.57 percent of the overall increase in population since World War II. This new-towns figure is smaller than the population in each of the planned new sectors on the outskirts of the big cities—such sectors as West Amsterdam, which has about 150,000 residents, and Pendrecht (in Rotterdam), which has 22,000. It is apparent that even in a country that has put enormous national effort into the development of new areas through a well-organized planning system, virtually all national urban growth is absorbed in existing towns.

However, by absorbing a part of the population settling in the reclaimed areas, new towns are having a regional impact; e.g., about a quarter of the population of the Northeast Polder lives in Emmeloord. The future growth of Lelystad, planned for over 100,000 persons, may signal a new role for Dutch new towns. Instead of being a provincial capitol with only a local role, it is going to absorb overspill population from the Amsterdam metropolitan area, thus becoming part of the outward expansion of the Rand-Stat, the urban rim of Holland.[5]

Urban development in Sweden is marked by a rise in living standards, a decrease in housing density (in 1966: 1.2 rooms per person; in the regional plan for Stockholm, 2.2 rooms per person), an increase in the number of families owning a second house, limited migration from small and medium-sized settlements to big urban settlements, and a low annual population growth (of about 50,000 per year). These characteristics of urban development help to explain the unique role of the new towns that are planned and built in and around the Stockholm metropolitan area. These are satellite towns with no concern for economic self-support. Rather they serve as overspill towns for the Stockholm population, maintaining very close connections of employment and commerce with the central city by means of an efficient mass-transit system. This process has also been facilitated by the political reorganization of the metropolitan structure, which has thrown a net around a number of the towns.

The new towns around Stockholm are organized in units of 15, 000 people, grouped into large units of about 60,000, and served by a main center situated in one of the units; e.g., Skärholmen, Vallingby, Farsta. There are 130,000 people living in the towns around Stockholm, representing 1.6 percent of the Swedish population.

Stockholm's new regional plan (1967) proposes larger new towns, consisting of units of 40,000-50,000 people, which combine to make groups of 200,000 residents. Consequently, as the plan is implemented, the relative importance of new towns within the total population of the Stockholm area (it is about 10 percent today) will be increasing.

Among the conditions that have proved to be critical in the successful implementation of the new-towns policy around Stockholm are the simultaneous building of the new towns and the transportation system connecting them to the central city, the farsighted policy of the Stockholm municipality in acquiring large tracts of vacant land in the outskirts of the city that were available for large-scale development in new-towns form, and a national policy that encourages reorganization of the metropolitan political and social structures.

A special place within a comparative study of new towns is occupied by the Soviet Union. The vigorous industrial development process undergone by the Soviet Union in the last 50 years has been accompanied simultaneously by the establishment of networks of new towns on a nationwide scale. Out of about 1,250 towns with over 10,000 residents (the 1959 census), there were approximately 400 completely new towns, set up on sites where previously no urban nucleus had existed. In 1966 there lived in these towns about 12 million people, constituting 5.2 percent of the total population in the country, or 10 percent of the total urban population.[6] The new towns in the Soviet Union play a highly important role in the economic development of the country and in populating its vast areas, mainly east of the Urals. The experience of the Soviet Union is of considerable importance in the international comparison of countries with a new-towns policy. Although it could be argued that this phenomenon of induced twentieth-century urbanization is analoguous to the American experience of "opening up the West" in the nineteenth century, particularly in terms of comparable spatial manifestations, the difference is, of course, that the Soviet process is a planned one and under the complete control of the state authorities.

It is of interest to observe that new-towns experiences in other countries in Eastern Europe are limited and rather insignificant in their urbanization and development processes. A typical example is Poland, which established a new-towns policy in 1950 but has not pursued it with energy and consistency. As of 1965, about 325,000 people lived in the new towns (of which Nowa Huta, Nowe Tychy, Stalowa Wola are the major ones), representing 1 percent of the total Polish population, or 2 percent of its urban population.[7] In a state that has control over the location of industry and centers of economic activity, this low rate serves as visible evidence of the limited enthusiasm and encouragement given to the new-towns policy on the part of the state authorities. A very similar picture can be found in Hungary, where the last new town was built in 1961. The new towns (the largest of which is Dunaujvaros) had a total of 190,000 people in 1967, which constituted 1.9 percent of the entire Hungarian population.

To complete this examination of new-town populations within the national total, I have chosen the most studied example of a new town in a developing country, Ciudad Guayana in Venezuela. Guayana had about 40,000 residents in 1960, upon the establishment of the Corporacion Venezuela de Guayana, and it had 122,000 residents in 1968.[8] In 1968 the population of Guayana constituted 1.3 percent of the total population of Venezuela, or about 6 percent of the total population increase in the country over the period 1961-68. However, Guayana's present growth rate, even though it is smaller than the one predicted by the planning team,[9] suggests that this new town will be significant in Venezuela's development process in the years ahead.

The examination of the share of new towns within total populations has been applied here to several of the countries that have new-towns policies; these countries are at various levels of economic development, with differing political regimes and urban systems. Against this background we could well conclude that, except in Britain, the Soviet Union, and Israel, new-towns policy is not taken as significant in the solution of urban problems in nations around the world. The meaning of this finding is that the achievements of new towns in various aspects, such as the quality of urban life, or excellence in design, actually pertain to a small population group within the overall urban population in those countries. Therefore it will be useful to examine the achievements of new towns in that very small number of countries in which they have had importance within the general urban system, on the assumption that these may be transferable and applicable elsewhere. This will entail an examination of the goals involved, the extent of accomplishment, and the relationship between the achievement of national goals and the well-being and welfare of the individuals living in the new towns.

SPATIAL AND ECONOMIC GOALS OF NEW-TOWN DEVELOPMENT

Goals for new towns tend to fall into three major groups: spatial, economic, and social—applied separately or in combination in various countries and under various local conditions. The first group of goals is national in scope and deals with changes in the spatial organization of the country. These changes are meant to bring regions with a development potential within the national activity system; mainly to populate vacant frontier regions in order to strengthen the national presence and sovereignty, and to tap resource potentials. These goals are normally found in countries with a relatively short history of development, an imbalanced population distribution, unexploited natural resources in distant and unpopulated regions, and a high political sensitivity to undeveloped areas in all parts of the country.

A considerable part of the Soviet Union's new towns, those of Israel and Venezuela and, to a certain degree, those of Canada, were established in order to achieve such national goals. The new towns in this group may serve as growth centers or as urban focuses in undeveloped or newly developed regions. The size and location of the new towns in this group is determined, to a large extent, by the random distribution of natural resources, by the structure of the transportation network, physical amenities, and the basic planning principles underlying the spatial organization of the economy.

It is important to note that a new town in the role of a growth center has to be built on a combination of industries with the following characteristics: "Large size and economic dominance, a rate of growth faster than that of the economy in which it is embedded and a high degree of interlinkage with other sectors."[10] The new town is liable to meet the two first conditions. An instructive example in this regard is Ciudad Guayana, the development of which is based on iron and aluminum industries. Yet it is difficult for the new town to tie into economic linkage system, which may be dispersed in all parts of the country and may not have a specific local spatial impact. The new town in the role of a growth center may also develop into a one-industry town, where the industry does not benefit from the advantages of external economics, and where the variety of employment opportunities is relatively limited. New towns aspiring to play the role of growth centers must probably reach medium size to permit the broadening of the economic basis, variegate the scope of opportunities, and raise the level of services. A medium-sized town may even develop a local political and social leadership, and thus influence change in the pattern of relations between the core and the periphery—between the big cities in the core and the new towns in the resource frontier. The larger the new town in a growth-center role, the better are its chances to be a focus of attraction for rural-urban or small-town to medium-sized-town migration as part of the stepwise migration process. This policy clearly necessitates an alteration of the concept of the new town as a small town with a rigid physical pattern, since this prevents the possibility of growing beyond a predetermined size.

Only by large-scale building, the forward planning of land uses, the provision of an efficient infrastructure system adequate for various industries, the appropriate timing of investments, and the creation of an image of rapid and vigorous growth, can the realization of the economic potential of a resource frontier be secured while creating a new spatial organization of the population in these regions. In addition to the example of Guayana, which serves the role of a growth center in eastern Venezuela and which is designed to reach a population of about 300,000 people around 1980, one may learn about the feasibility of this policy from a series of new growth centers in the Soviet Union and a number of Israeli new towns built in resource frontiers.[11]

An interesting example of overcoming the new-town problems that arise in the case of a single industry is that of Beer-Sheva. This town is the biggest of all new towns in Israel (1971 population, 81,000). Beer-Sheva is situated in the Israeli resource frontier, and it benefits from the advantages of the linkage effects of the other smaller new towns in this region. A considerable impact was given to the development of the town by the decision to develop tertiary and quartenary activities of a high growth rate; representative of this category are research institutes and universities. A major role in the present development of the town is occupied by research institutes (which, incidentally, are much concerned with the developmental potential of the region), and by a university that attracts students from all the southern portions of Israel. Aside from the economic part these institutions play in the development of the new town, there is a far-reaching influence on the image of the town, on its cultural and educational system, and on the formation of "reference groups" for the overall urban population.

By way of summary one may state that the new towns can serve as growth centers in countries that are in the second and third stages of the national development process; that is, the transitional and industrial stages. These towns may be of assistance in the economic development of resource frontiers, and in the absorption of population from the rural areas, by channeling migration streams. As they grow and reach stability, they may even change the spatial organization of political power by forming secondary cores in development regions.

A different facet of new towns in the role of growth centers lies in the policy of encouragement and development of lagging regions in developed countries. Such policy aims at closing the growth and income gap among various regions by using new towns as a helpful instrument in stabilizing backward regions and in slowing down the process of their impoverishment.

Thus Britain has developed a series of new towns designed to serve as urban growth centers within lagging regions. Relevant examples, in this context, exist in Scotland (especially Glenrothes and Livingstone),[12] in Wales (Cwmbran and Newtown) and northern England (Aycliffe, Peterlee, and Washington). In such regions, where the economic base had been concentrated on a declining industry, national efforts have been directed at broadening this base and preventing the migration of the active population. Government assistance to industries is provided through building grants, loans, and training subsidies. In addition, development of industrial estates is provided for by the development corporations of the new towns, which are simultaneously responsible for the provision of housing for the population arriving there. The combination of employment in modern industry, and decent housing in an environment of high urban qualities, explains the success of the new towns built in the relatively backward regions of Scotland and northern England. Since part of these towns' population has been drawn from a nearby metropolitan area (such as Glasgow), the towns could fulfill two purposes at the same time— serving as a growth center for a lagging region and providing a partial solution to the substandard and overcrowded housing problems of large metropolitan areas. The comprehensive responsibilities of the development corporations include building the industrial estates, providing living accommodations, furnishing the urban service system, and using the resources allocated to the development of the towns in a coordinated, time-phased process.

An important feature in the success of new towns in lagging regions in Britain has been the fact that the major part of living accommodations in these towns is rented. Since some of the people moving over to live in these towns are not sure of their economic future, the degree of their commitment to the new town is not especially high. The possibility of rented accommodations constitutes a very important means of adjusting to the new town and becoming absorbed in it. The renting itself is organized in graduated rent schemes whereby tenants of the development corporation with incomes below a certain figure may apply for lower rents, which are graduated by income and size of family, thus equalizing opportunities for decent housing for the whole population of the new town.[13] It is possible to conclude from this example that a new-towns policy may indeed have an important role in stimulating lagging regions within developed countries.[14]

To this point the discussion has dealt with new-town goals mainly within a regional framework. It is evident, however, that a national policy of building new towns could be directed toward an objective of a far higher level: a fundamental structural transformation of the urban system of the country. The Israeli experience may be instructive in connection with this goal and the feasibility of its realization. The Israeli policy for new towns has set two objectives in connection with the spatial organization of the Israeli society. These two goals have determined to a great extent the size and spatial distribution of the new towns in Israel. In this case the new towns were not built within a regional or metropolitan framework, but were designated to be an important part of the urban system as a whole and to bring about far-reaching changes in it.

Analyzing the city-size distributions of Israel from 1948 to 1967, it is possible to follow the changes that occurred in the urban system during this period. The analysis points to the conclusion that the goal of changing the urban system structure from one characterized by primacy (a single dominant center) to one characterized by the so-called rank-size rule has been achieved.[15] It seems that a vigorous new-towns policy with a deep national commitment could enhance the "trickle-down" mechanism and quicken the gradual changes toward rank-size structure in developing countries. The objective of changing the urban structure in this case had been based on concern over the effects of the primate city over the economic, social, and cultural systems of the country. Therefore the new-towns policy was accompanied by restrictions of the growth of the primate city (Tel Aviv), mainly by applying physical land-use control, preventing the conversion of agricultural land to urban use, and by not building subsidized housing for immigrants within the primate city. It should be emphasized that the induced changes in the structure of the urban system were crucial in facilitating the efficient operation of the "hierarchical diffusion" process within the urban system.[16] It is important to observe that the participation of the new towns in the diffusion process was differential, as it was highly influenced by the types of population both in the new towns and in the surrounding regions.

The change in the urban structure was designated mainly to bring the urban population distribution into greater balance between the primate city and the medium- and small-sized towns. The other national objective, that of regional integration, envisaged the new towns as service centers for the agricultural hinterland, enabling the agricultural population to get commercial services within their vicinity. The new towns had to fulfill an important economic role in the processing and marketing of agricultural products and in absorbing labor surpluses from the rural settlements. For the implementation of this objective, the size and location of a considerable number of the new towns were determined according to the so-called central place theory, under which is established a full hierarchical structure including five levels, from rural center up to the biggest town, with the new towns placed in the second, third, and fourth levels.[17] New towns in the role of service centers were designated to increase the efficiency of the marketing and distribution system throughout the whole country; they were also meant to decrease the economic dependence of the rural and small urban settlements on large towns. These two objectives—of creating integrated regional systems of rural and urban settlements and of increasing the economic efficiency of marketing and distribution, along with consideration of the accessibility pattern of the existing and planned road network—together determined the location of the new towns.

The idea of developing new urban centers in the role of service centers for an agriculture region has been implemented in the Northeast Polder and East Flevoland in Holland. The same concept, applied to developing countries, has been recently discussed in E. A. J. Johnson's study.[18] According to this approach the new urban centers could also serve as processing centers for agricultural products, as focuses of culture and entertainment, and as filters to reduce by absorption the flow of rural migrants to the big towns. The experience in Israel may indicate the degree of feasibility of this idea. During the period of over twenty years since new towns were first established, there has been a clear tendency to reinforce their role as service centers for their surroundings. Yet only a few towns have achieved their spatial potential and turned into regional focuses in terms of economic, commercial, and cultural activities.[19] Some of the reasons for this lack of success are unique to Israeli conditions. One is the cooperative structure of the marketing and purchasing networks of the agricultural settlement that connect these rural settlements directly with the big towns; another is the higher level of development of some of the agricultural settlements, mainly the kibbutzim, as compared to the new towns.

However, a number of conclusions could be relevant to other countries of a similar level of development. The reorganization of the spatial system of a country by using new towns to form a hierarchical system is a continuous and gradual process. The consumption habits of the population and the spatial activity system involve high inertia, and the adjustment to the new urban system, as effective as it may be, takes a considerable amount of time. A further conclusion concerns the rigidity of the new urban system. In Israel, and to some extent in Holland, the hierarchical system of the new towns has been determined by assuming, in addition to certain consumption and marketing habits, a certain motorization rate. The assumed motorization rate has proved to be underestimated, and consequently the average distance between the new towns is small—much smaller than the present average range of goods, even for low-threshold products. Hence the hierarchical system is now operating suboptimally from the point of view of goods-and-service distribution. The small distances between the new towns in Israel has necessitated the distribution of the population into a large number of towns—which has resulted in a small average size (about 15,600 people as an average for 1971). The small size of most of the new towns has made difficult the development of services and commerce of an appropriate level, thus diminishing the attractiveness of the new towns for the surroundings. The small size of most of the new towns has also prevented the formation of a variety of opportunities in employment or social activity.

New towns may successfully fulfill the role of service centers for an agricultural region, thus promoting regional integration and increasing the efficiency of marketing and distribution. This is true for a country in which there does not yet exist a complete system of service centers. This role of new towns demands great flexibility as to the planned size of the new towns, a datum that is liable to change with the changes in the consumption habits, mobility, and spatial behavior of the population.

An important point should be mentioned regarding the role of new towns in changing the urban structure, creating a complete urban hierarchy, and dispersing the population from the large metropolitan areas. These spatial goals may be translated into economic ones that encourage economic growth, either by speeding up the hierarchical diffusion processes within the urban system or by increasing the efficiency of marketing and distribution. Another economic motivation of the new-towns policy of dispersing population is based on the assumption that the average unit cost of public services grows with the size of the town. It is assumed that, for various public services, the average unit cost is a U-shaped curve, and hence the size of a new town should fit the trough of this curve.[20] It should be emphasized that even, if it were possible to overcome definitional problems and to determine the minimum point of the curve of the average unit cost of public services, this approach to minimizing public costs disregards the economic considerations of the firm benefiting from externalities and agglomeration economics with increases in city size. Nor does it consider the fact that the larger the city the more residents have opportunities for achieving higher personal income.[21]

This complex set of considerations undermines the long-accepted notion of small new towns and demands a thorough reevaluation of the preferred size as determined by economic considerations. The size of a new town in the role of a regional center could be critical, taking into account the frequently observed phenomena of the decline of central places at the lower levels of the urban hierarchy.[22]

To sum up, most of the spatial goals of establishing new towns prove to be beneficial to the national economy. This refers to the role of new towns in opening resource frontiers, in improving the marketing and distribution system by building up a complete urban hierarchy, in establishing growth centers in declining regions, in participating in the developmental process of transforming a primacy structure into a rank-size one, and in increasing access and range of opportunities to a larger portion of the population. On the other hand, new towns carrying out the goal of dispersion of population from large metropolitan areas still have to prove that, while they are decreasing the costs of services, they are not at the same time decreasing the efficiency of production and the level of personal income of their inhabitants. But even if this point is not proved, its relevancy in negating a new-towns policy is diminishing in importance because of the existence of another facet of new-town development—that of the social goals to be achieved.

SOCIAL GOALS OF NEW-TOWN DEVELOPMENT

Up to this point, attention has been focused on new towns with major goals in the economic and spatial realm. This kind of policy may be appropriate in developing countries going through the process of urbanization and industrialization, where new towns have an important part in organizing the country's spatial system and increasing its economic efficiency. On the other hand, an examination of the objectives of establishing new towns in developed countries suggests a quite different focus. New towns appear to be a means for equalizing opportunities in the realm of housing and employment, for bringing together population groups of different ethnic and income backgrounds in a physical framework that would encourage social interrelationships and integration, and for improving the quality of life through use of an efficient land-use pattern and imaginatively and attractively designed housing and public areas. The examination of the objectives in establishing new towns in Western Europe and in the United States shows a clear emphasis on these social and human implications. A typical example is the set of goals hoped to be achieved in Milton Keynes, a new town between London and Birmingham:

- opportunities and freedom of choice;
- easy movement and access and good communication;
- balance and variety;
- an attractive city;
- public awareness and participation;
- efficient and imaginative use of resources.[23]

This set of goals and their elaboration point clearly to the emphasis laid on the social and human implications of building Milton Keynes. An examination of the regulations of the U.S. Urban Growth and New Community Development Act of 1970 (July 1971) shows that the main objectives of the act are in the realm of equalizing opportunities, while emphasizing the administration of federal assistance to minority groups—e.g., Paragraph 4, "Increase for all persons, particularly members of minority groups, the available choices of locations for living and working."

This emphasis on socially balanced communities is one of the most important justifications for U.S. governmental support of new towns, such as Jonathan, Minnesota; Park Forest South, Illinois, and Flower Mound, Texas.[24] New towns are suitable for achieving social goals since they provide a variety of housing types and prices that cater to a wide range of income groups and life styles. Moreover, because they are built by one development agency, private or public, it is possible to avoid discrimination and to administer government support and subsidies to underprivileged groups. The control over the general physical layout and the timing of building public services enhance the possibility of achieving a high level of public services and amenities for all sections of the new town. Dealing with all facets of urban life in a comprehensive way, which is one of the basic characteristics of a new town, takes it beyond the realm of providing housing and puts it in a position to create a complete way of life, one with strong public emphasis on the level of education, health service, social activity, recreation, and amenities.

The sheer newness of a new town tends to bring an openness and receptivity to innovation in urban life and public services. It provides a fertile ground for social innovation, for testing the feasibility of new methods of providing public services, and for experimenting with new ideas on the relationships between physical layout and human behavior.[25] These functions require a fast and efficient monitoring system that will record, evaluate, and disseminate results from the new-town experience in order that they may be implemented in existing cities. As it is evident that new towns are not going to be the major solution to urban problems, their function as centers of urban innovation diffusion and physical and social experimentation is becoming more important.

There is empirical evidence indicating that the two goals—of a socially balanced community on the one hand and a high quality of urban life on the other—appear to be contradictory to the prospective new-town dweller.[26] To overcome this conflicting image, a clear settlement policy is needed in connection with the social mix of the new town in order to enhance the opportunity for creating an integrated community while preserving a high level of amenities.

The British experience of establishing the social balance of the new towns has emphasized the occupational balance of the new towns' population, as compared to the occupational structure of the total population of Britain. According to Heraud's follow-up study, "A considerable degree of class balance has been achieved in the town as a whole, but neighbourhoods have begun to take on distinctive class characteristics."[27] It seems that the goal of a socially balanced community is attainable when the balance is determined by occupational structure. The attainment of this goal faces grave problems when the balance is determined by ethnic structure, as in the Israeli experience, or racial structure, as in the American experience.

The Israeli experience may prove valuable in analyzing the social goals of new towns. In addition to their spatial, economic, and political goals, the Israelis' policy has three goals in the social sphere: (1) decent housing and standard of living for immigrants to the country, (2) integration of the various ethnic groups within the Israeli society, and (3) closing the gaps existing between the veterans and the newcomers to the country.

Contrary to the existence of a spatial policy, which has guided decisions concerning the location, size, and economic base of the new towns, a detailed social policy to direct the attainment of the social goals has not been formulated. Nevertheless it is possible to arrive at several conclusions regarding the achievements of social goals in new towns. Decent housing on easy terms has been made possible

43

by the government's providing land at low prices to the various public developers, and by building on a large scale. In addition a subsidied rent system has been established for the first few years of residence. The end result of these measures has been the achievement of a housing standard in the new towns that is quite comparable to that of the veteran towns.[28]

The evidence concerning the attainment of social integration is rather mixed.[29] Some of the new towns have achieved a social and ethnic mix comparable to the national one, but most others have gradually become dominated by one ethnic group as a result of a highly differential out-migration process to the large cities. This process, although contrary to the goal of social integration on the local level, has brought an unexpected result during the last few years. The new towns are beginning to fulfill a symbolic role, one of achievement for the new immigrants of Oriental origins. This sense of achievement, won through hardship and struggle, may prove to be the most important social gain of the new-towns policy, fostering social and political integration not so much on a local level as on a regional and national level.

A major obstacle in achieving a wide range of economic opportunities, and thus enabling a wide spectrum of social groups to settle in new towns, has been the concept of the self-contained new town. It assumes a closure of the labor market and a complete provision of employment opportunities for the whole active population within the new town. This concept, aimed at reducing commuting time and costs, considerably limits the range of opportunities, the choice of occupations and the range of income levels. The results of several studies in Britain[30] and Scandinavia[31] show that, even when the number of employment positions in a new town equals the number of employees in that town, there exists a considerable exchange of in-commuters and out-commuters between the new town and the region. In order to achieve the goal of a socially balanced community, there seems to be no point in insisting on the closure principle for employment, especially in the existing new towns of a small size.

The new town on the edge of a metropolitan region—a new-town-intown[30]—may provide employment to a considerable part of its population while at the same time, it enables residents to make a choice from among the larger employment opportunities within the metropolitan region.[32] This organization of the labor market, part of which is in the new town and part of which is in the metropolitan region, lies at the base of the new concepts of a renewed spatial organization of metropolitan regions. These concepts forsee development along main axes served by a mass-transit system that would efficiently and quickly transfer new-town residents to the metropolitan core and other employment centers.

The concept of a new-towns policy integrated within a regional plan for restructuring the spatial organization of metropolitan areas is incorporated to varying degrees in the plans of Washington, D.C., London, Stockholm, Copenhagen, Paris, and Moscow. This type of new-towns policy will help to facilitate the attainment of the social goals of new towns and, at the same time, not hamper the economic opportunities of their inhabitants. New towns, socially balanced, innovatively designed and administered, emerging as a central component in regional metropolitan development, may prove to be the most important contribution of a new-towns policy in the developed countries of the world.

NOTES

1. This definition is based on Shirley F. Weiss, "New Cities," Panhandle Magazine (Spring 1971), p.19.

2. Town and Country Planning, XL, 1 (January 1972), 36-53.

3. D. Amiran and A. Shachar, Development Towns in Israel (Jerusalem: The Hebrew University, 1969), p.6.

4. A. K. Constandse et al., Planning and Creation of an Environment (The Hague: Royal Institute of Netherlands Architects, 1963), p. 67.

5. A. K. Constandse, "The Ijsselmeerpolders: An Old Project with New Functions," Tijdschrift voor Economische en Sociale Geografie, LXIII, 3 (May 1972), 207.

6. C. D. Harris, Cities of the Soviet Union (Chicago: Rand McNally, 1970), pp.50-53. I. Smolyar et al., "The Experience of the U.S.S.R. in the Planning and Construction of New Towns," in Report of the United Nations Seminar on Physical Planning Techniques for the Construction of New Towns (New York: United Nations, 1971), p.6.

7. P. Merlin, New Towns: Regional Planning and Development (London: Methuen and Company, 1971), pp. 193-215; B. Malisz, Physical Planning for the Development of Satellite and New Towns (Warsaw: Institut Urbanistyki i Architektury, 1966).

8. Ciudad Guayana Transportation Study, Corporacion Venezolena De Guayana (Caracas, 1970), p. 20.

9. L. Rodwin, ed., Planning, Growth and Regional Development (Cambridge, Mass.: M.I.T. Press, 1969), pp. 84-87.

10. D. F. Darwent, "Growth Poles and Growth Centers in Regional Planning—A Review," Environment and Planning, Vol. I, No. 1 (1969), p. 20.

11. I. Smolyar, et al., op. cit., p.9.

12. I. Davis, "Scottish New Towns," Habitat, Vol. XIII, No. 2 (1970), pp. 10-16.

13. On the economic consequences of subsidized housing in new towns, see N. Lichfield and P. Wendt, "Six English New Towns—A Financial Analysis," Town Planning Review, XL, 3 (October 1969), 297

14. A different evaluation of this possibility is in N. M. Hansen, Rural Poverty and the Urban Crisis (Bloomington: Indiana University Press, 1970), Ch. 10.

15. A. Shachar, "Israel's Development Towns: Evaluation of National Urbanization Policy," Journal of the American Institute of Planners, XXXVII, 6 (November 1971) 370.

16. B. J. L. Berry, "Urban Hierarchies and Spatial Organization in Developing Countries," Rehovot Conference Proceedings (Rehovot: The Weizmann Institute, 1971).

17. E. Brutzkus, Physical Planning in Israel (Jerusalem: Minist of the Interior, 1964), p. 20.

18. E. A. J. Johnson, The Organization of Space in Developing Countries (Cambridge, Mass.: Harvard University Press, 1970), Ch. 7.

19. Two empirical studies of the regional role of new towns are Y. Cohen, The Hierarchy of Commercial Services in Southern Israel (Rehovot: Settlement Study Center, 1969); and D. Soen, Interactions in Nazareth, Afula, Migdal Ha-Emek (Tel Aviv: Institute for Planning and Development, 1970).

20. W. Z. Hirsch, "The Supply of Urban Public Services," in H. S. Perloff and L. Wingo, eds., Issues in Urban Economics (Baltimo The Johns Hopkins Press, 1968), p. 508.

21. W. Alonso, The Economics of Urban Size (Berkeley, Calif.: Center for Planning and Development Research, 1970), Working Paper No. 138, pp. 13-17.

22. B. J. L. Berry, Geography of Market Centers and Retail Distribution (Englewood Cliffs, N.J.: Prentice-Hall, 1967), pp. 114-1€

23. Milton Keynes Development Corporation, The Plan for Milto Keynes (Wavendon, 1970), pp. 13-18.

24. On the justification of public subsidy to the U.S. new-towns policy see H. C. Hightower, "New Towns Policy Objectives and Inner City Social Issues," in S. F. Weiss et al., New Community Developme Vol. I (Chapel Hill, N.C.: Center for Urban and Regional Studies, 1971), pp. 149-69.

25. W. K. Vivret, "Planning for People: Minnesota Experimenta City," in S. F. Weiss et al., eds., op cit., pp. 247-60.

26. C. Werthman et al., Planning and the Purchase Decision: Why People Buy in Planned Communities (Berkeley, Calif.: Center for Planning and Development Research, 1965).

27. B. J. Heraud, "Social Class and the New Town," Urban Studi V, 1 (February 1968), 33-58.

28. For the most comprehensive comparison between the veteran towns and the new towns, see A. Berler, New Towns in Israel (Jerusalem: Israel Universities Press, 1970), pp. 79-109.

29. E. Cohen, "Development Towns—The Social Dynamics of Planted Urban Communities in Israel," in S. N. Eisenstadt et al., eds., Integration and Development in Israel (Jerusalem: Israel Universities Press, 1970), pp. 587-617.

30. A. A. Ogilvy, "The Self-Contained New Town, Employment and Population," Town Planning Review, XXXIX, 1 (April 1968), 38-54.

31. Merlin, op.cit., p. 104.

32. H. Perloff, "New Towns Intown," Journal of the American Institute of Planners, XXXII, 3 (May 1968), pp. 155-61.

3

ECONOMIC OPPORTUNITY
IN NEW TOWNS
Nathaniel Lichfield

New towns must offer their residents more than economic opportunities, but it is clear that good economic opportunities are vital
to the residents and to the success of the very concept of new town.
By "economic opportunities" I have in mind both the production and
consumption sides—a reasonable choice of a means of employment
that provides job satisfaction as well a sufficient level of income for
a good standard of living, coupled with the choice of opportunities
for enjoying income and leisure time with regard to a wide range of
public and private consumer goods and services. Just what these
rather vague words mean will become clearer throughout this study,
in which I will consider the issues under three main heads: (1)
what economic opportunities can a new town be expected to offer;
(2) what the new towns of Britain and Israel, which have each initiated
about thirty new towns since the late 1940s, have in fact offered; and
(3) how in any particular new town such offerings can be enhanced
by ongoing socioeconomic development planning as a contribution
toward a general process of community development planning.

ECONOMIC OPPORTUNITY AS RELATED TO
NEW-TOWN CHARACTERISTICS

Since the typical features of a new town are not necessarily
uniform, it will be apparent that the economic opportunities of any
new town must depend upon its particular characteristies. A number
of these are particularly important.

Purpose

The opportunities available in a town must derive from the prime purpose for which it was founded, recognizing that there is usually more than one purpose. Some instances are the offer of new employment in a town founded to open up resources in distant regions (Kitimat, B.C.); the need for dispersal of population from an over-crowded city (East Kilbride and Glasgow), or for decentralization in a national context (Israel); the fostering of a growth point in an area of economic decline (Washington, in northeastern England); the need to relocate people from settlements where the employment base has gone, in order to avoid their emigration from the region (Peterlee, in northeastern England). .

Size of Town

On the whole, new towns tend to be somewhat small in the typical urban size distribution; even in the recently planned Mark III new towns of Britain, the planned growth does not exceed 250,000 people. Thus opportunities must be geared to towns of relatively modest size, recognizing that they cannot be as great as those available in larger towns. Just what size is best for maximizing such opportunities has been explored in the literature relating to "optimum city size," but usually with inconclusive results. Closely related is the question of the place of the town in the urban hierarchy. The economic opportunities of a town depend on its situation in the urban hierarchy of settlements, according to the principles in central place theory. The higher they are in the hierarchy—and therefore the greater the draw of population from outside the town—the greater the opportunities for employment and its rewards, and the provision of local services for consumption. In terms of job opportunity, this is significant not only because the amount of employment is relatively high compared with the resident population of the town but also because the nature of export services (e.g., government, headquarters of firms) is such that they offer posts that are more rewarding in opportunities for salary increases, intellectual content, and pay. The larger the catchment area the greater the appeal to the white-collar worker. In terms of consumption, the greater the catchment area the greater the level of services to be provided.

Distance Between Towns in Subregion

Another variable is the travel distance between the new town in question and other towns, new or old, in the subregion of which the new town forms a part. The nearer such towns are to each other the greater the economic opportunities afforded to the new-town inhabitants. This is the situation in certain new towns north of London (Stevenage, Welwyn Garden City, Hatfield and Hemel Hempstead) that are within reasonable travel distance of a number of established towns (Letchworth, Hitchin, Luton, and St. Albans). This geographical juxtaposition in so-called urban clusters enables the towns to perform economic and social functions as a group of local economies. These, together, could offer the opportunities of a town equal to the total size of the units, with the qualification that spatial dimensions and traveling distance impose a different kind of economic life on the total community.

Regional Policy

Where a new town is located in a region of a country in which the government wishes to foster or restrain development in pursuance of policies of regional balance, these policies themselves and the means taken to implement them will affect the nature of the employment opportunities that are established in such a town. In Britain, for example, a new town built in an area of economic backwardness will attract the special grants and subsidies given to all towns in that area. Thus factories established in such towns would not be there without government financial inducements. By the same token the new towns that have been established in the London region, for sub-regional purposes of population dispersal from the metropolis, have not only failed to receive such financial advantage but have had their freedom for economic growth restricted by location of industry policies that give first priority to underdeveloped regions. The result has been the long-standing apparent conflict between two policies of government: the one seeking to build new towns in the more prosperous regions with the aid of government money, and the other restricting the opportunities for factories to locate there, in the light of national priorities on industrial location.

Stage of Development in the Town

So far we have been describing the varying influences on the opportunities in the new town in terms of its situation when completed—its size, situation in the hierarchy, distance from other towns, etc. But the issues of interest in the new town are not those at the date of its completion (ignoring for the moment the very difficulties in the concept of "completion" of a town that must by definition continue to grow or stagnate or decline) as much as those in the building-up of the new town. When it has been substantially "completed," it becomes just another town.

While the process of economic growth and development in a town is not yet fully understood, there is no doubt as to the differences in the various stages in its growth from inception to maturity. Hence in relation to the Israeli new towns, for example, four stages have been suggested. In the first, only the means of livelihood and existence is available, with a large part of incomes coming from government grants. In the second stage, economic opportunities are widened and the foundations laid for greater scope of work, education, sociocultural facilities, welfare, and local government. For the third, there is economic security and a higher standard of living so that the way forward is seen in terms of personal advancement in the economic, social, and political spheres. And finally there is a an economic takeoff, when the town is capable of surviving on its own, without any aid distinguishable from that given to other towns in the region.

From this it follows that not only do the economic opportunities available to a new town depend on the array of influences described above but on the point during the stages of the town's growth at which these influences come to bear. Moreover it is not to be expected that every new town will go through these stages in the same order, or indeed that the stages are clearly definable and discrete. The predominately private enterprise towns of the Gold Rush and Silver Rush of the western United States were extreme examples of great economic opportunities and wealth in an industry sensitive to the blast of economic recession (e.g., from exhaustion of the resource base), with consumer outlets of an expensive and sophisticated kind but with miserable public facilities. At the other extreme the early growth of an Israeli new town in the desert catering largely to immigrants was made possible by public welfare but without much economic opportunity for production or consumption.

Development and Management Agencies—
Objectives and Constraints

Given the essential purpose of the new town, the manner of its development and therefore the opportunities available to it will be influenced by the nature of the agencies concerned with its realization and ongoing management. There will be a large contrast between an agency in the public sector and one in the private sector. But no new town is completely public or private. For example, the Rouse Corporation in Columbia, Maryland, requires the participation of the utility and education districts; the British Development Corporation invites the participation of private capital in industrial and commercial developments; the ministries in charge of the Israeli new towns look to private firms for employment. These agencies set the tone according to their objectives and constraints. The British new towns incorporate among their objectives the urban and regional planning policies of the government, and they operate under the constraint that the land must be bought and retained by the development corporation and disposed of only by lease. This could influence the kind of firm that will come to the new towns, and consequently the opportunities it offers. New Towns must also operate according to the standards laid down by central government as the condition for using government funds—such standards as those relating to minimum floorspace in housing.

An example from Israel illustrates the possible repercussions of management policy, this time in relation to the housing provided. The government subsidizes new-town housing so that it attracts people of low income who are prepared for this reason to put up with otherwise poor conditions. But the government aims at housing for sale and not for rent, which then inhibits mobility, for the sale price of a house in a new town is insufficient to buy comparable housing in the city. This lack of mobility is considered to be an index of failure of the new towns in that their people are not able to take advantage of the opportunities for advancement that are available elsewhere.

WHO ARE THE NEW-TOWN POPULATIONS?

The previous section showed how the particular features of a new town determine the economic opportunities available; this section postulates that, since the population of new towns is not composed of a homogeneous group of individuals (in terms of age, sex, and other demographic characteristics), the economic opportunities that should be available for them need to be varied accordingly.

Table 3.1 shows the situation diagrammatically for a new town at any one moment in time, the "x" indicating the presence of particular socioeconomic groups derived from demographic characteristics.

Not only is there a tremendous variation in the demographic structure of a new town at any one time—which in itself will cause a need for a variety of services and outlets—but also there is likely to be continuous change in the structure over a period of time. Thus economic opportunities for the new-town population must be visualized as in constant need of change.

This still presumes a given population confined within a given area, but it is an artificial concept, primarily because of interurban migration. This is of particular significance in Israel, which has

52

TABLE 3.1

Categories of New-Town Population in
Production and Consumption

Population	Producers			Consumers			
	Active	Po-tential	Re-tired	Col-lective	Per-sonal	Direct	Depen-dent
Pre-working age							
Males 0-16		x					x
Females 0-16		x					x
In higher education							
Males 16-21		x		x	x		x
Females 16-21		x		x	x		x
Working Age							
Males 16-64	x			x	x	x	
Females 16-64	x			x	x	x	x
Retired							
Males 64+			x	x	x		x
Females 64+			x	x	x		x

seen a rapid turnover of population in the new towns, as immigrants have been directed or attracted to them. Then, after a period of assimilation, many have chosen to go elsewhere, frequently to the larger cities. The number of arrivals in the new towns taken as a whole over the years of town growth is three times the number of those remaining, after deducting for natural increase; in particular towns that are exposed to hostile conditions on the borders, the throughput has been as much as eight times greater.

Where there are nearby major urban centers, not only is there the need to consider their regional relationships when the new town is completely built, but also during the intervening years of the buildup, when the mutual work-commuting and service-center flows will change. It is surprising, therefore, that in Britain and Israel the planning studies for new towns have placed quite inadequate emphasis on the location of the town in its varied subregions, or on the implications for its growth on the competing and attracting forces in those subregions. In the new towns in Israel this has been particularly unfortunate, and the understandable assumption that they would be service centers for the surrounding rural areas has not been realized. This has been due to the very highly centralized institutions for marketing the products of Israeli agriculture, thus denying to the new-town residents the economic opportunities of providing services for the surrounding rural areas.

ECONOMIC OPPORTUNITIES COMPARED WITH WHAT?

The previous sections have reviewed what could be called the determinants of economic opportunities in new towns that give rise to differences between such opportunities in different towns, or within any country or between countries. These determinants will influence the discussions proceeding in the United States as to whether or not to build new towns and whether or not they should be part of a national urbanization strategy. Once it has been decided to build a new town, the determinants will figure in the regional and economic studies leading to the preferred location and design of the town in the planning stage. They should also be present in any assessment that is made of the success or failure of a new town in affording economic opportunities to its residents.

In these discussions and assessments, consideration will be given to efficiency (best use of resources) and equity (fairness in distribution). In both cases the comparison must be with welfare in the foregone alternative situation (the option that has not been taken), not only with the new-town population itself but also with other people who would be affected by the absence or presence of the new town. It is here that concepts of equity become pressing, for the question is whether or not there is a "widening of the gap" in distributive terms as between the alternatives.

If, for example, it is not feasible for lower-income groups to live in a new town, will conditions be easier for them—in terms of house filtering, congestion, etc.—in the metropolis that has been vacated by the higher-income groups? And if the higher-income new-town needs public subsidy of some kind, is it equitable to spend public money in this direction rather than to subsidize the poor? Or is the relevant consideration the "perceived" impact of opportunity denied, and thereby hardship to the underprivileged city population? In the Israeli situation, a reverse process is seen. Many of the new towns have former immigrants who had little choice in the past other than to settle where directed in a new town; then they could not afford to move. This government policy toward the new towns has thus denied these people the opportunities of city living.

New-Towns Programs in the National Context

Instead of comparing specific populations affected by the new town, directly or indirectly, the repercussions could be considered in terms of the country as a whole. The new-town program could have been influenced by government regional or national policies regarding location, regional development, etc; for example, to leave a greenbelt between the London new towns and the metropolis, or to open up the country as in Israel. Then, any limitation in economic opportunities of the inhabitants must be seen as part of the price they are paying for their contribution to the overriding government regional or national goals and policies aimed at the welfare of the whole population.

A clear example of this is in the Israeli new town of Qiryat Shemona, some few miles from the Syrian border, which is exposed to raiding attacks. The diminution in daily life suffered as a consequence of those attacks is part of the price the residents pay for the greater security of the state as a whole. In other words the Israelis of that new town have benefited in the national sense (given the correctness of the national goal of population dispersal) even though they have suffered by comparison with other Israeli citizens in other parts of the country.

This last consideration poses the question in quite different terms: what would happen to the people concerned, and to the national interest as a whole, if a new-towns program were not introduced at all. To find this basis for comparison some attempt must be made at prediction. This needs assumptions. To begin: in the absence of the new-towns program would the alternative be the absence of any national policy to influence the pattern and size of urban settlement? This could happen to the United States if no progress is made under the Housing and Urban Development Act of 1970. Should the assumption be nonetheless that the location and size of urban settlements would be under some form of control, such as under the British Town and Country Planning Acts system, or would the assumption be the sort of midway course likely to arise in Israel, where there are indeed national and district plans for the distribution of population, even if rendered somewhat ineffective by undercoordinated means of implementation.

Whatever the appropriate assumption, the essential question concerns the opportunities available to the people who would be located other than in new towns. This could be in the metropolitan areas toward which it is likely that the potential new-towns people would be attracted—thus posing a comparison of life in a small town with that in a large one, with residents being in suburbs (where the additional population must be housed) and employment and other opportunities being distributed elsewhere in industrial and commercial areas. But perhaps another comparison should be between life in small new towns and life in small established towns. This would be logical, given the proposition that people who are prepared to accept a small town are opposed to metropolitan way of life.

This comparison is in terms of the opportunities to the new-town population. But as indicated above, another comparison is important: the implications for the nation as a whole of differing patterns of urbanization. This is significant for both Britain and Israel, where the new-towns program has introduced a different hierarchy and distribution of urban settlements than would otherwise have existed, with implications for nationwide costs and benefits.

In England, for example, it is interesting to question what would have happened to the London metropolis had the dispersal policies not been undertaken. In Israel the same question applies to the country as a whole: what would have happened if there had been an even stronger buildup of the coastal belt, where the official Ministry of Interior plan still expects some 44 percent of a total population of 4 million in 1983, after some 35 years of a national dispersal policy?

Comparison with Intentions

Another possibility for comparative purposes in assessing the achievements of a new-towns program is that of intention. Regardless of whether the individual is better or worse off compared with where he might have been, the important question is whether he is as well off as he should have been, given the new-towns program and the intention behind it.

In Britain an early intention of the London new towns was that they should provide homes for the underprivileged in the London metropolis—those who were homeless or living in squalid conditions. However this aim was soon abandoned as impracticable, in that, given the intention and the need to build-up the industrial base of the new towns and attract employers, it was necessary to permit the industrialist to take with him and find locally employees of the kind that he needed, rather than saddle him with the necessity of manning his factories with people who had been selected for the new towns on the basis of residential underprivilege. This led to the Industrial Selection Scheme, whereby the residents of the town were largely those who chose to move from London to take up employment with an industrialist who was moving, or had already moved, to a new town. Thus, judged in terms of the former objective, the new towns have not succeeded; there is limited place for the underprivileged of the metropolis in the London new towns.

In Israel, difficulty arises in attempting to determine the formal goals of the government in establishing the new-towns program, and in attempting to trace the changes since then. Notwithstanding this, two simple goals have been maintained throughout the whole period of Israeli independence-the continued absorption of immigrants and the continued dispersal of population throughout the country, although there is difficulty in defining just what dispersal is, as well as its quantitative measure.

Comparison with Average

It will be apparent from the discussion that, while the "alternatives foregone" can be readily visualized, they cannot be so readily defined, forecast, and measured. In these circumstances, where the comparison is needed, it tends to be with some "average man," — national, regional, or urban. But while not answering all the questions, such a comparison is nonetheless revealing. It is the basis of the following discussion on the economic opportunities that have arisen in two countries with major new-town programs—Britain and Israel. For the latter there is reliance on two recent publications that cover all the new towns, whereas in the former, there being no such coverage, the reliance is on various isolated studies.

ECONOMIC OPPORTUNITIES IN
BRITISH NEW TOWNS

Standard of Living

It is sometimes forgotten that the prime reason most people in Britain go to a new town is to have better housing, and that the contrast between where they came from and where they now are is really very great indeed. For example virtually all people (between 95 percent and 98 percent) in the Hertfordshire new towns (outside of London) have exclusive use of an internal toilet; the comparable figure for Greater London is only 73.9 percent, and that for the inner boroughs is less than 66 percent. This kind of comparison could be extended to such things as hot water, bedrooms, and gardens, making the change from old to new very radical. The new-town residents are also better off in terms of car ownership: in the London new towns the average is 61 percent; in the outer metropolitan area, 59 percent; and in the Greater London Council Area, 42 percent.

These signs of the better life, however, do not come cheaply, and the financial burdens on the inhabitants are often very pressing. Rent is obviously going to take a higher proportion of net income. In Crawley and Stevenage the figure is 13.6 percent, against a national average of 9.2 percent. Also, as housing costs escalate, rents will have to rise. In the Mark II new towns, rents are likely to take about 20 percent of net income. And larger houses mean higher bills for heating and electricity.

If new-town families have come from furnished accommodations, their hire-purchase (time payment) commitments are likely to be heavy. In a survey carried out in 1968 in the Sutton Hill area of Telford, only 14 of 153 families were not buying goods on some form of credit scheme. In the same area, 10 percent of the families had rent arrears of 4 weeks or more. The strain on them, and on others who make ends meet only with difficulty, must be considerable. Life in the new towns, therefore, despite the seeming affluence of the cars and houses, can be quite burdensome.

Employment Prospects for Women and School-Leavers

No new town in its first generation of growth could hope to offer the range of employment available in the conurbation of origin. However the policies pursued by the development corporations make it unlikely that for the males who first emigrated to the new towns there will ever be a serious risk of unemployment on a scale abnormal to that of the population in general. These policies, however, were not necessarily designed for the employment of wives, nor were they primarily concerned with the problem of schoolchildren. Significant divergences from the national pattern in this respect could well have been expected. However, the rate for women in employment in the London new towns was, in 1966, exactly the same as in Greater London 37 percent. Thus it seems that, for whatever reasons (which may include an element of need greater than in "old" towns) there is work available for women.

One of the fears in the early days of the new towns was that there would be a huge surplus of labor when the children of the first immigrants reached school-leaving age. Lack of suitable job opportunities would, it was felt, force them to leave the new town for the old city. In view of these often-expressed fears, it is surprising that there has been no major survey of this aspect of new-town development. In fact the issue seems to have become forgotten. This, however, is perhaps a measure of the fact that it does not seem to be a problem. The factories of the first wave of incoming firms— typically engineering firms—have been followed by enough office-centered concerns to prevent this exodus. This increase in office and service industry will also extend the opportunities open to women, both mothers and school-leavers. The new town of Harlow feels capable of saying "The vast majority of school-leavers wishing to find employment in the town have been able to do so." The problem is, of course, a continuing one, and the "bulge" will be evident each year for every year of the town's rapid growth. But it does seem that, if the children want to stay in the town, there will be opportunities open to many, although, as in Stevenage, a substantial number of those who leave school early lack the skills required in the town and are compelled to seek employment elsewhere.

Social Mobility

Career building also appears to have happened among the adult population. Table 3.2 shows that inhabitants tend to move up the socioeconomic scale after entering a new town.

TABLE 3.2

Harlow: Mobility of Occupation—Heads of
Households Only, 1970

Classification of Occupation	Number	
	At Date of Survey	On Arrival in Harlow
Professional managerial	707	522
Intermediate professional and managerial	2,229	1,556
Skilled	10,150	9,138
Partly skilled	3,003	3,666
Unskilled	457	642
Not employed (incl. schoolchildren)	2,079	3,101
Total	18,625	18,625

Source: Report of the Harlow Development Corporation, 1972.

59

As the table shows, there has been an increase in numbers of the professional, managerial, and skilled, and a decrease in the partly skilled and unskilled. Clearly, therefore, there are opportunities to progress toward higher status jobs.

A similar situation, although achieved by different means, is happening at Corby. There, as a matter of policy, the local steelworks the major employer—takes on unskilled workers and trains them for semiskilled and skilled jobs. Thus the intake for the new town include 16 percent from the unskilled classes—twice the national average—with nearly all of these people moving into a higher socioeconomic grouping after training.

ECONOMIC OPPORTUNITIES IN ISRAELI NEW TOWNS

The Israeli new-towns program was massive by any comparative standard and was carried out at a time of great economic and political difficulty, absorbing population from up to 80 different countries. Inevitably it encountered many problems. This led to widespread discussion and debate on the future of the new towns, and Mordechai Bentov, then the minister of housing, asked for a study leading to a report on achievements and the current situation, suggestions as to alternative strategies that could be pursued, and a recommendation following an evaluation of the alternatives. In addition, recommendations were requested regarding improvements in the practice of developing new towns in Israel, with emphasis on the improvements needed.

The study included a comparative review of the achievements of the new towns in socioeconomic development, leading to a statement of the problems that need to be tackled in devising strategies.[1] In this review the following factors were examined: the absorption of immigrants, the growth of population, the ethnic character of the population, age and family size, incomes and ownership of durable goods, labor force and patterns of employment, output of labor and capital, investment in industrial facilities, investment in human resources, consumption and purchasing power. Some of the pertinent conclusions that follow are necessarily in a summarized and generalized form, which cannot give an accurate picture for each new town; furthermore since the emphasis was on the problems, the successes in the towns are concealed. The conclusions are:

1. The most characteristic trait of an Israeli development town is the unusual composition of its population, a predominant feature being the large number of post-1948 immigrants. Within the two major ethnic groups of immigrants (European-American

60

and Afro-Asian), there is a mixture of "foreign" social and cultural backgrounds, which gives rise to difficulties in adjustment to Israeli society. However, through the dynamics of out-migration, a consistent trend toward social as well as ethnic homogeneity is evident.

2. The average family size in the new towns is four persons; it is estimated that there is one wage earner per family.

3. Average income per wage earner was 246 Israeli pounds per month in 1968, compared with a national average income per urban family of I£665. Average income per capita is I£112.5 for new-town residents, compared with I£200 for urbanites.

4. Labor force participation in the new towns is low but increasing.

5. Rates of employment are high in industry and agriculture, and low in services.

6. In most of the new towns there is a high rate of friction unemployment.

7. Productivity tends to be low. Since there is a positive correlation between capital per worker and output of the worker in the new towns, and no significant relationship between productivity and size of industry, differences in productivity are explained by external or internal advantages or by differences in the quality of the manpower in the towns.

8. Opportunities for education in the new towns have been limited. Little has been achieved in the improvement of the education and social advancement of the older residents, as opposed to their children. Those who are able leave as soon as possible, to seek advancement in other settlements.

9. Since the educated and the skilled tend to emigrate from the towns, the socioeconomic level of new-town populations consistently declines. Thus the towns tend toward an ethnic, educational, occupational and income homogeneity on the lower socioeconomic level.

10. The generally downward trend in the towns tends to be self-perpetuating. The decreasing attractiveness of the towns continues, which in turn leads to further out-migration. Those who can offer leadership, mainly the middle classes and the young people after completing military service, require improved services, increases in purchasing power, and better labor opportunities.

11. The towns' failure to function as regional focuses has repercussions on the establishment of their economic base, since they are deprived of agricultural processing and related services. While employment in mining and mineral processing provides a substantial part of the economic base in some of the towns, the agricultural sector employs only the least skilled of the urbanites, who contribute little of the towns' income.

The principal general conclusion that emerges with regard to the new towns is that they are unable to compete successfully with the large cities, in terms of the opportunities for standard of living and level of affluence they provide for their populations. Among the major reasons for this situation is the newness of the towns, most of which have not yet approached the point of economic takeoff, their geographical location vis-à-vis the country's urban centers, and a lower level of economic productivity.

Evaluation of Alternative Development Strategies for the New Towns

As mentioned above, one objective of the study was the recommendation of a strategy for the future planning of the new towns, following evaluation of alternatives. This is of interest here since the evaluation itself brings out the difference in the potential socioeconomic opportunities in the new towns under the different strategies.

Regarding the constraints on the recommendations that could be made (closing down none of the towns and setting up no new ones), the alternative strategies revolved around the disposition of the expected growth of population in the country as between the new towns and the rest of the country, and as between the new towns themselves. This expected growth in the new towns is significant, amounting approximately to 400,000 more between 1969 and 83, 500,000 more by 1993, and 500,000 more by the year 2000.

From these population figures, the consequential implications and repercussions were worked out in terms of three planning strategies that were alternatives to the official plan of the Ministry of Interior. These strategies were planned around the concepts of urban clusters, growth centers, and axial development. In addition, a strategy was developed under the name of "existing trends," based on the proposition that past and present development trends and implementation policies would not be altered. There were thus five alternative possibilities for evaluation. Each possibility was specified as a package of urban developments (housing, jobs, roads, etc.).

The evaluation of the alternatives with a view to recommending a preference assumes as a datum for comparison that existing trends would continue. As indicated earlier, the evaluation was carried out as far as practicable in relation to what would have happened otherwise. The methodology was planning balance sheet analysis. Although there is no call in this study to discuss this evaluation process, the overall result is of interest.

Compared with the projection of existing trends, each of the planning hypotheses put up by the study team was superior in terms of net community benefits; of these hypotheses the urban clusters strategy was clearly the best. But when comparing this with the Ministry of Interior's official plan there were seen to be advantages for the latter (largely economic output) and advantages for the former (largely social). Thus the evaluation led to the conclusion that neither of these two could be judged to be the better on the information available. Therefore the recommended course was that the urban clusters hypothesis be put forward for detailed study, alongside the official plan, with a view to evolving a sixth strategy that cuts out the disadvantages of both and combines their advantages.

THE NEED FOR SOCIOECONOMIC DEVELOPMENT PLANNING

In discussing the repercussions of typical features of a new town on its economic opportunities, reference was made earlier to the question of management. We return to this now in reply to the following question: once the planning has been completed and the town started, how can its growth be managed in such a way as to enhance the economic opportunities that will be available to its people, however such opportunities are defined? It is in this sense that we refer to the need for socioeconomic development programs.

The initiation of a new town begins with some plan and program of development, based on the studies that have been undertaken, including the economic planning studies. The program is concerned with several factors. First, there are the factors associated with the attempts to bring to the town the productive enterprises of all sectors indicated by the economic plans. This involves setting up appropriate conditions in the town (in terms of good environment, space for building, communications and utility services, means of access, and labor in appropriate quantity and skill), as well as attempting to attract such enterprises by means of dissemination of information, promotion, and establishing active links with investment agencies and cities where there could be firms wishing to decentralize. The latter presupposes the necessity for accumulation of information about the town, its potential and plans, which would be of interest to inquiring industrialists.

In many of the towns, the initial aims are simply the attraction of any employment opportunities. But as the towns grow, their needs in terms of employment opportunities should also influence the search for employers. For example there are such matters as levels of income that can be paid, prospects of growth in the industry in question—and therefore prospects of a bright future for its employees, career and training prospects within firms, the possibility of mutually benificial linkages between established and new firms, diversity of employment to minimize the impact of economic recession, and freedom from environmental pollution. As time goes on, each of the towns can be regarded as an industrial complex with a dynamism of its own, always of course in relation to the surrounding area and the nation. Another interest is the attraction of firms that are export-orientated, in the sense that they will be producing goods and services for consumption outside the town and so attract income to the town. This of itself increases the multiplier effect by attracting dependent jobs.

As a counterpart to the attraction of employment, it is necessary for the town to prepare its labor force for its objectives. This involves vocational training programs with a view to retraining those whose skills can find no outlet, and also the training of others for the kinds of skills that employers are seeking—for example, in the management and operation of modern plants and in the white-collar skills that are necessary for efficient administration. The broader education that equips people for wider responsibilities must come alongside this vocational education.

So far we have been dealing wtih management of the town's economic program in the sense of production. But there is also the corresponding need to manage the town's social program in the sense of ensuring that opportunities exist for different kinds of consumer services on which residents will depend: those they can command directly by expenditures from their pockets, those they can demand collectively through the expenditures of taxes, and also those provided outside these two in the form of voluntary services. These are part of what can be called the social development program. In passing, it can be mentioned that the adequate provision of such services could fall as much on those concerned with the economic, as opposed to the social, development plan, since the need is to promote and attract the appropriate enterprise, private or public.

In relation to the community facilities described, there are many needs. First, an agency must be found to undertake the provision of various facilities. Where there is no existing institution for the purpose, then some alternative means must be found, either through the promotion of an appropriate institution or through local initiative. In general terms the role of those responsible for building the new towns is seen as catalytic in this sphere by ensuring that all are aware of the need for the facilities, by promoting their provision through official bodies and voluntary associations, or in the last resort by their undertaking the responsibility themselves. Such stimulus is needed to ensure not only that the facilities in question are provided but also that they are provided when needed in the life of the community—and not delayed in their provision, as is so often the case with nonremunerative services.

TOWARD COMMUNITY PLANNING AND
PROGRAMMING FOR NEW TOWNS

Socioeconomic development programs for new towns would go a long way toward ensuring that economic opportunities, in the full sense described in this study, can be advanced for the new-town residents to the greatest practicable degree. But such programs would still be only part of the effort needed to create a healthy and happy community in building the towns. To do this the concept of socioeconomic development planning and programming needs extension.

However different the purpose, location, and institutional setup of the various new towns, there is one common purpose that is generally accepted: the introduction of improved ways of building new communities. Indeed new towns throughout the world are taken as opportunities to demonstrate how urban life could be conducted, in contrast to the way that it is conducted in older areas, particularly metropolitan areas. Pushed further this common purpose could be described as aiming at advancing the development of human beings in these towns—as human development. This in itself recognizes that the human being is, at one and the same time, an individual, a member of a close or extended family, and a member of a different array of groups that we call communities. And if the conflict between national and local goals in new-town building is borne in mind, the local community is also part of the national community. In all these respects the individual needs opportunities to develop the human qualities with which he is endowed.

The degree of advancement possible is necessarily geared to opportunities, not only in the economic sense, however broadly this is interpreted, but in other senses too. The resultant is currently being described as "quality of life." This need has been recognized in the British new towns with the appointment from the outset of social development officers alongside other members of the corporation staff teams. The role of such an officer is seen as being that of social adviser in the initial design, and one who helps in the continuing work of developing conditions that provide maximum satisfaction of the residents. His duties are varied: to collaborate in the planning stage of the town from the social planning viewpoint; to stimulate the widest possible provision of community facilities; to provide public relations and information; and to carry out research on the population coming to and leaving the town.

Although the British new towns have had social development officers from the outset, they have only just begun to appoint development officers to carry out comparable tasks in respect to the economy of the towns themselves. This function is performed, if at all, by so-called estates officers, who are comparable to real estate

65

consultants in the United States. The economy of the town is thus seen through the eyes of land economics.

The lack of this type of specialized assistance is even more pronounced in the Israeli new towns. For one thing, there is no development corporation or similar centralized body essentially responsible for the new towns themselves. The responsibilities are spread throughout various ministries, with the Ministry of Housing taking the primary role. One result of this is the absence of a multidisciplinary team that can collaborate on the planning and development of the new towns; teams that do exist are heavily oriented toward physical development (architecture, engineering) rather than the social sciences.

Thus there are gaps in these respects in both the British and Israeli programs. This has led to the proposals in the Israeli study for advancement on the following lines.

First, the need was seen not only for socioeconomic development programs but also for widening the concern of such programs toward the broader concept of human development, for which was evolved the term "community development"—recognizing that the term had various meanings and was used in various ways. For the purpose of the study, it was taken to mean the creation of an organization in which people can be happy according to their own lights. This organization would aim at the socioeconomic development programs referred to above, the right kind of local government machinery for an ongoing community, the need to coordinate the various activities carried out under the heading of community development, the need to monitor the happenings in the community with a view to evaluation feedback and review, and the need for public participation.

But if such organization for community development were to prosper, then its operations would need to be considered both in planning the town and in carrying out the town's physical development. Put more precisely, if planning for people is to be taken as a reality, then the plans for the welfare of those people in the broadest sense must be put at the forefront of the planning process for a new town. Thus the report also went on to show how the various processes— plan making, physical development, and community development— should be considered as one interrelated process concentrated on the provisions of a healthy community life.

Thus we turn full circle to the opening of this study. Economic opportunities are certainly not the sole need for the inhabitants of a new town, but they are important, particularly if their provision is seen as part of the wider opportunities that people need as human beings. It is the role of community development planning to make provision for these wider opportunities, including economic opportunities.

NOTE

1. Arie Shachar, "The Development Towns of Israel: A National Policy of Urbanization and Spatial Organization," Rehovot Conference Proceedings (Israel, 1971).

BIBLIOGRAPHY

British New Towns

Cooke, R. L. "An Analysis of the Age Structure of Immigrants to New and Expanding Towns," Journal of the Town Planning Institute, Vol. 54, (1968), pp. 430-36.

Howard, Ebenezer. Garden Cities of Tomorrow. Rev. ed., London: Faber and Faber, 1965.

Moss, Jennifer. "New and Expanded Towns: A Survey of the Demographic Characteristics of Newcomers," Town Planning Review, Vol. 39 (1968), pp. 117-39.

Osborn, Frederic J. and Arnold Whittick. The New Towns: The Answer to Megalopolis. London: Leonard Hill, 1963.

Reports of the British new-town development corporations.

Rodwin, Lloyd. The British New Towns Policy. Cambridge, Mass: Harvard University Press, 1956.

Ruddy, Sheila A. Industrial Selection Schemes, An Administrative Study. Birmingham: Centre for Urban and Regional Studies, University of Birmingham, 1969. Occasional Paper No. 5.

Schaffer, Frank. The New Town Story. London: MacGibbon & Kee, 1970.

Seeley, Ivor H. Planned Expansion of Country Towns. London: George Godwin, 1968.

Speigel, Erika. New Towns in Israel. New York: Praeger Publishers 1967.

Thomas, Ray London's New Towns: A Study of Self Contained and Balanced Communities. London: Political and Economic Planning, 1969.

Town and Country Planning, Vol. XL, No. 1 (January 1972).

Israeli New Towns

Amiran, D. and A. Shachar. Development Towns in Israel. Jerusalem: The Hebrew University, 1969.

Berler, Alexander. New Towns in Israel. Jerusalem: Israel Universities Press, 1970.

Shachar, Arie. "The Development Towns of Israel: A National Policy of Urbanisation and Spatial Organisation," Rehovot Conference Proceedings. Israel, 1971.

4

CAN THE UNITED STATES
LEARN FROM THE EXPERIENCE
OF OTHER COUNTRIES?
A COMMENTARY
Neil C. Sandberg

Much of the dialogue on new towns has been advanced from polarized positions, with critics tending to be strongly for or against them. Some have opposed U.S. investment in new towns because the towns have not fulfilled their promise. Others have supported them, believing they represent an opportunity to start anew in dealing with the problems of a rapidly urbanizing society.

The essential need, it seems to me, is for a realistic appraisal of what has been promised, what has been delivered, and what has not been attempted at all—at least in any meaningful way. To begin with it should be recognized that the creation of planned new towns is a relatively recent phenomenon, with most efforts of any consequence dating from after World War II. Hence the analysis of successes and failures must of necessity concentrate largely on the experience of only one generation, a rather small time frame from which to make longterm judgments. Furthermore the much-heralded social experimentation and innovation of new towns is, on closer examination, more the illusion of unfulfilled dreams than the reality of actual implementation. There are, to be sure, a number of new-town models that represent important contributions to the study of social, economic, political, and environmental factors. It is important, however, to assess these ventures carefully and selectively, so that our conclusions reflect thoughtful considerations rather than sweeping generalizations.

THE REALITIES OF SOCIAL DIFFERENTIATION

One of the most widely held notions of new-town observers is that such towns have been centers for experiments in social differentiation that have usually ended in failure. While it is true that the rhetoric of new towns has been and is today focused on the concept of a balanced population, few serious attempts have ever been made to fully achieve this ideal. In Letchworth, Welwyn Garden City, and many other places, we find that the realities of social stratification were accepted from the beginning through the structuring of separate neighborhoods based on income. And even in the most utopian scheme it was not really assumed that the upper classes would give up their life styles to move to new towns. The real problem has been with the lower-income groups, which usually have not received the social and economic supports needed to attract and maintain them in a new milieu Given these limitations, therefore, it seems fair to say that most new towns have a reasonable representation of the working, middle and upper-middle classes, which make up the greatest proportion of the general population.

With respect to achieving a mix of incomes, both in new towns and elsewhere, the United States has much to learn from Britain and other countries. Public housing provides nearly 50 percent of new housing annually in Britain and accounts for 28 percent of the total stock of housing units. (Over two-thirds of the dwellings in new towns receive government subsidies). Since public housing is not looked down upon, it serves people of varied incomes. The key element is that people whose incomes go up are encouraged to stay on at higher rentals, as opposed to the U.S. practice of removing the upwardly mobile, thereby creating a caste of impoverished problem families.

In Israel the situation has been quite different, with those from the lowest socioeconomic groupings representing the bulk of the new-towns population. Although the Israeli experience has been one of the most serious attempts at social and ethnic differentiation, the Israeli new towns have not been able to provide the economic, cultural, and social amenities needed to attract and hold a middle-class population It was only after they began to utilize improved social planning approaches, selecting skilled persons who were given housing and tax subsidies and were offered challenging employment, that a measure of balance was introduced in such places as Arad.

The mix of socioeconomic groupings has been encouraged in a number of other countries with varying degrees of success. In the Finnish new town of Tapiola, with substantial government backing of mortgage loans, there are unskilled and skilled blue-collar workers and white-collar and professional people living in close proximity, many in the same multiple structures or in adjacent housing. In Sweden half of all families with children receive state and local housing allowances, with a system of rent control and housing grants to low-income families and government loans to builders; in Denmark more than half the population of the new town of Albertslund benefit from rent supplements.

Most of those who have moved to new towns have been relatively young, although over time the age distribution has tended to equalize with that of the general population. As a means of securing an earlier and more representative proportion of the elderly, a number of promising experiments are being conducted. In Thamesmead, a new-town-intown type of development in London, and Skärholmen, one of the satellite towns of Stockholm, clear social objectives are being emphasized through the creation of high-rise apartments for the elderly, including nursing services and systems of "wardens." These are located in the central parts of the towns near shops, services and, most important, younger people. Other new towns also have buildings for the aged but they are frequently separated from the center and isolated from communal activities.

In Tapiola, individual units have been placed adjacent to a school-yard, so the elderly can enjoy watching and listening to the children at play. Telford, in England, is also encouraging the integration of age groups both in housing and recreational areas, using a center and the schools as places for age-related recreational activities. Some new towns distribute the elderly throughout the community; and in Harlow, connected apartments are available for grandparents wishing to maintain the extended family. All of these efforts should be studied carefully over time to see which of them prove to be most successful.

THE DELIVERY OF SERVICES

A broad complex of social services is provided for all segments of society in a number of foreign nations. Hence there are satisfactions in new towns and elsewhere in having full social care throughout the life cycle. On the negative side, a high tax base has been developed to pay for these services and there are overstructured public bureaucracies that often adversely affect delivery systems. Thus, while health care tends to be very good, a six-month wait for a dental appointment in Tapiola or a lengthy crosstown trip for a pediatric examination in Stockholm suggest that public programs can be a mixed blessing.

One of the major problems of new towns is that health and welfare services, recreational opportunities, and other amenities are not usually available in the early stages of development. This may well be an important factor contributing to some of the social and psychological malaise so frequently observed in new towns. The trend in Britain toward building on already existing towns promises to alleviate this situation somewhat, since a variety of services is available immediately in the older areas. Thus we find attractive shopping centers and other amenities in Telford, Peterborough, and elsewhere serving an early need in the evolution of these communities.

THE NEED FOR SOCIAL PLANNING

One of the striking anomalies of a number of the European countries and Israel is that social planning is not very advanced. This is particularly interesting for, as a consequence of their socialist orientations and the creation of a broad complex of social welfare programs, it could well have been expected that meaningful social planning processes would have been developed. We find instead, with some exceptions, that planning for new towns is geared to physical and economic concerns and less to social needs, particularly the problems of the poor and the minorities.

Social planning (as distinguished from social welfare) may be defined in Perloff's terms as "an interrelated system that introduces socio-economic and human behavior considerations into the making of governmental and private group decisions." The critical need is for the integration of physical, economic, and social planning at the national level, because social gains often depend on the use of the power of the national government. This can facilitate the establishment and ranking of social goals, the creation of programs for human resources development and problem solving, and the collection of data for systematic analyses of social indicators that can tell us how new towns may be improved.

In Britain, despite the provisions of the Town and Country Planning Act of 1968, there is only marginal emphasis on the social environment. This may be related to the fact that social development officers in new towns have great responsibility for a variety of social programs and services, but they have very little power, limited resources for long-range planning, and no budgets of their own. Their efforts are not supported by the national leadership and usually depend on the whim of the corporation manager of each town. Those who work in the field tend to be knowledgeable and skillful but are locked into a political situation locally and nationally that makes it extremely difficult for them to be effective. Consequently, in the effort to integrate social and physical planning, the social end is submerged and social planning is often considered unmentionable.

Despite these limitations a number of the social development people have created innovative and useful programs. Officials of Milton Keynes have moved into the Lambeth section of London, an area predominantly poor and black, to aggressively recruit such families by offering better jobs and housing, while seeking to overcome fears of the new environment and attachments to the old. And within the towns themselves, the social development officer is frequently a powerful force for improved communication and community organization. Thus we find a Pakistani-Anglo community relations committee in Telford, a cooperative pub in Thamesmead, and a children's play council in Peterborough—all of which serve as important vehicles for involvement. Social development was also reinforced in Peterborough by having community workers on the job before any newcomers arrived.

RESEARCH ON SOCIAL FACTORS

A serious limitation of planning and programming in many European countries is the virtual absence of useful social science research. This may be due in part to the tendency to think of cities as physical structures with populations and technological bases rather than as systems of social organization and social relationships. The real deficiency has been the inability to understand and deal with the attitudes, ideas, and personalities of those who live in the cities and who are engaged in the processes of collective behavior. This is especially true with respect to the paucity of data available for social planning for the poor and the minorities. There is some evidence to suggest that we tend to deal with that which is easiest to measure rather than the less discernible aspects of life quality and human need. It is also apparent that actions are frequently taken without the benefit of adequate studies and data.

The problem is underscored by the fact that academicians and public officials in Britain and Scandinavia manifest relatively little interest in intergroup relations and research, frequently ignoring the ethnic diversity of their respective societies. Moreover they tend to overlook the ongoing processes of migration and mobility that in recent years have motivated many individuals to seek economic opportunity in foreign countries.

With the onset of declining economies and rising unemployment, competition for jobs has contributed to serious tensions between the native and foreign populations. Thus, for example, in the new town of Tensta near Stockholm, there are problems stemming from the belief of some Swedes that foreign workers from Southern Europe and North Africa are parasites exploiting the economy. This is compounded by cultural and language differences, which often make communication and social interaction difficult.

In Britain, the situation is even more complex, with some 1.5 million Asians and blacks and large numbers of Italians, Poles, and others, many of whom live in enclaves. These ethnics tend to have limited power with only marginal political representation and influence. Moreover their efforts to have a more significant voice in matters of group interest are leading to conflicts, including race riots—conditions that focus attention on the inadequate mechanisms for dealing with intergroup relations.

A contributing factor was the shortsighted view of the Conservative government, which saw little need for social science inquiry and which crippled the nation's research programs in the 1950s. More recently, however, as a consequence of growing societal conflicts as well as the need to understand the rapid processes of change, new research efforts have been initiated under the auspices of such groups as the Center for Environmental Studies.

Although its efforts are very largely oriented toward physical and economic concerns, the Center recently completed a study of the factors that inhibit the movement of disadvantaged minorities of new towns. (The "minorities" are defined as blacks, Asians, the elderly, the disadvantaged, and the unskilled.) These factors include the desire of some racial and social groups to remain with others like themselves; the element of prejudice; the lack of information on available opportunities for housing and jobs; and the tendency for ethnic groups to be unskilled, which is related to the lack of suitable jobs and training opportunities.

Only recently, the Social Science Research Council's Unit on Ethnic Relations was established to fill the glaring gap in the study of ethnic groups and intergroup relations. Among the unit's early projects are investigations of identity problems among first-generation Asians, the structure of the majority community in Leeds, and the factors pertaining to discrimination in housing. While these studies should prove useful in the shaping of British public policy, they will have less meaning for the United States, where social science research has had significant support over many years.

THE CASE FOR GOVERNMENT PARTICIPATION

It has been suggested that the strong political authority of national government is a critical ingredient in the process of creating new towns and achieving national urban goals. Some believe the leadership of government may be needed, because private developers often lack the ability to take care of vital social, economic, and political requirements. These requirements include the planned move of industrial and commercial enterprises from the cities to the towns, with appropriate incentives and supports; the use of public funds for financing—particularly for low-income housing and essential public services; the reorganization of existing political jurisdictions into comprehensive regional mechanisms; and the assemblage of land and the creation of a system through which workers may be placed in job-linked housing.

Government-sponsored new towns can also be helpful in changing current patterns of urban and suburban growth, particularly if viewed in the context of regional development. They can influence the housing

74

supply for low- and moderate-income families, provide for optimum use of space and recreation areas, stimulate the economic and social development of backward regions, and contribute to an orderly growth process in which environmental quality is a paramount value. Consequently government participation in the planning and building of new-towns may be the critical factor in accomplishing a broad range of social and human goals.

The involvement of government is not an unmixed blessing, however, for both at the national and local levels in a number of countries the major policy decisions are often made independent of elected local authorities and without citizen participation. Nationally the Department of Environment in Britain exercises enormous power in the allocation of resources, so that, for example, the desires of Harlow and Welwyn Garden City to expand are effectively thwarted. Locally the partnership of new-town development corporations and urban district councils (as well as other jurisdictions) is an unequal one in which the corporations have the major power. Even after reaching maturity, some of the towns are guided by the New Towns Commission, an arm of the Department of Environment. This benign influence is reinforced by the devices created to assign people to housing through government ownership and control of rental property.

THE PHYSICAL ENVIRONMENT

Although social motivation has been a primary concern of many new-town builders, the emphasis has been on a kind of environmental determinism, in the belief that the physical surroundings would have a sociocultural effect. This is evidenced in such places as Tapiola and Stevenage, where it was felt that the physical neighborhood would generate social cohesion and community. However, as a result of differences in life styles and changing patterns of physical and social mobility, we have observed complex processes of social interaction across large physical areas.

Nonetheless experiments aimed at providing more satisfying physical and social environments are continuing. They hold out the possibility if not the promise of creating meaningful places for living on a human scale. This was the basis of the "integrational habitational unit" developed in Kiryat Gat, Israel, where the use of a variety of building types placed around open malls and parks, with walkways, playgrounds, and public spaces, provided a psychological and architectural focus for the integration of diverse elements. Thus the close proximity of functions on a manageable scale was seen as a means of reforming rather than rejecting city life.

Not enough is being done to study the impact of the environment on human behavior and to see if space can be used therapeutically for the alleviation of physiological, psychological, and sociocultural stress in a technological society. It may be useful to ask if a physical environment can be planned to help us deal with the cultural shock of interacting with others who are different, the association of mental health difficulties with mobility, the belief that alienation may be influenced by rapid change, and the impact on human health of such physical stressors as noise.

The emphasis on the physical environment has also been reflected in those new-towns where natural and man-made beauty have been viewed as essential to an urban community. We have seen a variety of efforts ranging from the greenbelts and open spaces of some of the British new-towns to the creation of a skyline in Kivenlahti in order to distinguish it from Tapiola as one comes in from the sea. Regrettably, and possibly as a consequence of economic considerations, the trend in the more recent new-towns appears to be toward environments of concrete. This tendency is opposed by young people in Sweden and elsewhere who are pressing for environmental quality and better life styles. In effect they are asking if market factors and growth needs require the rape of the environment, or if change can be effected in a more humane way.

CONCLUSION

The comparative study of new-towns tends to support the belief that the new-towns idea is still vital—despite many errors of omission and commission and the differential accomplishment of various countries. If we in the United States accept the view that there is something to learn from those who have had years of new-town experience, and if we approach the subject prudently and selectively, then we have much to gain in our own programs. If, on the other hand, we reject the large body of knowledge available to us purely on the basis of structural and ideological differences, then we have much to lose.

In the next few decades we can anticipate a growth in the U.S. population of an estimated 50-100 million persons. As a result already congested urban areas may well be affected by a rapidly deteriorating environment and from the human and social problems stemming from social dislocation, changing patterns of family and group living, overcrowding, and intergroup conflict.

The view that we can continue indefinitely the current practices of mismanaging and abusing our urban environments seems shortsighted. At the same time it is foolish to expect that new-towns will solve all our urban problems.

What is needed is a realistic appraisal of the opportunities they present, as well as their shortcomings. It is also important to recognize that they represent only one avenue for urban reform and renewal, and that an even greater commitment is needed to our existing urban areas, particularly the inner cities that hold the victims of poverty and prejudice. It is to be hope that these will not prove to be mutually exclusive options.

THE EVOLVING
FEDERAL
NEW COMMUNITIES
PROGRAM

THE FEDERAL
NEW COMMUNITIES PROGRAM:
PROSPECTS FOR THE FUTURE
Hugh Mields, Jr.

The federal New Communities Program passed into law in 1968, and made its first loan guarantee commitment in October 1970 to the satellite new town of Jonathan, located 20 miles southwest of Minneapolis, Minnesota. By October 1972, the U.S. Department of Housing and Urban Development (HUD) had approved twelve more new community developments in seven additional states (see Table 5.1). The projected aggregate population at peak development of these thirteen HUD-approved new communities is estimated at well over 700,000 people. They are expected to produce over 244,000 new dwelling units, some 60,000 of which are planned to be for low- and moderate-income families.

It is still not clear just how these thirteen new communities, plus the ten to twenty more that HUD is expected to approve within the next two years, will ultimately affect the quality of urban life in the United States. There is by no means universal agreement or optimism concerning the potential of the new-towns program, nor is there any certainty that the bureaucrats who are responsible for its administration will deliver as Congress intended.

It is the purpose of this study to present the case that the Title VII new towns show promise of being a desirable new generation of communities in America, and are a significant social and environmental departure from the large developments that marketed themselves as "new towns" in the 1960s.*

---

*Only a handful of the 63 large developments analyzed by HUD in 1969 had industry and were socially integrated, and not one had any substantial amount of low- and moderate-income housing.

It is also the purpose of this chapter to point out that the program is under way, and that the next five years should provide enough action and experience for proponents and critics alike to subject the program to evaluation based on practice, not hypothesis; thus what is important is that the program be given a fair measure of support and resources, and thereby a fair chance to succeed as Congress intended.

WHY A NEW-COMMUNITIES PROGRAM?
CONGRESSIONAL INTENT

Congress intended that the new-towns program encourage a new style of community building as an alternative to the conventional, disparate residential tract-shopping center-industrial park development that has characterized urban expansion and renewal in our metropolitan areas in the past. The basic objectives of the New Communities Program as expressed by Congress in Title VII of the Housing and Urban Development Act of 1970 were to encourage the creation of planned, largely self-sufficient communities, developed in an orderly manner consistent with the need to protect the environment and with the anticipated growth or renewal needs of the area in which the communities are located. These communities would offer a full range of social and cultural services; provide jobs for a substantial number of residents; be open to all, regardless of race, creed, or color; and provide a reasonable range of housing opportunities for low- and moderate-income families.[1]

It is fair to say, I think, that most serious students of the urban scene in the United States would have little reluctance in agreeing with the findings and in supporting the intent of the Congress. Few would, I believe, question the desirability of the new communities program in terms of the Congressional goals stated above. The act itself does not profess to offer any pat solution to "the urban problem." It was enacted to "encourage" action that would result in decent housing in an improved pattern of urban development and renewal.

While Congressional interest in the program since its enactment in 1968 has not been intense, it has been positive. Title VII of the Housing and Urban Development Act of 1970 served to augment and strengthen the program considerably. During the past two years, comments on the program, as they have appeared in the Congressional Record or in hearings before the Banking and Currency and Appropriations committees, have been almost totally supportive and encouraging.[2]

There is no lack of interest in the program, either from public or private developers. Apparently there has been very little fallout

TABLE 5.1

Summary of New Communities Guaranteed by the U.S. Department of Housing and Urban Development

Community	Guarantee Commitment Amount ($'000) Date	Guarantee Issues Amount ($'000) Date	Interest Rate (%)	Population (Projected)	Dwelling Units (Projected)	Location
Jonathan, Minn.	21,000 2/70	$ 8,000[a] 10/70	8.50	18,000 in 10 years	5,500 in 10 years	20 mi. SW of Minneapolis
St. Charles Communities, Md.	24,000 6/70	$ 18,500[a] 12/70	7.75	75,000 in 20 years	25,000 in 20 years	25 mi. SE of Washington, D.C.
Park Forest South, Ill.	30,000 6/70	$ 30,00 3/71	7.00	110,000 in 15 years	35,000 in 15 years	30 mi. S of Chicago
Flower Mound, Tex.	18,000 12/70	$ 14,000 10/71	7.60	64,000 in 20 years	18,000 in 20 years	20 mi. NW of Dallas
Maumelle, Ark.	7,500 12/70	$ 2,500 12/71	7.62	45,000 in 20 years	14,000 in 20 years	12 mi. NW of Little Rock
Cedar-Riverside, Minn.	24,000 6/71	$ 24,000 12/71	7.20	30,000 in 20 years	12,500 in 20 years	downtown Minneapolis
Riverton, N.Y.	12,000 12/71	—	—	25,600 in 16 years	8,000 in 16 years	10 mi. S of Rochester
San Antonio Ranch, Tex.[b]	18,000 2/72	$ 12,500 5/72	7.125	88,000 in 30 years	28,000 in 30 years	20 mi. NW. of San Antonio
Woodlands, Tex.	50,000 4/72	$ 50,000 9/72	7.10	150,000 in 20 years	49,160 in 20 years	30 mi. NW of Houston
Gananda, N.Y.	22,000 4/72	—	—	82,500 in 30 years	17,200 in 20 years	12 mi. N of Rochester
Soul City, N.C.	14,000 4/72	—	—	44,000 in 30 years	12,096 in 20 years	45 mi. NW of Raleigh-Durham
Lysander, N.Y.	6/72[c]	d	d	18,000 in 20 years	5,000 in 30 years	12 mi. NW of Syracuse
Harbison, S.C.	13,000 10/72	—	—	23,000 in 20 years	6,500 in 20 years	8 mi. NW of Columbia

[a] Guaranteed under Title IV; all other guarantees under Title VII.
[b] Contingent on water-protection studies.
[c] Eligible for 20-percent grant from HUD, supplementing thirteen basic federal grant programs.
[d] First to receive a determination of eligibility for grant assistance rather than federal guarantee of its debt; receives federal assistance under Title VII, Housing and Urban Development Act of 1970.

Source: Department of Housing and Urban Development, as of October 4, 1972.

so far on the part of potential developers as a result of HUD's current critical staff shortage and its inability to process existing completed applications in an expeditious manner.

The new-town developers themselves have organized into the League of New Community Developers, and they are exercising a growing, largely constructive influence on the program, both in HUD and in Congress. The Urban Land Institute has created the New Communities Council, and plans to devote an increasing share of its resources to new-towns issues.

Indicative of this level of support is the House of Representatives Banking and Currency Committee's report on the Housing and Urban Development Act of 1972,[3] in which the committee restated its continuing support and concern for the program:

> The New Communities Program, as expanded and recast by title VII of the Housing and Urban Development Act of 1970, was intended by the Congress to serve a number of extremely important purposes . . . achieving more efficient and economical use of land; . . . more efficient design and construction of site improvements, public facilities, and residential, commercial, and industrial structures . . . preserving or enhancing the natural environment; creating new forms of urban opportunities for employment, civic and cultural activities, and recreation.
>
> At the very least, a proper use of the New Communities Program would multiply the choices available to our growing population as to where and how they may live and work and enjoy their leisure time. Also, as our population continues to grow and to seek the benefits of new and expanding technology, it is inevitable that urban growth strategies will be more consciously adopted at the national, regional, State and metropolitan levels so that the potential benefits of growth may be attained and the all too familiar problems of growth avoided. The New Communities Program will surely provide one important element for use in the emerging urban growth strategy.

The House committee also indicated its concern that not enough effort is being made by the administration to encourage new-towns-intown. The report states:

> The Congress also intended, as is clear from the text and the legislative history of title VII, that the program include major additions to existing communities, both large

and small, and new-towns-in-town. Thus, new communities to be developed on blighted inner-city sites are eligible both for urban renewal assistance, including grants to write down the cost of land, and for guarantees and grants under the new community provisions of title VII [author's emphasis added]. Questions have arisen as to the desirability of providing a full measure of benefits under both the urban renewal and new community programs. The committee believes it appropriate to combine full benefits under both programs as now written so that new-towns-in-town are encouraged. It should be noted that under the block grant provisions embodied in chapter IV of this bill, the city is entirely free to use its grant funds to write down the cost of land in blighted or inappropriately developed areas, thereby giving, if the city so desires, maximum additional assistance to any new-town-in-town development being aided under title VII of the 1970 Act.

The intent of Congress with regard to expansion of the new communities provisions of the 1968 and 1970 acts is suggested by proposals included in a 1972 bill (H.R. 16704), even though the bill itself was not passed. The House bill provided for, among other things:

1. An increase of another $500 million to the present $500 million authorization for new-community development guarantees;

2. A requirement that the Secretary of Housing and Urban Development reserve such available housing assistance funds as appropriate for new communities to make certain they receive their fair share of such funds;

3. An offer of additional interest grant incentives to attract public developers to the program;

4. An authorization for the Secretary of HUD to set aside community development block grant funds for use where appropriate in new communities. This means that once the legislation is passed, new communities approved under Title VII will be able to receive grants for open space, parks, and infrastructure, as well as for supporting social services.

Finally the report on the bill also included language urging the Urban Mass Transportation Administration to consider one or more of the approved new communities as suitable sites for transportation sytem research and demonstration projects.

MORE SUBURBS—NO INNOVATION?

How innovative, self-sufficient, and attractive can the socially and economically integrated—i.e., "balanced"—new communities

85

envisioned by Title VII be? Can the satellites among them amount to something more than middle-class enclaves?

It is probably worth noting here that the record of a few of the nonfederal new towns in attempting to innovate is not too bad. The Utopian new town of New Harmony, Indiana, it may be remembered, which was begun in 1825, produced the first kindergarten, high school, free library, and trade school in the United States. Park Forest South, Illinois, pioneered in the provision of rental housing in the Chicago suburbs, and in the use of regional-type shopping centers to support the community's tax base as well as its retail service needs. Columbia, Maryland, pioneered open classrooms within the Washington metropolitan area, and experimented extensively with internal transportation systems (with some assistance from the federal government) and a community-wide health-care program.

As for the Title VII new communities, they are now, among other things, actively engaged in exploring and testing the possibilities of advanced health-delivery systems, solid-waste collection, disposal and recycling systems, and wide-band cable television systems tied into health, educational, and public-safety needs.

Nevertheless, in terms of the American and European experience so far, it is clear that the potential to innovate—on the scale and with the diversity called for in the language of Title VII—and the probability of actual innovation is and will be largely dependent on government or foundation sponsorship and/or support.

To innovate is to do something different—and being different may adversely affect the ability of the developer to market his homes and the new community itself. There are unquestioned risks that innovation brings, especially when what you propose to do runs counter to conventional wisdom and established life-style patterns.

For example neither Congress nor HUD intends that Title VII new towns neglect the needs of the low- and moderate-income families. The new-town developers are obligated under the law and their contractual agreements with HUD to produce such housing in agreed-to proportions, and on a continuing basis, throughout the life of the new town's development. Requiring such a mix is innovative in of itself; to achieve it may well require some further innovation on the part of the developer in marketing the community.

HUD requires, as a part of the project contract agreement, that the developer build an open community and pursue an affirmative action program to make housing and job opportunities available to all, regardless of race, creed, or color. The population profile of the new community must be comparable to that of the metropolitan area in which it is being built. That is, if the population of the metropolitan area is 25 percent low- and moderate-income families, then the new community must also try by all legal means to develop a similar occupancy pattern consistent with projected supply and demand, and projected employment within the project.

Considering projects approved or projected for approval, it is anticipated that Title VII new communities over the next five years will provide roughly 23,000 dwelling units of subsidized housing, which will serve some 100,000 people (based on current income limits for 235 and 236 assisted housing). On the average about 25 percent of all housing to be provided in Title VII new towns will be for low- and moderate-income families.

WHAT KIND OF NEW COMMUNITIES?

The program is beginning to achieve some diversity in terms of sponsors, as well as in the types of projects approved and geographic coverage. The thirteen approved Title VII new towns involve eight states and include ten satellites, of which the tenth, Lysander, New York, is the first state-sponsored new town to be approved. (It will be developed by the New York State Urban Development Corporation.) Included in the program is a privately sponsored new-town-intown: Cedar-Riverside, Minnesota; a freestanding new town— Soul City, North Carolina; and a major addition to an existing town— Harbison, which will constitute a large-scale addition to Columbia, South Carolina. Harbison is also the first nonprofit-developer approved town; the sponsor was organized by the Presbyterian Church.

Satellite new-town developments seem destined to assume the largest share of Title VII activity for the next few years. This is consistent with urbanizing patterns reported in the last census, which estimated that 80 percent of future population growth would occur in suburban portions of metropolitan areas. Demonstrating economic feasibility requires private developers to choose land where growth is happening, often uncontrolledly, and show why controlled growth will prove socially and environmentally better, while remaining in competition with trend development in the area. Only a limited number of intown and rural new communities sponsored by private developers can meet these tests.

Nevertheless, new-towns-intown should get an increasing share of the action in the future. The House Banking and Currency Committee, as noted above, has clearly indicated to HUD that it expects more emphasis on inner-city needs. In addition, while the cities have been slow in recognizing the potential virtues of the new-town approach, there are a fair number of communities with public and/or private groups actively contemplating new-town-intown projects, including among others Newark and Paterson, New Jersey; Welfare

Island, Sunnyside Yards, Jamaica Center, and South Richmond, New York City; Chicago, Illinois; Philadelphia, Pennsylvania; Atlanta, Georgia; New Orleans, Louisiana; Little Rock, Arkansas; San Diego and Los Angeles, California; Youngstown, Ohio; Flint, Michigan; and San Antonio, Texas.

There have been some fears expressed that the program as presently constituted will divert federal resources from the needs of the central cities. In part this concern is based on the assumption that satellite new towns will somehow be favored by the federal government, and thus will capture an inordinately large share of Title VII aid and other grants from federal programs such as water and sewer, Open Space, 235 and 236 assisted housing (which is in short supply), mass transportation, hospitals, education, etc.

First, it should be noted that Title VII aid consists almost exclusively of loan guarantees—not subsidies. Second, the law calls for the program to be applied to the needs of the inner city. Congress takes note of this fact in the House report on the 1972 bill, and it is my firm belief that this means we can expect HUD to give intown projects greater attention in the future, and in addition make renewal grant funds and other assistance available to help support intown projects.

Based on our past experience with redevelopment and renewal, it seems virtually certain that, in order to succeed, intown new towns will require subsidies for land write-downs of some considerable magnitude. It also seems virtually certain that the only possible source of such grant funds will be the renewal program. It seems equally certain, based on eligibility criteria in the law, that no renewal money will go to satellites or freestanding new towns. Since renewal funds constitute by far the largest single source of grant funds to local governments, it is hard to see how the New Communities Program can conceivably act to divert grant assistance from our older cities to newly developing areas.

As for the other grant programs noted above, their resources are allocated in a variety of ways, usually based on formulas calculated to achieve a relatively even geographic distribution, and with some effort to recognize need and to equate size of grant with number of people to be benefited. Should not citizens of federally approved new-towns-intown, satellites or otherwise, which have met the highest kind of environmental, housing, amenity, and occupancy standards, be entitled to share in such grants? As a matter of fact it could be argued that, because they do have to meet such high standards and because they are open communities and must serve low- and moderate-income families, they probably should be given preference for federal aid.

Finally, while public-service grants are authorized under Title VII to cover "start-up costs," and to assure reasonable levels of public services from the beginning of the occupancy of the new town, such grants would be made available equally to intown projects as well as satellites.

Accelerated growth centers, both within and outside of standard metropolitan statistical areas (SMSAs), seem at this juncture to offer the least potential for the future. Local governments of smaller communities may lack the capability, capacity, and imagination to use Title VII tools to guide and control their future development. This may remain a major problem until HUD and the states provide some reasonable level of technical assistance. Moreover, many such communities now feel that additional development may be costly and inimical to the environment—and therefore unwise. Finally, Title VII forbids discrimination, requires an affirmative action program for involvement of minorities, and demands a suitable input of low- and moderate-income housing as part of the process; such requirements probably act as a deterrent even where the desire for growth is otherwise positive.

ENVIRONMENTAL PROTECTION

Both Columbia, Maryland, and Reston, Virginia, have helped to pioneer in environmental protection. They have done credible jobs in building and achieving—without significant adverse environmental impact—physical environments rich with amenity.

All Title VII new communities must file detailed environmental inventory and analyses with HUD, which in turn must circulate and clear an environmental impact statement with all other affected departments and the Council on Environmental Quality. Woodlands and San Antonio Ranch, two new communities in Texas approved by HUD, and Pontchartain, the Louisiana new-town-intown located within the eastern boundaries of the City of New Orleans, which has an application pending, have produced three of what will probably by judged the most sophisticated, ecologically based plans ever developed in the United States for a community. Riverton, New York, is working with the New York State College of Forestry in developing a program that will monitor on a continuing basis the impact of the new community on the environment. All Title VII new communities approved so far are devoting from 18 percent to 27 percent of their total land areas for recreation and open space.

PLANNING AND PERFORMANCE STANDARDS

It is important to realize that new community planning and development under the federal Title VII program is far more comprehensive and complete that when an independent private developer undertakes to build conventional tract housing, or even a planned unit development. Title VII requires the developer's involvement with a host of federal, state, and local governmental agencies and his encouragement of the new community's citizens to participate in the planning process, not to mention his need to assure provision for a full range of community services that are not ordinarily a part of the old-style tract housing development—such services as education, health and public safety systems, to name a few. Many developers will find these kinds of requirements onerous and burdensome.to the point that they will avoid the program entirely.

But it is not likely that Title VII will continue to be unique in imposing such high standards. Like it or not, almost all future urban development will be increasingly subject to more government intervention and scrutiny from a variety of groups concerned about growth, particularly as concern for protection of the physical environment becomes more acute, and as local governments—especially more affluent suburban jurisdictions—become more conscious of the increasing costs that conventional new residential development bring to them.

GOVERNANCE

Contrary to the view expressed by some critics of the program the Title VII New Communities Program is not designed to encourage or support monopolistic enterprises that regulate the lives of citizen residents, or limit their legitimate rights to protect their own interests and those of the larger community. HUD has and continues to insist on the citizen's right to be heard and to participate in the development of policy affecting the welfare of the community. HUD's regulations, and the developer's acceptance of those regulations as a condition of receiving federal assistance, guarantees a greater citizen potential for involvement than is probably the case in any other old or new community in the United States.

In the area of intergovernmental relations and local government reform, new communities are increasingly becoming instrumental in developing innovative approaches to community governance in a way hardly conceived of in the past. Moreover they can and have served as a catalytic agent for existing governments, which they have persuaded to improve quality of services, to extend control

90

on land use, and generally to take a more realistic and comprehensive view of future growth and the development of appropriate strategies to deal with it.

New towns in America are in fact, as Royce Hanson has suggested, "Laboratories for Democracy," and under federal auspices they may be even more so than if only privately developed.

SUMMARY

The Title VII program is in fact functioning, innovating, and uniquely trying to help meet the housing needs of our less affluent families in the context of a community, rather than a tract of homogenized housing. The next four years will be crucial in terms of the program's ability to grow and produce high-quality communities in significant volume. To have a fair chance to succeed, the Title VII program will require greater involvement of the renewal program, release of special planning and public service grant funds, much more staff support from HUD, and a much higher priority in the administration's scheme of things. Other federal departments also need to become involved in a more purposeful way. The program's clients, its supporters, the public-interest groups, and the program's constructive critics should continue to urge that the program try different approaches, try experimenting, and also run risks. Even if 5 or 10 percent of these projects flounder and the federal government has to pick up the pieces, the experience involved has to contribute something to our store of knowledge of how to do it right.

The Title VII New Communities Program offers one of the best possible opportunities the nation has to test, on a large scale, the potential viability of a community that has staked its future on good planning and a need to safeguard its environment, and that has accepted social, economic, and ethnic integration as a stated goal. The federally assisted new communities are probably the only major developments taking place in the United States where such goals are presumed essential elements of the community-building effort. If there is any hope at all that we will be able to pioneer a significant number of new and improved ways of providing opportunities for good, safe living environments equitably, for all our citizens, it most clearly seems to lie with the federal New Communities Program.

NOTES

1. The full text of Title VII is worth reading and study. See the Housing and Urban Development Act of 1970, 84 Stat. 1770. Approved December 31, 1970.

2. For example, see "HUD-Space-Science-Veterans Appropriations for 1973," part 3, in Hearings before a Subcommittee of the Committee on Appropriations, House of Representatives, Ninety-second Congress, Second Session.
3. Report on H.R. 16704, 92nd Congress, 2d Session, House of Representatives Report No. 92-1429.

6

RHETORIC VERSUS PERFORMANCE: THE NATIONAL POLITICS AND ADMINISTRATION OF U.S. NEW-COMMUNITY DEVELOPMENT LEGISLATION

Francine F. Rabinovitz
Helene V. Smookler

New communities have been hailed in the United States as a settlement style that could bring about significant innovations in the way people live in urban areas. The underlying thesis appears to be that new communities can help solve many of the social and eco-logical problems confronting America. However not all developments that claim the status of new communities are justified in so doing. It is generally acknowledged that there are several factors that contribute strongly to the determination of whether a development will be an exciting new community or just another suburb.[1] Such developments "must include most of the activities normally associated with a city or larger town. In addition to housing, they should provide balanced and harmonious facilities for commerce, industry and recreation, creating an attractive environment for those who live, work and shop there."[2] Rarely are all these elements present. In the United States there are close to 100 large-scale private develop-ments completed or under construction. Of these only a handful have any industry or other major specialized functions associated with them. None have substantial low- or moderate-income housing.

There are many reasons why private developers have not taken on the challenge of new-community development. New communities need the type of financial backing that serves to define the nature of the community and ensure the probability of longterm monetary success. In addition the developers must have the ability to attract business and industry to the community, which will help raise property values and provide employment. Perhaps the most difficult chore

We are grateful to Paul Halpern and Robert Hill for comments on earlier drafts and to Lawrence Susskind for materials and dis-cussions.

is finding a racial and economic mix of residents that is both socially and economically viable. Planning for socioeconomic mix in housing is certain to hurt any guarantee for financial success. The largest obstacle, though, has been the reluctance of investors, due to the heavy investment in site preparation and the long period before there is any return on the outlay. Only in very rare circumstances could such a new-community development be carried out on the usual profit calculus. This is the reason why the major housing builders in the United States are not involved in new-community development.* The fact that the private sector does not think of problems of design and resource allocation in terms of social need, and that social objectives are neither profitable nor entirely feasible in the open-market system, provides justification for government involvement.

Congress has passed two pieces of legislation that could, in theory, enable such innovations to occur: Title IV of the 1968 housing act and Title VII of the 1970 act. By October 1972 commitments for $240 million in guarantees had been made under these acts to build new communities. Yet, as Pressman and Wildavsky indicate in their study of the Economic Development Administration, the student of urban policy has a sense of having heard it all before; Congress passes a piece of legislation, which in this case is supposed to save the cities and the suburbs. However, years later, although the program has been announced with great fanfare, and funds have been authorized and appropriated, muckrackers reveal that the goals of the original program have not been met; the results are disappointing and controversial, serving some interests for which they were only marginally intended, serving others—presumably the targets of the program—not at all.

Is the federal government's new-communities program likely to be another in the already long line of urban policy disappointments?

A partial prediction can be made from an investigation of two parts of the process in which an early warning of breakdown may appear: the creation of new-communities policy in the legislative arena, and the national-level administration of that legislation once is has been passed. The question we address is this: irrespective of whether new communities are economically, socially, or

---

*Builder Eli Broad, for example, "believes that tying up money in long-term land holdings is wasteful and inefficient. K. & B. never buys property until it is ready to use it; usually within six to nine months of acquiring land, the company is selling houses on it." Kaufman and Broad's main concern "is mass producing and selling a product that happens to be housing but could just as easily be bed springs or toenail clippers." ["Broad Builds Up," Time (July 17, 1972), p. 66.]

esthetically a good idea, what do the patterns of politics and administration associated with the legislation and its administration suggest
about who will realize what benefits from the planning and developing
of new communities? Our summary answer is that the politics of
pluralism out of which the program arises will not make possible
the reshaping of urban communities as implied in the legislation.
One reason is that this is a program that will fail because it rests
on very weak political support; it is designed to do quite grand things
in an atmosphere in which some powerful interests are hostile, and
others indifferent, to its major goals. Another reason is that the
new-communities program is likely to go awry because the task
assigned is beyond the limits of what can reasonably be expected from
a public organization that is under pressure to innovate in a field
where little is known. But even more fundamentally we will argue
that the prognosis for success is poor because this is a program
with multiple and conflicting goals stemming from contradictions in
interests arising from the structure of American society and embodied
in a political system that insulates some of these interests from
change.

THE WEAKNESS OF POLITICAL SUPPORT

At the outset the federal government's new-communities program
suffers from potentially fatal weaknesses vis-à-vis political support.
This is a program that was either opposed or ignored by important
interests. A capsule history of the program in its various forms
appears in Figure 6.1. The first bill—Title IV—guaranteed the loans
of private developers for new-community development and provided
supplemental grants for up to 80 percent of the cost of water and
sewerage facilities. However, market conditions were such in
1969-70 that private developers could not raise the necessary money
even with a guarantee; the money for the supplemental grants for
this program was never appropriated. The Advisory Commission
on Intergovernmental Relations, the New Towns Task Force of the
American Institute of Planners, the Domestic Affairs Council and
Democratic legislators in the House and Senate all seemed engaged
in a race to produce an expanded program.[3] Suddenly, though, in
1970 the President's version was suppressed as concern for the
economy grew.

Representative Thomas L. Ashley (D-Ohio), a member of the
housing subcommittee of the House Committee on Banking and Currency, continued, however, to push for new-communities legislation.
In order to get exposure for the bill, Ashley held public hearings
supported independently of the House Committee, under the aegis

FIGURE 6.1

History of New-Communities Legislation

1964—President Lyndon B. Johnson proposes, in an omnibus housing and community-development program, that legislation provide federal insurance loans to private developers for acquisition of land for planned subdivisions, and make public-facility loans available for advance land purchase. Congress authorizes only grants to localities in planning public facilities in community developments.

1965—President Johnson calls for federal insurance for private loans for entire new communities, and aid to state land-development agencies for acquisition of land, installation of facilities, and resale to private developers.

1966—President Johnson takes the recommendations of the Urban Task Force headed by Robert C. Wood and calls for a massive demonstration-cities program for inner cities, supplemented by federal assistance to new-community development. Late in the year Congress passes Title IV of the Demonstration Cities and Metropolitan Development Act of 1966, which expands the FHA Mortgage Insurance Program (Title X of the National Housing Act of 1934) empowering the Secretary of HUD to insure loans to private developers for new-community development.

1967—The Presidential Task Force on Suburban Problems and the Subcommittee on Executive Organization, Senate Committee on Government Operations (see the Federal Role in Urban Affairs), 90th Congress, 1966-67, identify problems of the meager program.

1968—President Johnson recommends expanded program. Housing and Urban Development Act follows his recommendations with minor revision, adding Title IV (Public Law 90-448) to the 1968 act. Earlier Title IV emphasis on land development is here expanded from first-mortgage insurance to cash-flow financing; HUD is also authorized to make supplementary grants for water, sewerage, open space, beautification, and historic preservation.

1969—Numerous proposals are made for expansion by the Federal Advisory Commission on Intergovernmental Relations, the Task Force on New Communities of the American Institute of Planners, and the National Committee on Urban Growth Policy.

1970—Congress passes the Housing and Urban Development Act of 1970, including Title VII (Public Law 91-609), which creates a Community Development Corporation in HUD to provide guarantees to private and public developers as well as loans for interest payments on indebtedness, and extends supplementary grants for public facilities to mass transportation, airports, public health, water pollution, education, and public works. It also authorizes funds for planning assistance. Title VII also includes a provision for an "Urban Growth Report" by the President.

1972—HUD has, as of July, issued a total of $240 million in guarantees and commitments to eleven new communities. The housing subcommittee of the House Committee on Banking and Currency submits new titles to increase guarantees to $1 billion and to increase the interest differential payments to public-development agencies.

96

of an ad hoc subcommittee on urban growth.* A wide range of groups
with potential interests in new-community development were exposed
to the subject in the hearings. Reactions were favorable for the most
part. Even the minority report, under the name of the ranking Republican, William Widnall (R-N.J.), while generally negative, opposed
only small portions of the new-communities program rather than the
basic guarantee and grant-in-aid extensions at the heart of the bill.
The Senate version of the bill also eliminated a series of appended
provisions. Ashley's strategy was to maintain enough differences
between the House and Senate versions to push a good deal of the
decision-making into the conference committee. After initially losing
in the House (less than 200 Representatives and only a few Democrats
were on the floor), the issue went to the Senate, which passed a compromise version by voice vote. With the liberals back on the floor
the bill also passed in the House. The conference committee retained
the expanded guarantees and also a provision, to which the administration was opposed, requiring a biennial report on urban-growth
policy. Only by attaching the program to other sections of the housing
act vital to the continuation of national housing programs, particularly
the FHA mortgage-insurance programs, did sponsors assure President
Nixon's signature. The act was signed on December 31, 1970, the
day Congress adjourned.

The 1970 act provided a significantly expanded program of
assistance for new-community development. The new program, Title
VII, raised the ceiling on loan guarantees to $500 million (with a
$50-million limit per development), and the program was extended
to public developers. Title VII also authorized developers to be
eligible for grants-in-aid from fourteen programs, including mass

---

*Ashley represents Ohio's 9th Congressional District, which
includes most of Toledo. He has been a strong supporter of civil
rights and urban and housing legislation. He is considered by many
to be an expert on housing and is one of the founding members of the
National Committee on Urban Growth Policy. Part of his interest
in new communities can be traced to his involvement in the Redevelopment Authority of Lucas County, which is proposing to build a new
community west of Toledo. Ashley sees in the use of the county's
redevelopment powers a precedent that others could follow to assemble land and develop new communities. Voluminous testimony relating
to new communities can be found in The Quality of Urban Life, Hearings, a record of the hearings held by Ashley under the aegis of an
ad hoc subcommittee on urban growth, Committee on Banking and
Currency, U.S. Congress, House of Representatives, 91st Congress,
1st and 2d Sessions, Part 2.

transportation, highways, airports, hospitals, recreation, open space, beautification programs, water and sewerage facilities, and other public works.

Title VII would not have passed through Congress without the support of large-city mayors, whose concern was mainly to save the provision for a national urban-growth policy. But while the bill was supported by the mayors and numerous public-interest groups, it was virtually ignored by the AFL-CIO, and by the National Association of Homebuilders, the National Association of Real Estate Boards, savings and loan associations, and the American Bankers Association—all of which normally lobby intensively on urban-housing legislation. They saw themselves not affected by the potential new-communities housing market, since in reality large land-investment concerns and financial conglomerates were the natural clients of the program.

Even more important, the President's domestic advisers opposed the program on the grounds that it was inflationary, despite Republican support in the House for some expansion. One would presume that no President is likely to encourage the creation of a powerful organization to administer ab initio a policy he opposes. This is in fact what has occurred with the 1970 legislation. The early history of the new title has to do with the effort to emasculate the independent features of the new-communities agency. The original Title IV program was administered through the Metropolitan Development Division of HUD, in its Office of New Communities. Under this system however, a major locus of decision-making on the program was the Urban Affairs Council's cabinet-level Subcommittee on Land Use and Development, headed by Transportation Secretary Volpe. This subcommittee, together with Volpe's department, would be affected by the supplemental contributions provision. Under this arrangement the department made no commitments for loan guarantees at all, hamstrung in part by the reluctance of other agencies to surrender any of their own funding or autonomy to HUD. In 1969 the Metropolitan Development Division was reorganized; the program was moved into HUD's Community Resources Development Administration, and then into the open as a separate division reporting directly to the assistant secretary for metropolitan planning and development. Separation was coupled with expansion; the staff jumped from three to seventeen, mainly organized into a project development and management division whose job it was to identify and nurse along developers with potentially acceptable projects. A small application review division and an even smaller public-industrial liaison division also existed on paper.

Under Title VII, however, a five-person New Community Development Corporation (NCDC), appointed by the President and confirmed by the Senate, was required. The corporation was to be located in HUD but was supposed to be independent. The reasoning was that the new-communities development process must be visible and separated from the world of housing mortgage finance. Jonathan B. Howes, director of the Center for Urban and Regional Studies at the University of North Carolina, says that "the people who drafted the Ashley bill don't like HUD.* They feel HUD has a banker's mentality and that it ought to stay in the banking business. Anything new and likely to represent new initiatives is going to have to be done by somebody completely different. Originally, their proposal was to create that corporation outside of HUD entirely. . . ."[4]

The intent of the legislation to make NCDC independent has been partially subverted. In the first place, three of its members are officers of HUD, a fourth is undersecretary of the Department of Transportation, and there is only one public member, a New York financial consultant. Second, the corporation has no independent staff and no finances. Finally, while NCDC was supposed to set policies for the Office of New Communities, and guarantees and commitments are issued in its name, it does not approve the preliminary applications whose negotiation is the heart of the guarantee process.

Dependent administrative structure notwithstanding, Presidential policies continue to be paramount in the implementation of the new-communities program. Presidential policy is played out in the activities of the Office of Management and Budget (OMB). The new-communities program potentially conflicts with three Presidential concerns—the preference for private over public operation of new developments; the preference for introducing general or special grants to replace categorical grants-in-aid; and the emphasis on regional control of federal programs. In each of these areas OMB has managed to turn the program toward Presidential ends.

First, given the Presidential preference for private initiatives, OMB has refused to compensate applicants for increased interest rates on the obligations of bodies guaranteed under the act, resulting from loss of the exemption of interest from federal income taxes. The only agencies that would have been eligible are public-development corporations. Thus of the seventy pre- and granted applications in process, the only public agency to receive a grant is the New York Urban Development Corporation, a quasi-public body; the City of New Orleans and a special district in one Texas new town participate in two other communities, but with private agencies.

Second, given the Presidential push for general revenue provision rather than categorical grants to cities, OMB has held up

---

*Howes was formerly director of the Urban Planning Assistance Program in HUD, and director of the Urban Policy Center of Urban America, Inc. (later the National Urban Coalition).

$5 million earmarked in the program for innovation in new communities. It argues that it does not wish to allow spending in new categorical grant areas while the campaign to replace categorical aid with general revenue sharing for cities takes place.

Third, given the prominence in President Nixon's 1971 executive reorganization program (the Ash Council) of efforts to regionalize executive agencies, New Communities Office pressure for more staff has been denied. In the Nixon plan all departments were asked to appoint regional directors to represent the secretaries in the field, so that resolution of conflicts can be achieved without recourse to Washington. Although the new-communities program is a central-office function, requests to increase its Washington staff are rejected on the grounds that a heavier concentration of personnel at the national level is contrary to administration efforts to regionalize urban policy.

Fourth, given the generalized opposition to the program in the White House, the $3.5 million in application fees collected by the Community Development Corporation from applicants has been impounded by OMB and there is some doubt that a line-item approval for spending these funds to expand staff would be approved.

In his testimony on the new-communities program in 1971, HUD Secretary George Romney provided an accurate summary of the consequences of Presidential opposition to legislative programs for the implementing process.

> . . . in the process of enactment of the legislation the
> administration was opposed to some of the provisions
> and made its opposition known. And when you get into a
> situation such as the one we are in, where the OMB has
> the responsibility of cutting back appropriations to live
> within outlined ceilings, the probability is that when
> those things have been enacted and involve some obliga-
> tions of actual outlays, they are the things that are going
> to suffer first. . . . There were aspects of the program
> that the administration opposed in the process of the
> enactment of the legislation in the first place . . . And
> confronted with budget problems, why those were the
> victims. Now that is what it gets down to.5

THE LIMITS OF GOVERNMENTAL INNOVATION

Advocates of the new-communities program may well argue at this point that its political history tells us much about a given administration but little about problems inherent in the program. The hope held out would be that at other times, with different administrative priorities, such a program might do much to fulfill its initial promise. We would suggest, however, that even if the political difficulties of the new-communities program were not present, accomplishment would be difficult. As James Q. Wilson has recently argued:

Persons easily convinced that the government is not acting rightly tend to assume that it is because the government is not righteous; if industries are being regulated wrongly, then [in this view] it must be because bad people are doing the regulating. . . . [But] the problem . . . is not wholly a problem of clientelism, political meddling or agency incompetence; in substantial part it is a problem of the nature of the tasks which we have given agencies. These tasks probably could not be performed well even in theory, and amid the practical realities of confused ends and ambiguous standards they are, through the fault of no one in particular, performed abominably.[6]

The unwieldiness of task in the new-communities program arises from two conflicting tendencies, which have also been identified by Pressman and Wildavsky in their study of the Economic Development Administration. On the one hand there is constant pressure to build communities rapidly. In 1969 the National Committee on Urban Growth issued a report calling for the development of 110 new cities by the year 2000. This target seemed conservative when a Senate Banking and Currency Committee report predicted that ten new communities would receive guarantees in each fiscal year starting in 1969-70.[7] But, on the other hand, given that not much is known about how to make new communities work, HUD declared itself committed to a go-slow approach. Secretary Romney testified that "what we felt we ought to do in this early stage is to undertake to get under way different types of new communities, enough of them so that we get some feeling of the extent to which one is more successful than another, or what the problems are in connection with different types."[8] While HUD regards delay as required for learning, Congress regards delay as a political effort to sap the program of its strength. The exchange between Representative Ashley and Secretary Romney quoted below is illustrative of the tension:

Mr. Ashley: I don't really understand the emphasis that you put upon the experimental aspect of this kind of development. We are really talking about an alternative to the piecemeal fragmented development process. . . .
When you look at Cedar Riverside, what we are saying is

101

that there are 100 acres that have been developed as a
coherent integrated entity. . . . There really is nothing so
dramatically experimental about this it seems to me. . . .
  Secretary Romney: . . . I want to say that a new
town is so much more complicated that. . . . [It] is not
realistic to expect our department to just rush pell mell
into approving a lot of new towns around this country. . . .
  Mr. Ashley: It seems to me that you are a little
cautious about this, a little more than I would think was
justified. . . . [The] facts seem to me to be that we have
had various considerable experience, most of it fairly
bad.[9]

The combined pressures to spend, produce results, and to vary
carefully the conditions under which guarantees are given suggest the
notion that government is engaged in an experiment. But government
is in this case an unwieldly vehicle for experimental design.
  First, experimental design requires sophistication about the
range of choices to be made.[10] The Office of New Communities in
HUD had to develop the guidelines for this experiment. The office
first had to decide on what constituted a new community, and then
presumably how U.S. new communities should be distributed. Inex-
perienced, rushed, faced with 200 inquiries, criticized because no
guarantees had been approved a year after Title IV funds were available, the office wrote guidelines by looking at the applications under
review and then asking the client-constituent industries to comment
on the set of regulations and guidelines drawn up.[11] Client-responsi
regulations are a problem because clients do not turn out to be very
innovative or very concerned with national urban-development direc-
tions. The lowest-level experimental justification for the new-
communities program is that it would stimulate progress and innovat
in housing and hardware design. Most of the applications received
are not strong even in this kind of innovative planning: "The private
developer is by definition interested in profit and concerned with the
risks to profit. This means without special incentives, it is difficult
to encourage innovative planning in dealing with private developers."
HUD has reinforced this conservatism by its concern that federally
supported new communities be not only experimental but financially
sound. "The pressure to make a killing or to avoid a disaster drives
out most high risk activities and provides powerful reinforcements
for hard boiled, conservative, not to mention backward and prejudice
judgments as to what will work."[13]
  Second, another problem with the experimental notion is that
successful pursuit of experiments in design and in racial and econom
integration probably depend on large expenditures of funds in selecte

areas. If urban programmers have learned anything about Congressional politics from the Model Cities experience, it is that it's almost impossible to develop a national program in which benefits go to only a few projects or regions. Without wide dispersal of projects it is very hard to maintain a new program over time and through administrations.

Third, experiments also require mechanisms for using the new experiences in experimental communities to correct the program as it develops under varying conditions in a set of sites. Probably the point at which the new-communities development process will depart farthest from experimental notions has to do not with selection but with the effects (or lack thereof) of evaluation. The federal government is committed by a major investment in each community. The guarantee implies a high probability of following loan assistance with grants. New communities consultant Robert Tennenbaum comments that "in St. Charles, getting the grants is as important as getting the guarantee. There's no doubt in the world that Marcus [Flower Mound] could go out and get financing in Dallas just as Columbia did with Connecticut General. But what he is getting is this backup on the grants and 20 percent add-on for the town."[14]

Robert E. Simon, developer of Reston and Riverton, agrees:

The most important of Title IV is not the insurance, but the grants that go with it. The grants can make this difference: housing has to cost more in a good community where the developer provides amenities than in a community where the developer does not provide them. . . . The grants for roads, utilities, open space acquisition, planning and certain amenities can allow you to produce housing in new communities which will cost less than other housing.[15]

In such an environment it is unlikely that any commitment will or could be withdrawn.

Donald T. Campbell, commenting on the difficulty of conducting social experiments under government auspices, states that what is needed to make such experiments possible in government is a shift in political posture, namely:

the shift from the advocacy of a specific reform to the advocacy of the seriousness of the problem and hence to the advocacy of persistence in alternative reform efforts should the first one to fail. This political stance would become: "This is a serious problem. We propose to initiate Policy A on an experimental basis. If after five years there has been no significant improvement, we will shift to Policy B." By making explicit that a given problem solution was only one of several that the administrator or party could in good conscience advocate, and by having ready a plausible alternative, the administrator could afford honest evaluation of outcomes.[16]

The difficulty is of course that this experiment involves attaching individuals and investments to projects that will be difficult to dislodge, once they have been developed over time periods sufficient to undertake evaluation. Second, there is the assumption that criteria are clear for determining success and failure. Third, a subtle shift takes place in which the problem, which was once central-city congestion in Representative Ashley's definition, becomes the variable structure of new communities themselves, in Secretary Romney's definition. Each new community is thus a separate experiment; the program itself, then, is not seen as one solution to a particular problem alongside which others also could be advanced. At the same time, though, the experimental notion is unavoidable when, as here, we do not and cannot know precisely what to do.

THE DEVELOPMENT OF MULTIPLE GOALS

Following the lines of the argument thus far would suggest that if in the year 2000 we were to judge the federal government's new-communities program a failure, the explanation would lie partly in the properties of Presidential politics and partly in the realities of bureaucratic organization at the national level. There is a third difficulty, however, and it is one that we suspect subsumes the other two. Today when programs fail the most frequent explanation is "the bureaucracy problem"; i.e., the impact of an otherwise good program was perverted in the translation of legislation into administration. If we wish to avoid this occurrence, the objective must be clear at the outset. "The only point at which very much leverage can be gained on the bureaucracy problem is when we decide what it is we are trying to accomplish. When we define our goals, we are implicitly deciding how much, or how little, of a bureaucracy problem we are going to have. A program with clear objectives, clearly stated, is a program with a fighting chance. . . ."[17]

To pass the new-communities program it was necessary to violate this condition almost from the outset, placing within the program two sets of goals that conflict. In initial conception the program was designed to be in aid of public advance land acquisition. Attempts were made as early as 1963 to interest Congress.

104

President Johnson's personal concern led to a provision in 1966 for FHA-insured mortgage-loan guarantees for the purchase of raw land and the development of improved building sites in large suburban-type tracts. While this provision attracted little attention, discussion of it did prompt the first confrontation of program proponents and the nation's mayors. The mayors were afraid that financial aid for new communities would discriminate against the older cities and promote further disparities between central cities and outlying areas.

There was also concern on the part of the U.S. Conference of Mayors that creation of new communities would lead to a proliferation of more units of local government. On the whole, the mayors felt new communities were not a solution to ghetto problems. However President Johnson was able to move the mayors from a position of strong opposition to one of support, albeit weak support. He first deprived the mayoral conference of its ally in the National League of Cities by convincing small-city mayors to support a bill. If it were passed, they would be able to absorb the new towns as members. He then agreed to provide more money for urban renewal and for a program of rent supplements, implying that new communities were part of a strategy that included the provision of low- and moderate-income housing for inner-city residents.

City chief executives continued, however, to try to keep attention focused on the urban crisis in their own jurisdictions. By 1967, in the wake of the urban riots, Charles Haar, then assistant secretary for metropolitan development, was able to get through a separate new-community provision, Title IV of the Housing and Urban Development Act of 1968, which provided for federal guarantee of cash-flow debentures sold by private developers to finance new-community development. He did so, enlisting President Johnson's strong backing by including a provision for experimental new-towns-intown, as well as the more customary peripheral developments which brought the mayors reluctantly on board.

The multiple goals of the program became locked into it at this juncture. Its suburban goals suggest that the new-communities bill is designed to improve the heretofore fragmented process of sub-division development. Clark and Mode,* describing HUD's posture, have stated that "Title IV . . . is just for large scale subdividing . . .

---

*Clark and Mode served as consultants to the Kaiser Commission on Urban Housing and worked on the report which led to the formation of the National Housing Partnership under Title IX of the 1968 Housing Act. Both are attorneys involved in consulting for developers of new communities, including Fort Lincoln and Jonathan.

[The] Title IV developer should purchase, plan, put in sewers, grade and sell as if these were not separate functions removed from the organic growth of a community."18 The urban goals of the program suggest that there will be benefits not only for the suburbanite seeking a better environment, but for the urban dwellers seeking better housing. This can happen in two ways: first, through the construction of housing in peripheral new communities that is open to and economically feasible for central-city dwellers; second, through the program's provision for new-towns-intown. In contrast to Clark and Mode, Robert M. Paul, special assistant to the director of HUD's Community Resources Development Administration, has stated that "Title IV provides assistance to private developers in building new communities, which is an uneconomical thing to do, and in return we hope to meet some national goals for low- and moderate-income housing. Title IV is not a national new towns policy. It is a method of getting some more moderate income housing in return for a federal loan guarantee."19

Of course the issue of class and/or racial integration in the suburbs is very sensitive. Suburbs have traditionally used their zoning powers to protect the fiscal and social homogeneity of the community. It has been noted that suburban Americans in particular have reacted to the changing nature of black participation and black demands by becoming increasingly fearful for their personal safety and seeking political leaders who promise a defense against "outsiders." Policies outside the new-communities package that seek to introduce low-income housing into the suburbs and attack the so-called snob zoning provisions that narrow the range of housing opportunity have met with resistance. Locating the problem on a new site does not make the conflicts disappear.20 Thus the marriage of suburban improvement with the introduction of moderate- or low-income housing, if class or racial integration is implied, produces a program with overall objectives that are potentially conflict-generating.

The central-city dweller in need of better housing can also be served within the program by new-towns-intown. Descriptions vary of what such communities would be like. It is noteworthy that a recent assessment of the idea suggests that the purpose of new-town-intown is to revive the inner-city economy by introducing business and high-income families. Rodwin and Susskind predict that "basically such developments will seek to revitalize sagging inner city economies. They will also try to attract high income residents back to the central city and to promote racial integration."21 Again we are talking about housing low-income, inner-city dwellers as well as about rehousing suburbanites—but this time in the inner-city; low- and moderate-income housing would be a possible side-payment from the program.

What is the likely result of operating within a program that by virtue of its creation contains grand but dual objectives involving conflicting interests? Martha Derthick, examining a program for new towns on surplus lands that bore a similarly messianic tone, has observed that "federal officials stated objectives so ambitious that some degree of failure was certain. Striving for the ideal, they were sure to fall short."22 A lapse from original intentions as suggested by Derthick would hardly be surprising here. However the more interesting problem is just how programs will be adapted, in that, despite pronouncements of imminent failure, new-communities guarantees are being issued, applications approved, and supplementary grant funds earmarked.

We have attempted to trace the process of adaptation with regard to the three sets of goal conflicts we perceive in the program: the pressure to build peripheral new towns versus that to build new-towns-intown; the pressure to improve suburban development versus that to construct low-cost housing in peripheral new communities; and the pressure toward racial, as distinct from class, integration in new communities.

One set of goal conflicts in the program is between peripheral towns and new-towns-intown. In theory both types of development will be funded; in fact planners are well aware that intown development is likely to be harder and slower, particularly in the absence of powers of eminent domain through which to condemn and thus assemble large tracts of land. At first, HUD made an effort to force both peripheral and core-city developments to proceed in tandem. The notion of "pairing" was adopted in which each suburban new town would be linked to a community in a core city, so both could proceed apace and benefit from technological discoveries in the other. Thus the first loan guarantee went to Jonathan, Minnesota, which was later paired with Cedar-Riverside, a 100-acre development near the center of Minneapolis. However, as time passed and the difficulties of building or planning intown new towns were encountered, the Office of New Community Development began increasingly to concentrate on places where projects could be built faster. As of early fall 1972 only one additional new-town-intown—on the east side of New Orleans— of the seventy applications considered to be serious grant possibilities was being actively pursued.*

---

*We use the seventy applications or pre-applications then being evaluated as a proxy here for what will be done. We suspect this is a realistic index; since it costs $10,000 to apply for a guarantee, only those developments likely to be approved are in fact allowed to fill out formal applications. The observations we make about the universe

107

The Presidential Task Force on New Towns in 1967 concluded that the main reasons for federal involvement in new-community development were the "clear indications that unaided private entrepreneurs will not satisfy any national commitment to foster new communities of the right kinds in the right places at the right time."[23] It stressed the need for 360 intown new communities to be built in the 1970s. The areas with the greatest need included those in Los Angeles, New York-northwestern New Jersey, Chicago-northwestern Indiana, the San Francisco Bay Area, and metropolitan Detroit. Today, when other offices in HUD talk about bailing out cities, they still talk about new-towns-intown for Detroit or new-towns-intown for St. Louis. Yet the Office of New Community Development apparently does not.

The practical downgrading of intown developments is not a matter of articulated intent but in some sense one of survival. Pressman and Wildavsky note a similar process occurring in EDA, where at the outset two goals—construction and employment—were designed to be pursued simultaneously. "But as time passed and the training programs became hopelessly stalled, there was pressure within the agency to concentrate on getting construction completed. After all, a spending agency has to keep moving money and building projects or Congress will suspect it is not doing its job."[24] Faced with a constant barrage of criticism from Democrats that hesitation and procrastination, measured by the failure to issue guarantees, were sapping the new-communities program, the Office of New Communities Development similarly has begun to move the money—to the city's periphery.

A second set of conflicts inheres in the pressure to use the program to promote the construction of low-cost housing in peripheral developments. The legislation contains, and HUD guidelines ask for, provision of subsidized housing for the poor in all new communities. HUD guidelines base the fraction of subsidized housing required, in plans, on the profile of the standard metropolitan statistical area (SMSA) in which the community is located, and simultaneously on the marketability of such housing and the availability of employment for its anticipated residents. It is important to recognize that, in a typical SMSA, subsidized housing occupants can approach incomes of $10,000 per year. For example, in Park Forest South, Illinois, a guaranteed development adjacent to the community about which Whyte wrote The Organization Man, 25 percent of the residences would have to be for those with incomes below $7,500, 25 percent

---

of seventy are supported if one looks at the smaller group (eleven) of guarantees that have formally been made.

for those between $7,500 and the SMSA median (here $10,800), and the rest for any income group. Even given the $7,500 figure, only one community that has received a guarantee, St. Charles, currently plans to provide more than 80 percent low- and moderate-income housing. Moreover, these priorities are counterbalanced by the desire to achieve marketability and financial stability in the communities guaranteed. In consequence an informal guideline has developed suggesting that housing provision can be staged and the projected income-mix need not be achieved till after the first five years. Rodwin and Susskind suggest that this delay will end up making the provision of low-income housing impossible:

> To meet financial strains during the early stages of development, even the best intentioned developers will decide to build a high percentage of high revenue producing housing first. Once the initial wave of high middle and middle middle income families have been served, however, resistance to the construction of housing and facilities for low and middle income families will heighten. And so, most new communities twenty five years hence will have ended up catering to a clientele not much different from the customary suburban development.[25]

A further indication of the slippage on the issue of subsidized housing inheres in the structure of earmarking such housing in the HUD programs associated with the initial loan guarantees. The assistant secretary of housing production and management has refused to earmark funds under the section 235 and 236 programs, which are the leading rental and home-ownership subsidy instruments available to HUD for single-family housing for low- and middle-income owners and renters. Thus, for future housing allotments in staged new communities (including those that will not begin construction until 1975), each developer will have to apply at that time and take his chances with the availability of subsidy funding. In contrast the office handling community-development programs has earmarked both open space and water and sewerage grants—crucial to development over extended areas—with such alacrity that some grants have been forfeited already because communities have not geared up in time to use them.

A third conflict exists with regard to racial integration in new communities. HUD guidelines base racial standards on the conformity of a new community to the existing SMSA profile; officials point with pride to the fact that in Jonathan, as in Minnesota, 2 percent of the residents belong to minority groups. Developers are also required to have affirmative marketing plans for the sale of housing. Since the majority of the seventy applications under consideration would

109

place new communities in the South, the profiling principle provides different pressures in different areas. The structure of the plan for a new community near Atlanta suggests that in the South even the standards created by profiles will be relaxed.

But the crux of the integration issue may well turn not on federal but on local action. In St. Charles Communities, which is located outside Washington, D.C., the county government has threatened to halt water- and sewer-line construction into the area. Since each new community must file an environmental impact statement and since water and sewer inadequacies makes the building of St. Charles environmentally damaging, the county will bring construction to a halt. The goal of racial integration here will not be determined by federal policies but by the actual execution of individual new-communities plans. Given the limited benefits of low-income, black new communities to most areas, it is difficult to see how federal resources could be brought to bear effectively in such a setting.

Yet while the cards appear stacked against new-towns-intown, against the provision of low-income housing, and against racial integration, at least two new communities that will be largely black have received guarantees (Soul City and St. Charles); one new-town-intown has been funded (Cedar-Riverside), and another is close to final approval (Pontchartrain); and some low-cost housing may be built in peripheral towns. In short, while HUD seems unconcerned with the indivisible benefits produced by prodding all new communities with federal backing toward racial integration, officials are rigorous in seeing that benefits are distributed to some black towns as well as to white towns in the total of projects.

RHETORIC VERSUS PERFORMANCE

How should we evaluate the "real" new-communities program that is emerging out of the legislative and administrative process? One possibility is that we would conclude that the honing-down of objectives is a process well adapted to the pressures of governing a very large and very heterogeneous nation. Another viewpoint is that the program in operation is a struggle against the initial untenable goal structure, rather than as an example of the abandonment of any effort to house the central-city poor. James Q. Wilson catches the flavor of the operating success so interpreted:

> The agency and its staff wish to be able to achieve partic-
> ular goals in particular cases. Though the goals may be
> ambiguous and the cases all different, the general desire
> to realize a particular state of affairs is more important

to the agency than the desire simply to insure that the rules
are followed. To continue the analogy it is as if the base-
ball umpire desired not just to see that the game was played
fairly, but also that a certain number of runs were scored
(so that fans would be happy), a certain number of pitches
thrown (so the pitcher would get a good workout), and a
certain price charged by the owners (so they would be
either happy or unhappy, depending on his intentions).[26]

A less-benign view would be that different goals in the program
represent the interests of different groups and that, as the agency
and the program seek to maintain themselves, some groups receive
largely symbolic recognition of their demands while others receive
the tangible benefit.

Though undoubtedly new communities will be constructed, our
impression is that: (1) as indicated in our discussion of support, the
office will be captive in HUD, not fully independent of the "bankers";
(2) as indicated in our discussion of bureaucratic limits, the technology
will not be innovative;* (3) as indicated in our discussion of goals, the
housing is not likely to be integrated in all communities; and (4) as
indicated in our discussion of new-towns-intown, the location will
be primarily suburban and the impact on central-city population and
problems marginal. How much change new communities will make
in patterns of suburban development is also a subject of some concern—
even the inclusion of industrial with residential development is in some
doubt. Jonathan is said to have too much employment. Other new
communities rely heavily on the typical commercial development
of suburban areas. As Pressman and Wildavsky observe of EDA,
when a program is characterized by so many contradictory criteria,
antagonistic relationships among participants, and a high level of
uncertainty about even the possibility of success, it is not hard to
predict or to explain the failure of the effort to reach its goals. The
wonder is not that the program may flounder but that anyone thought
it could be implemented at all.[27]

The reality, it seems, is that the careful balancing of interests—
the mayors, the inner-city organizations, the black and the white
private developers, the investment companies, the public-interest
groups—is arranged so as to include all parties. But when all is

---

*Several of the guarantees are conditional, based on the de-
velopers' ability to solve specific technological problems (e.g., San
Antonio Ranch is faced with the situation of polluting its underground
water supply); on the whole, though, no widely applicable break-
throughs are being looked for or planned.

said and done, this inclusiveness has the effect of leaving the holders of guarantees to develop guidelines and indeed communities, according to criteria quite similar to those they used before—while they are receiving public guarantees and grants. The symbolism of "balance," "pairing," and "planning" reassures both blacks and whites; some tangible rewards to each are also available. But guarantees and grants are issued not to such mass publics but to very large private corporations in the insurance, investment, or mineral-development fields—corporations with priorities and definitions that ultimately define new-communities development.*

The idea of planned new communities is in many ways appealing. Federal efforts to prod the private sector toward new concepts involving coordinated development is also laudatory, for here government steps into a breach created by the difficulty of fulfilling the function through the market alone. Policy is made to fill the gap. But the policy process contains not only a policy-making but an implementing stage. Thus far in the new-communities program, government seems unable, once it has pointed out in legislation what might be done, to act in ways that change the basic nature of the private sector's activities. Instead, government relies on firms to flesh out the new programs and adopts private investors' concerns with marketability and fiscal soundness—and in the process it sacrifices innovation and integration. No one seems to have intended that this be so, yet no useful purpose can be served by denying that this program is going through the implementation process in a way that suggests that the new-communities program will one day be added to the list of federal policies failing to deliver the results their public proponents fought so hard for in the policy-making arena.

NOTES

1. The case material herein is interpreted in light of, and is heavily dependent on, the theoretical notions developed by three rather disparate sets of observers of bureaucracies: Jeffrey Pressman and Aaron Wildavsky, Implementation: How Great Expectations in Washington Are Dashed in Oakland; Or Why It's Amazing That Federal Programs Work at All, This Being a Saga of the Economic Development Administration as Told by Two Sympathetic Observers Who Seek to Build Morals on the Foundations of Ruined Hopes (in press, Berkeley,

---

*A separate investigation would be required to specify clearly the implications of this kind of corporate participation in the new-towns development process.

112

Calif.: University of California Press); James Q. Wilson, "The Bureaucracy Problem," The Public Interest, No. 6 (Winter 1967), pp. 3-9; and Robert R. Alford, "The Political Economy of Health Care: Dynamics Without Change," Politics and Society, II, 2 (Winter 1972), 127-64.

2. New Communities, U.S. Department of Housing and Urban Development, Publication No. M/IP 109 (June 1969), p. 3.

3. The History of Title IV can be traced through Legislative Research Council, Report Relative to New Towns, Commonwealth of Massachusetts, House Report No. 6192 (July 20, 1970); and Suzanne Farkas, Urban Lobbying (New York: New York University Press, 1971). An interesting view of the contents of Title IV before its trip through Congress is contained in Mortimer Zuckerman, "The Zurban Report" (a confidential memorandum prepared for the President's Task Force on the Development of New Town's Legislation, Fall 1967). On the development of Title VII see Hugh Mields Jr., "The Politics of Federal Legislation for New Community Development," in Shirley F. Weiss et al., eds., New Community Development: Planning Process, Implementation, and Emerging Social Concerns (Chapel Hill: Center for Urban and Regional Studies, University of North Carolina) (New Towns Research Seminar, October 1971), pp. 242-62. For an analysis of the legislation, see Charles L. Edson, "The Housing and Urban Development Act of 1970," The Urban Lawyer, III, 1 (Winter 1971), 142-48. See also National Housing Goals, Hearings, a record of the hearings held by the housing subcommittee of the Committee on Banking and Currency, U.S. Congress, House of Representatives, 91st Congress, 1st Session, 1969; Housing and Urban Development Legislation of 1970, Hearings, a record of the hearing held by the housing subcommittee of the Committee on Banking and Currency, U.S. Congress, House of Representatives, 91st Congress, 2d Session, Parts 1 and 2; and William Lilley III, "GPR Report/Parties, Agencies Scrambling to Shape Future of New Communities Program," National Journal, II, 14 (April 4, 1970), 726-35.

4. Jonathan B. Howes, "The Shape of Federal Involvement in New Community Building—1970," in Weiss, et al., eds., op. cit., pp. 161-92.

5. Housing and Urban Development Legislation of 1971, Hearings, a record of the hearings held by the housing subcommittee of the Committee on Banking and Currency, U.S. Congress, House of Representatives, 92d Congress, 1st Session, Part 1 (August 5, 1971), p. 326.

6. James Q. Wilson, "The Dead Hand of Regulation," The Public Interest, No. 25 (Fall 1971), p. 39.

7. Housing and Urban Development Legislation of 1969, Senate Report 91-392 to Accompany S. 2864, 90th Congress, 1969, pp. 23-24.

8. Housing and Urban Development Legislation of 1971, Hearings, p. 304.

9. Ibid, pp. 304-305.

10. The role and conditions of government as experimenter are developed in Pressman and Wildavsky, op. cit., pp. 187ff.

11. Independent Offices and Department of Housing and Urban Development, Hearings, a record of hearings held by the housing subcommittee of the Committee on Banking and Currency, U.S. Congress, House of Representatives, 91st Congress, 2d Session, Part 3, 1970, p. 296.

12. William J. Nicoson, "The Role of the Federal Government in New Community Development: Present and Projected," in Weiss, et al., eds., op. cit., p. 454.

13. Lloyd Rodwin and Lawrence Susskind, "New Communities and Urban Growth Strategies," (unpublished manuscript).

14. Robert Tennenbaum, "New Communities for the Seventies, Part I: St. Charles Communities, Maryland and Flower Mound, Texas," in Weiss, et al., eds., op. cit., pp. 413-50.

15. Robert E. Simon, "New Communities in the Seventies, Part II: Riverton, New York," in Weiss, et al., eds., op. cit., p. 201.

16. Donald T. Campbell, "Reforms as Experiments," Urban Affairs Quarterly, VII, 2 (December 1971), 136.

17. Wilson, op. cit., p. 8.

18. Reuben Clark and Paul J. Mode Jr., "Transfer of Power in New Communities," in Weiss, et al., eds., op. cit., pp. 30-31.

19. Robert M. Paul, "The New Town Development Process: Public and Private Venture," in Weiss, et al., eds., op. cit., p. 83.

20. See Frederick Wirt, Benjamin Walter, Francine Rabinovitz, and Deborah Hensler, On the City's Rim: Politics and Policy in Suburbs, (Lexington, Mass.: D. C. Heath, 1972). See chapters 8, 9, 13, and 14 for summaries of findings on attitudes toward racial and class integration in the suburbs and the results of federal dispersal-oriented policies.

21. Rodwin and Susskind, op. cit., p. 2.

22. Martha Derthick, New Towns In-Town: Why a Federal Program Failed, (Washington: The Urban Institute, 1972), p. 91.

23. 1967 Report of the Task Force on New Towns, Office of the Assistant Secretary for Metropolitan Development, HUD, pp. iii, 1-2.

24. Pressman and Wildavsky, op. cit., p. 155.

25. Rodwin and Susskind, op. cit., p. 5.

26. Wilson, op. cit., p. 51.

27. Pressman and Wildavsky, op. cit., p. 124.

PART

III

HUMAN
CONSIDERATIONS:
LIFE STYLES,
INTEGRATION,
AND GOVERNANCE

CHAPTER

7

NEW TOWNS TO SET
NEW LIFE STYLES
Margaret Mead

An examination of the mass of experience on new towns points
to many purposes—new towns to develop new areas, to house special
populations, or simply (it is to be hoped) to serve as experimental
models for new planning. In analyzing the literature I was struck by
two things: (1) the socioeconomic emphasis in which people are
thought of in large groups or categories of race, class, age, and
income level, with the possible assumption that individuals are
interchangeable within such categories; and (2) the relative absence
of any explicit tracing of the connections between actual physical
design—size and shape of a house, design of the streets, kind of
amenities and how they are housed and located—and the quality of
life. Partly in response to the need for this emphasis, and also in
response to the importance of dealing with the human factor, I want
to emphasize these two points, which seem to me to have been severely
scanted. I also want to discuss the way in which the pressures to
modify our way of life that come from the recognition of the environmental crisis may provide the necessary frame within which needed
changes may be undertaken.

To date, public plans for the design of cities or towns, or
private plans for the design of mansion houses, or rows of tenants
or workers' cottages, have been responsive to a series of constraints,
including the amount of resources available, and the social doctrines
of the period—the way in which it was appropriate to lay out a city
in honor of a monarch or a newly created state, or suitable to provide
housing for the necessary poor (those who tilled the fields, worked the
mines, unloaded the docks, or lived in slave quarters on plantations).
Architects and planners worked, on the one hand, to enhance the prestige and glory of noble or wealthy patrons, and on the other to econo-
mize and still house the poor.

117

It has been in rare instances that whole towns have been laid out for all those who were to live in them, providing shelter and security, dignity and participation for all. Even in the egalitarian and town-conscious days of our colonial forefathers, there was a grading of residences closer to the center for the more prosperous who might be the least likely to move on. Cities and towns around the world have been marred by the disregard, the contempt, or the downright hostility of those who planned for some of the people who lived just within or just without the gates. Now, as much as any time in the militaristic and imperialistic pasts, the same tendencies prevail; whole towns are built to someone's glory, need is rated low, and there is very little participation by those who will live there.

Yet I think it is very clear that unless a town is planned by and with, as well as for, those who will live there, we will continue to be plagued by the evils of which we have such an abundance at the present time. It is true that our own condition is exacerbated by the long history of immigration and the contemptuous relegation of the new immigrants to the worst housing, by the virulence of our racial prejudices, and by a class system in which the status of members of each class is endangered by the close presence of members of a lower class. It is also undoubtedly true that these factors, combined with the influx of unskilled and unwanted labor into the cities, and the exodus of both affluent families and the newer, cleaner and more affluent industries from the cities, have contributed to the present crisis. But in the course of our preoccupation with the desperate social, political, and moral evils that have accompanied our present urban arrangements (all of them derivative of and worsened by the automobile), we have become so preoccupied with one set of consequences—the condition of rural and urban slums—that we end up forgetting that the terrible conditions of any part of a population reflect directly upon all the rest.

I believe that the present growth of suburbs—residential units homogeneous by age, class, and race primarily designed as bedrooms—is itself a reflection, cause, and condition of our planning priorities, in which no one, except the occasional wealthy man who can employ an individual architect, has any real choice in how a couple and their children will live. Hunting for a house in a strange city where one has found a new job is as unrelated to genuine human values as trying to find half a room in a slum or half a kitchen in an Eastern European country with a housing shortage. For all the appearance of affluence in many of our upper-middle-class suburbs, and for all the appearance of adequacy in the gadget-filled house with garage available to many members of the working class, we are nevertheless all trapped in a no-choice residential world as far as fundamental human values are concerned.

In a situation as desperate as the urban crisis in the United States, with the kind of tie-in between government and private industry in which radical change is very difficult to bring about, there is a tendency to overestimate one set of factors. So, in the UN Ad Hoc Expert Group Meeting on the Role of Housing in Promoting Social Integration, held in Stockholm, May 8-13, 1972, integration was seen as the proper aim for every society, and the right of people to associate closely with their own kind—with those who shared the same manners and aspirations—was only grudgingly accorded as something that might be permitted, but certainly should never be assisted in any way by public funds. Yet integration, while emphasizing the need to permit disallowed minorities the choice now permitted majority or affluent groups, also carries within it an implicit endorsement of the values that are presently being denied to the poor and the racially disallowed. It carries the same kind of self-regarding ethnocentrism that any other doctrine of integration carries; the extension, to those who are not like them, of a better chance to be like the majority group. If the children of the minority group can play on the same street and attend the same school, if in fact the neighborhood is integrated, or microintegrated (as Herbert Gans uses the term), they will, it is assumed, be better off.

It is also assumed that segregation automatically carries with it poverty, disease, educational disability, and crime, which in turn make those who emerge from segregated areas unable to compete in the larger world. The argument then proceeds that, because new towns seem to offer very little in the way of mitigating racial and class segregation and little for the very poor, they are automatically not worth building and can contribute nothing that is needed in our harassed society.

I would maintain, however, that if we abandon our class-centric attitudes, which presume that whatever the most affluent of us have is good, and say instead that there are virtues in diversity and virtues in similarity, that both need protection, and that our cities are bad cities because neither value is adequately recognized, we may approach closer to the ideal of designing towns for all the people who are going to live there. If people are not given some device through which those with common social and cultural backgrounds can live close together, share each others cooking smells and lullabys and jokes, there is no hope of their children growing up with a relationship to their pasts that they will be able to transmit to their children. Single households of Germans or Irish or Eastern European Jews or Southern blacks cannot transmit their version of their ancestral culture to their children. To do this takes a neighborhood where the children must come in at the same time to supper, or are allowed to play all night in the street. Under the guise of attempting to remedy the terrible conditions to which we have steadily reduced the poorest and most helpless among us, we are still insisting, in the old patronizing strain, that they should be forced to accept the majority values, along with jobs, security, and decent homes.

Actually, though, our policy of segregating the newly arriving poor—in the past those who had another version of European culture and, today those who have another version of American culture and are distinguished by physical differences—has deprived all Americans of choice and of their rights to shared diversity, and has resulted in segregating the whole country. Only in the small towns that are rapidly vanishing do we have anything like a society where there is a place for everyone. All go to school together and each has an opportunity, even in the acrimoniously prejudiced present, to find that others are human because they are like themselves, and interesting because they are different.

Those who lack interest in new towns because they seem unlikely to solve our massive problems fail to emphasize the large number of inhumanities that now characterize our present-day residential arrangements. If new towns would give us an opportunity to develop social forms and architectural styles that would make life more human again, then they could make a great contribution—one that is wholly disproportionate to the amount of capital or effort that goes into them, or the number of people they house.

I am speaking here of a new town as being any newly built community in which comprehensive planning for all aspects of life can be included, whether it is a new town staked out in a meadow, a new area of city where the old buildings have been mainly or partly demolished (a new-town-intown), or a well-designed new town erected on top of an old one. None of the contributions I wish to emphasize are restricted to any one of these. What is needed is a new conception of what a community is and how it can be designed and built with and for its residents. Any one of these three kinds of new towns can be used for experiments in meeting human needs.

A community is a group of people with ties to each other, ties of kinship and friendship, ties of shared work and shared responsibility and shared pleasure. The nucleus of any community is people who know and value each other. Therefore the first requirement for constructing a new community is to devise a way in which people who already know each other can form the nucleus. It has been argued that in a completely new town the inhabitants are not there yet and so cannot take part. But the residents of new towns, even of some single-industry town in a remote wilderness, are not recruited from the moon. And in most cases the people who will move into a new town already live and work somewhere nearby under somewhat less satisfactory circumstances. They could be recruited early, to come as friends and neighbors and kin, to plan how they would like to live, how close or far away from each other they would like to be, how they would like to provide for privacy, one from another, and for shared pleasures within the generations. Yet little consideration is given to the fact that friends may just possibly like to live near each other; that although a family does not want grandmother in the house they would enjoy having her down the street, comfortably on her own; or that the best friends a boy has may turn out to be the children he played with in a sandpile years before.

Paying some attention to creating the conditions in which people who enjoy taking vacations together or working together could also enjoy living within easy visiting distance of each other would accomplish several objectives: provide a planning nucleus of participating residents, provide a base for citizen responsibility, and create a very different life style.

It was this life style, where people lived around the corner and married daughters saw their mothers several times a day, that was wrecked in England when the first new housing was built. This is the destruction of life style that is lamented by inhabitants who remember an earlier Harlem, and which third-generation Czech and Polish and Italian communities are complaining about all over the United States. Poverty and crime and misery in the inner city, and planned one-class, one-age, one-occupational style suburbs, have robbed people of the right of living close together. Neither the block where the poor, living on welfare, move in and out, nor the suburb where the newcomer knows no one (and thinks he wants to know no one), meet this need. Moving among strangers, such people are wary of strangers. In some of the new developments outside Sydney, Australia, residents said they kept themselves to themselves so that a collection agent who came snooping about after a time-payment could not get any information.

In these noncommunities, where everyone is a stranger and equally lost, there is no basis ever to become friends, except when there are children who play together. The idea that this is the way to plan for living is as stupid as the notion that it is good for college students to be assigned roommates as freshmen, and only allowed to choose roommates as upper classmen. What happens more and more is that, coming from a nuclear family without close kin or neighbors, the boy or girl is so unprepared for sharing anything with anyone that a year of living with a stranger prepares them only for a desire to live alone, or with one mate replicating their parents' home. Forced propinquity does not make people into community members.

A second defect of our present system of residential non-choice is that suburbs and apartment houses in so-called developments are constructed in such a way that young people have no expectation of living anywhere near where they now live. Part of the furious repudiation by young people of their parents' way of life—the more affluent, the more furious—comes from growing up in segregated suburbs in which they themselves will not be able to live, and from which their wealthy parents will have to move when they retire. Equally, the widow who has lived for twenty years in a modern suburban zoned community will have to move because the town does not have any apartment where she can live. Here we see a clear case of the way in which the kind of zoning designed to keep "undesirable people" out of a town—because they are poor or black, have a lot of children to burden the school system or would rent and contribute less to the school tax—ends up with depriving the very people who have participated in the exclusionary zoning and contributing to a segregated, fragmented way of life.

For community we need three generations. We need a place that the young can grow into, where the adults move about, leave and return to, and where the old can live out their days close to children, in a familiar landscape. We need adequate provision for young people to have haunts of their own, where the noise they have invented to encapsulate themselves does not deafen the ears of their elders. We need places where those in need can find work because they are close to those who need them—to clear snow, baby-sit, or provide daily household or garden assistance. We need places where young beginning professionals, teachers, and white-collar workers can live close by the places where they work, near the schools and banks and public offices that serve members of other income groups and other occupations.

A second human need, as important as the need for community, is the need for continuity, which is strongest in infancy and early childhood, essential for the sanity of the old, and essential too for the humanity of all ages. Where infants and children just learning to talk are concerned, this means that no professionally manned day-care center can substitute for the continuing care that can be provided by an individual who knows what that child saw and heard yesterday. Where mothers work, only communities where there are older people, free to spend time with children, can provide such continuity. And only in communities where the housing and neighborhood plans are designed to accommodate diversity can such needs be met.

So the intimate relationships between town planning and meeting human needs for community and continuity become immediately clear. If members of different generations are to live near each other, certain kinds of housing needs must be met. There must be provision for older people to walk to shopping centers, to visit each other, and to visit the playground or the nursery; there must be housing which they can afford and manage without undo strain, and where they will be safe. The special needs of older people, both men and women, can be determined only by careful observation combined with a chance for them to participate in the planning process. If our old people were properly provided for, we would no longer have to shunt them off into retirement ghettos where they have to smile and pretend they are content when their children come long distances to visit them.

So community is something that demands that there be diversity of housing types—housing for the young, the old, the middle-aged and the single—and services that permit people to live in these different ways close together. It requires meeting places where a meal can be shared, places where casual meetings with people one knows are always possible—as there were and still are on the streets of a small European town. It means that a young couple should not have to buy a large house, rattle around in it until their children are born, and cling on to it after the children have left home. It ought to be possible to move just a few blocks or miles away, as life situations change, or find a home again after having been abroad or in another part of the country for a decade. We need to invent much lighter ties to the ownership of a particular dwelling and much stronger ties to a community, so the ownership of a particular house would constitute a sort of residential charter, rather than just a material asset to be narrowly guarded, or a liability that limits freedom and association.

A further human need is the one for women to have a place in the world that is comparable in dignity and importance to that of men. This was provided for historically by the expectation that every woman would devote her entire life to the tasks of homemaking and child-bearing, being busy and troubled over the needs of the next generation, and supporting the efforts of a husband to devote his talents and strength to that next generation also. When people lived at a sub-sistence level, neither men nor women had time or energy to spare for anything other than mere subsistence. When agriculture was invented, society could support a few men who did other things besides seeking for tomorrow's food but women remained dedicated to child-bearing and childrearing.

The population explosion has changed all this; society now needs a stabilized population, not an ever-increasing one, and this in turn means that only a small portion of the working life of either men or women will be devoted to rearing children. Many people will have none children, others only one or two. Our present residential style—the single house with its expensive use of energy and space, and its isolation from others—is designed for the single family with several children. We now need entirely new designs, ones that make new provision for privacy for parents away from children, for care of children in groups, for houses that do not demand the continuous attention of a woman, and for services that can be obtained centrally. We need designs that permit families with children to find appropriate housing, but do not force everyone to live as if they had four young children throughout the whole fifty years of an active adult life.

But most of the modern world is covered with attempts to provide each family with a self-contained house, and new housing everywhere treats the family unit of parents and children as if it could move anywhere, unencumbered by other ties, not even intimately related to the place where the husband works, and with no provision at all for the place where the wife might work or for a home that can be maintained without her continuous presence. It is a human need today to provide for modern changes in the career line, to make it possible for women to contribute to public life as individuals, to construct the physical relationships between residence and work so that both men and women may be able to combine work, avocation, and residence in ways that are much more economical and humane.

Human beings, especially children, need closeness and familiarity with all of life, with their own bodies and the bodies of adults, with birds and beasts and blades of grass, with changes in the seasons and movements of the stars, and with the quiet that is invaded by no mechanical sound, where they can listen to their own heartbeats. Yet we have built in such a way that much of this is denied to them. Instead we are providing for a kind of vacation in which people, moving in hoards, descend upon and destroy our few remaining large pieces of natural wilderness, rather than building parks, pools and small wildernesses, and farms and gardens within the limits of the city.

These are demonstrated human needs—the people's need for community and continuity, their need for participation in constructing their own communities, their need for choice in where and with whom they will live, their need to remain or leave or return to places they have lived before, and their need to provide their children with closeness to the natural world.

But all of these needs appear in far more diverse forms than the needs for nutriment that are so easy to demonstrate, with physiological tests of the body and chemical tests of the food. It is difficult to draw blueprints for mass production that can fit human needs; it has been much easier to mass produce dwellings that are straight-jackets within which human beings fitted willy-nilly, to put people into the mold that is now continually described as middle-class, selfish, narrow, prejudiced, xenophobic and egocentric—all characteristics that have been nourished by the residential life that has grown up in the last hundred years and become intensified in the last twenty-five.

It is clear that new towns would give an opportunity to experime in change. Earlier participation in planning, delaying the completion of some parts or sections of a town, postponing the exact location of a path until footsteps have worn it, designing units that are convertible into different sizes, designing neighborhoods in ways that produce clusters of ethnic or life-style seclusion within larger areas that provide contact with many other kinds of people, allowing for choice of neighbors and friends instead of for atomization—all this could be done, and done more easily in a new town than in an old one. Nothing is harder to convert into a community than a well-zoned modern suburb where there are not even sidewalks on which people can walk, if there were anywhere to walk to.

But several questions remain. Where does the demand for such ways of life come from, and has it enough strength to meet the intention of planners if that intention were in fact there? Will people indeed simply echo what they see pictured on the ads today, stating, for example, that they are willing to give up a dining room for a family room—(which simply reflects the disappearance of servants in the upper-middle class and the revolt of the middle-class wife against playing the role of a servant)? Will they demand replicas of what they see on television, the homes which the poor rightly despair of ever attaining, so that many of them turn to crime instead? Will all the resources of the market, not only of available funds but of manufacturing and employment styles, foil any attempts even to experiment architecturally and in town-planning with such innovations in making our residential arrangements more human?

These are basic objections and they are advanced in terms of several kinds of rationale. One objection is the intractability of human nature; tastes are deeply engrained, and those people who have been reared within the lack of neighborhood in our segregated world will want just that and be unable to change; they will reconvert whatever is built into a replica of the old.

Our belief that this does not have to be so, is based on many kinds of observed change, where change in social expectations has established a new style, as when the wealthy deserted their great houses that required an army of servants, and moved into small apartments that could be run without servants—a change that was completed very rapidly during the 1940s in the United States. We have seen Puerto Rican immigrants, highly resistant to changes in nutritional style at home, become amenable to suggestion when their entire physical circumstances were changed by living in high-rise flats in mainland cities. We have seen experiments showing that people are much more willing to accept a new food in a new container than either an old food in a new container or a new food in an old container.

As a field anthropologist I have followed in detail a Melanesian people—the Manus—who took their entire cultural style into their own hands, redesigned every bit of it—village plan, house, furniture, social organization, village responsibility—and with this across-the-board change were able to skip centuries into the modern world. But there were several essential ingredients in their success: they overhauled everything; no slight detail escaped scrutiny; they did it themselves under their own power; and they brought all three generations with them, leaving no old-fashioned people to pull them back. The implications of this historical experiment for new towns is obvious: the town would be new, everything could be rearranged, the residents could participate in the planning, three generations could be welcomed in.

But the case of the Manus contained one other element—a remarkably intelligent and charismatic leader. In the contemporary world, such single leadership is being replaced by teams that are able to diffuse a knowledge of what they have done. A new town that met these needs sufficiently dramatically, but in ways that are not as strikingly different and as unacceptable as Buckminster Fuller's original dymaxion house, would catalyze building and planning throughout the country and the world. It is particularly important to realize that every innovation in town-planning and styles of housing, good or bad, reverberates around the world; new towns designed for new countries are built by international firms, using models from their own countries. Experiments must be conducted and popularized with all the reservations that will protect those who would wish to copy them whole. What is needed is not to popularize a particular kind of housing or housing mix or town plan, but to popularize the idea that there can be kinds of housing and housing mixes and participant planning that will suit other situations.

Ideas like these can be spread; the whole notion of "do-it-yourself" during the 1960s was a case in point. Ideas such as slow completion with resident participation, house designs that can be altered easily, access to different kinds of housing for different life periods, the need to include homemaking styles and accessibility to a labor market for women as well as for men—all these could be experimented with and then diffused.

There are also other changes coming that should make such experiments more viable. One of these is the demand for the rationalization of power lines, communication lines, and highways so that properly planned utility corridors will make it possible to lay out space that is no longer controlled by small recalcitrant local governments, and guarantee the possibilities of building and locating industry within such a matrix. This should make it possible to translate the inventions made in planned new towns into the planning of less controlled and more market-directed housing.

A second change is the demand of young people—the style-setting upper-middle-class young people, who had such an influence on the life styles of the 1960s—for a more humane, more diversified kind of society, where people live closer together and depend upon each other more, where there is more joy and less competition. These are the young people who are looking for more human places to live and who may become early participants and creative style-setters in planned new towns.

A third change is the whole ecological movement, which demands a more economical use of energy and use of biodegradable materials. These demands reinforce attempts to design more human, less artificial, more interdependent ways of life, where power and machinery can be centralized, energy conserved, space allotted to protected open areas, transportation rationalized, and dependence upon the automobile minimized. All of these demands, dramatized in an enormous number of activities, are favorable to the kind of experimentation and diffusion I have been discussing.

The time seems to be ripe for experiment; those who could participate are clamoring for new life styles and recognizing that, without a well-designed structural basis in town-planning, regional planning, and new architectural forms, the kind of life style they would like to see will be impossible. If each experimental component is examined in the light of criteria for providing community and continuity, choice of association of friends and relatives and colleagues, ability for people to move within a community and not merely into and out of it, conservation of resources and protection of the environment, then the chances of diffusion of innovations will be enormously enhanced.

BIBLIOGRAPHY

Doxiadis, C. A. City for Human Development. Athens: Athens Center of Ekistics, 1972.

_____. "Networks: Movement of People and Public Services: 1967," Ekistics, XXXIII, 197 (April 1972).

Garvan, Anthony N. B. Architecture and Town Planning in Colonial Connecticut. New Haven: Yale University Press, 1951.

Gordon, R. E., and others. The Split-Level Trap. New York: Geis; Toronto: Random House, 1961.

Hall, Edward T. The Hidden Dimension. Garden City, N.Y.: Doubleday, 1966.

Keniston, Kenneth. The Uncommitted: Alienated Youth in American Society. New York: Harcourt Brace, 1965.

Keniston, Kenneth. Young Radicals. New York: Holt, Rinehart and Winston, 1968.

Mead, Margaret. "Broken Homes," Nation, CXXVIII, 3321 (February 1929), 253-55.

_____. "Cross-Cultural Significance of Space," Ekistics, XXXII, 191 (October 1971), 271-72.

_____. "Cultural Discontinuities and Personality Transformation," Journal of Social Issues, Supplemental Series No. 8 (1954), pp. 3-16.

_____. "Cultural Factors in the Housing Patterns of the United States," Ad Hoc Expert Group Meeting on the Role of Housing in Promoting Social Integration, May 8-13, 1972. Stockholm, Sweden: in press.

_____. Culture and Commitment: A study of the Generation Gap. Garden City, N.Y.: Natural History Press/Doubleday, 1970.

_____. "Energy Changes Under Conditions of Cultural Change," Sociometry and the Science of Man, XVIII, 4 (December 1955), 201-11.

_____. "Ethnological Aspects of Aging," Psychosomatics, VIII, Section 2 (July 1967), 33-37.

_____. "Megalopolis: Is It Inevitable?" Transactions of the Bartlett Society, III (1965c), pp. 23-41.

_____. New Lives for Old: Cultural Transformation—Manus 1928-1953. New York: Morrow, 1956; reprinted 1966.

_____. "Outdoor Recreation in the Context of Emerging American Cultural Values," in Trends in American Living and Outdoor Recreation, pp. 2-25. Washington, D.C.: Government Printing Office, 1962.

_____. "Problems of the Late Adolescent and Young Adult," in Children and Youth in the 1960's: Survey Papers Prepared for the 1960 White House Conference on Children and Youth, pp. 3-12. Washington, D.C.: Golden Anniversary White House Conference on Children and Youth, 1960.

_____ . "The Crucial Role of the Small City in Meeting the Urban Crisis," in Richard Eels and Clarence Walton, eds., Man in the City of the Future, pp. 29-57. New York: Macmillan, 1968.

_____ . "The Pattern of Leisure in Contemporary American Culture," Annals of the American Academy of Political and Social Science, CCCXIII (September 1957), 11-15.

_____ . "Towards More Vivid Utopias," Science CXXVI, 3280 (November 1957), 957-61.

_____ . "Values for Urban Living," Annals of the American Academy of Political and Social Science, CCCIV (November 1957), 10-14.

_____ . "Working Mothers and Their Children," Manpower, II, 6 (June 1970), 3-6.

Mead, Margaret, and Muriel Brown. The Wagon and the Star: A Study of American Community Initiative. Chicago: Rand McNally, 1966.

Myers, Dowell. "Forest Hills: The Function of Scattersite Housing in the Integration Process." Unpublished manuscript, 1972.

Pettigrew, Thomas F. Attitudes on Race and Housing: A Social Psychological View. Washington, D.C.: National Academy of Science, Division of Behavioral Sciences, 1971.

Schwartz, Theodore, and Margaret Mead. "Micro- and Macro-Cultural Models for Cultural Evolution," Anthropological Linguistics, Vol. III (1961) pp. 1-7.

Waddington, C. H. "Space for Development," Ekistics, XXXII, 191 (October 1971), 268-69.

Waddington, C. H., and others. Biology and the History of the Future, IUBS/UNESCO Symposium. Edinburgh: Edinburgh University Press, 1972.

8

SOCIAL PLANNING,
PERCEPTIONS,
AND NEW TOWNS
Marshall Kaplan

Social planning remains more a moral imperative articulated by a few federal staff people and academicians than a body of reasonably understood and accepted techniques. National and university rhetoric on the subject has plainly outrun the professional's capacity to deliver. We know amazingly little about varying individual or group perceptions of space and services occupying space, and we do not have the type of information needed to plan realistically for new-town populations.

With the above as caveats, I would like to take you through a recent (and, I think, innovative) attempt to relate household needs/ priorities to community planning and development efforts associated with the new town of Flower Mound, Texas, through a survey designed specifically to find out about such needs and priorities. I believe our efforts were significant in that the methodology used seems to extend previous efforts at linking behavioral patterns directly to planning processes. Equally important the results of our efforts played a major role in shaping the developer's plans.*

Essentially we initiated two extensive interviews—one a highly structured mail questionnaire directed at visitors to assumed competitor models and employees at the present airport** the second a

---

*The study was carried out by the firm Kaplan, Gans and Kahn. Credit must go to Raymond D. Nasher, developer of Flower Mound, near Dallas, for his willingness to use the development as an urban laboratory. His commitment to making the new town come as close as possible to anticipated resident needs and desires was clearly articulated to those of us who served as staff, advisers, and consultants.

**Visitors to models were thought to come close to the characteristics of "first residents"; airport employees were sampled because of the imminent opening of the new regional airport near the site.

lengthy face-to-face interview directed at selected subgroups within the Dallas/Fort Worth populations. The total sample size of the first group was close to 1,400; the second, 600.

Both questionnaires were oriented toward determining resident perception of existing services, and resident toleration for new services (as well as delivery of services). The "face-to-face" survey also sought to gain a fix on life styles of varied class/caste groups. Each survey was capable of generating multi-variate analyses. (A special subset was directed at nonmarket participants, lower-income households, teenagers, blacks, chicanos, etc.)

The characteristics of those who participated in the mail survey (close to 12 percent) paralleled profiles of market households by the Federal Housing Administration and the Bureau of the Census. The sample interviewed in face-to-face sessions replicated returns for the mail questionnaire. While many of the survey's general conclusions supported conventional wisdom concerning perceptions held by a population weighted heavily in favor of low-moderate and moderate-income households ("traditionalism," conservation, automobile orientation, use of television, etc.), several findings seem to depart significantly from accepted norms. These indicated that:

1. Although the terms "neighborhood" and "village" remain popular (among consumers and at HUD), individual household life styles and perceptions of needs seem to mute the social and economic importance of these terms.

2. Household perceptions of space and value of space vary considerably by income and race; in effect, the importance of "place" and a sense of place appear to vary significantly by income, race, and household status. Certainly the definition of community begins to take on nonspatial connotations as one's income and mobility options increase.

3. Most nonpoor would willingly tolerate—indeed, in some areas, demand—modifications to existing social services and the delivery of services. (This varies by type of service; e.g., changes in health services are more acceptable than changes in education.)

4. Integration would be accepted by most people, as long as income differential is not too severe. (Tolerable class differences, however, appear narrower in Texas than in many other parts of the country.)

5. The safety-and-security issue is all-pervasive, affecting all groups in the population and generating considerable tension with respect to purchase and rental decisions.

6. Planner's jargon and value-laden premises concerning new towns and planned environments must still be "sold" to skeptical parties in the market. For example, as one's income increases, new towns lose their merchandising value unless defined in terms of options

131

for "exclusivity" and nonregimentation. Clearly new towns are viewed by moderate-income families partially in terms of equity protection.

IMPLICATIONS OF THE SURVEY

The survey provided many details on perceptions and preferences, most with significant planning ramifications. They suggest the patterns that can be expected to emerge in the new towns.

General Life Style

Most of the initial population attracted to Flower Mound will be married and in their twenties or early thirties. While the largest number of households will have annual incomes in the mid- to upper-teens, incomes will range from very low to very high. Although children will be a common sight in Flower Mound, smaller families will be the rule, rather than the exception.

Nearly one out of every three wives will work at least part-time, with the proportion tending to increase with income. Many heads of households will work longer than a 40-hour week. Those having higher incomes will have one job and those having low and moderate incomes will frequently have two.

Nearly 100 percent of the households will own an automobile, 50 percent will have two, and approximately 10 percent will have three. Automobiles will be the preferred mode of travel for most types of trips, irrespective of the quality and availability of public-transportation alternatives.

Almost 50 percent of all working individuals will be willing to travel between 11 and 25 miles to get to work. Over 10 percent will accept a journey to work that extends beyond 25 miles. Upper-income individuals will, as a rule, be accustomed to traveling less distance to work than lower-income individuals.

Housing

Ownership will clearly be the preferred type of tenure for households of all income levels. Households with few or no children and those households with incomes above $20,000, however, will find an amenity-oriented, well-designed, and conveniently located rental unit competitive. Although they will prefer ownership, lower-income families will accept rental status.

132

Detached units will find most acceptance among most early households attracted to the site. Attached and multi-family units will be preferred, however, by an increasing number of young singles, marrieds without children, and the elderly. Multi-family units will also become increasingly competitive with single-family detached units as incomes and numbers of children increase.

Because they will be concerned about the safety of children and the nearness of friends, young marrieds with small children will accept clustering of residences more readily than will other households. More affluent families will prefer and pay for less organized housing environments; golf course and lake-frontage sites will be highly desirable housing locations for them.

"House for the money," defined in terms of space, room size and resale value, will be a principal ingredient in the purchase decisions of those initially attracted to the site. Planning will be viewed primarily in terms of its protection of future resale value and equity.

Different income groups will demand different ingredients in their housing. For example, while family rooms, rather than dining rooms, will be preferred by moderate-income groups, dining rooms will be preferred by the more affluent. Room arrangements will be relatively more important to upper-income than to moderate- and lower-income groups.

Mixing of housing types will be easier to achieve at the micro-scale than the mixing of divergent housing prices and rent levels.

Recreation

Unstructured or unorganized play will be preferred by most adults and young children. Passive recreational activities, such as short walks and picnics, will be more popular than active ones. Rates of recreational participation will generally vary with the level of household income; the lower the household income, the lower the participation rate.

Although television and movies will clearly consume more hours than any other recreational activity, many households will want to engage in hobbies and the performing arts. The opportunities to attend formal spectator art programs, such as the theater and ballet, will be desired by a sizable minority, particularly those whose incomes approach $20,000 a year.

Religion

Nearly three out of four of the early residents of Flower Mound will be interested in participating in religious activities. Many will apparently accept interdenominational sharing of a single location, but resistance will increase if sharing a location leads to sharing facilities. The church, particularly among low- and moderate-income families, will be a center for a wide range of social activities.

Education

Classroom size will be of more concern to residents than school size. Also, most families will be concerned more with the quality of education than the location of the school. Quality will be defined differently, however, depending on income. Lower- and moderate-income families will seek traditional facilities and teaching processes directed toward "a basic education" and the "three R's." Affluent households will more readily approve innovations in both facilities and teaching processes, such as open classrooms, team teaching, and new educational technology.

Most households, regardless of income, will want their children to do well in school and to continue their education. Approximately 85 percent of the high school seniors will want to continue their education at the post-secondary level.

Adult and continuing education opportunities as well as pre-school opportunities for youngsters will be viewed as valuable adjuncts to community life. Should these options be available, however, intensity of use will vary by income unless special assistance is provided.

At least one-quarter of the adult population will wish to attend adult education classes of one kind or another. The higher the population's educational attainment, the greater will be the demand for continuing education opportunities.

Health

Given its projected income and age characteristics, Flower Mound's population can be expected to be relatively healthy. Most new residents will be covered by some form of private or group insurance, although many will find coverage and costs less than satisfactory.

Choice of doctors will be premised first on the quality of the patient/physician relationship; second, on the expertise of the physician, and finally on the costs of professional services. People will be willing to travel reasonably lengthy distances to find a doctor or dentist they like. Preference for selected facilities and services will clearly vary by income and education.

Safety and Security

Choice of Flower Mound as a place to live will in part be linked to perceptions of it as a safe environment. Fully 70 percent of the survey respondents listed a safe environment as being the most important or secondmost important factor in their decision to locate in a given area. Property damage rather than bodily harm will be a more pervasive fear among all income groups.

Positive perceptions of the role and functions of the police will be prevalent among those whose incomes are classified as moderate to affluent. Without special police-community programs, lower-income groups will be more likely to articulate criticism of the police.

Commercial

People will prefer large centers providing a variety of stores and goods; small convenience shopping centers will be relatively unpopular with the population. Trips by car will be favored over trips by foot, even if the facilities are close enough to permit pedestrian access.

Community Involvement

Most residences will be uninvolved in the traditional processes of local government. Civic and social organizations will, however, stimulate political activities for all income groups. For lower-income groups, these organizations will tend to be work-related or class-oriented; for the more affluent, they will tend to be communitywide in nature and issue-oriented—like the Parent-Teachers' Association and League of Women Voters. Concern with commitments made or believed to be made in the new town will continually activate varied reactions among existing residents and new residents of the area.

CONCLUSIONS

What does all this mean in terms of planning for the new town? The following observations appear in order:

1. Given the pace at which life still seems to be changing, at least for some, we ought clearly to try to emphasize planning processes rather than plans. (In effect, political and institutional factors may dictate "hardness" in terms of early documents, yet consumer perceptions and cash-flow needs suggest keeping options open.)

2. More priority should be given the space around the residence and the space included in larger commercial facilities than heretofore. Rigid adherence to a hierarchical organization of space (neighborhood, village, etc.) is outmoded and irrelevant from both a social and economic perspective.

3. Clearly the number, type, and location of community services need not be premised on traditional or conventional standards. Specific needs of specific individuals and groups should govern definition of services. Criteria premised on accessibility and choice seem preferable to criteria governed by centrality and/or hierarchal structure.

4. A range of housing types and prices will be difficult to achieve at the cluster scale, but possible to achieve at a large scale (grouping of clusters). Even at the larger scale, variations in price and type will of necessity, however, require careful attention.

5. "House for the money" may be a more compelling competitive attribute for certain income groups than amenity, recreation, etc.

6. Clearly, for some time in the future, the automobile will be the dominant and preferred way of travel. Recreational preferences will vary by class and caste. Romantic notions relative to the popularity of walking, of golf, etc., may lead developers astray. Pathways should be short and purposeful.

While such findings do not provide definitive answers to all the issues that are certain to arise in the building of the new town, they do at least provide a useful framework for the planning that will guide its development.

9

THE POSSIBILITIES
OF CLASS AND RACIAL
INTEGRATION
IN AMERICAN NEW TOWNS:
A POLICY-ORIENTED ANALYSIS
Herbert J. Gans

The myth of the new is a persistent element of American culture, and many Americans believe that significant social change can be accomplished simply by adding or superimposing something new on to the status quo. For example it is often suggested that pollution can be ameliorated by new technological inventions, that the problems of the cities can be solved by adding a new government agency in Washington, and that the communication blocs in society can be removed by adding a new mass medium, such as cable television. Like all myths, this one is not entirely inaccurate, for social change does require novelty. But novelty alone is insufficient; it must be preceeded by other changes that make old solutions unworkable and create receptivity for new solutions. Thus setting up the U.S. Department of Housing and Urban Development (HUD) was not enough to alter national priorities toward urban problems; these priorities were altered more when the ghettos erupted in violence, which made it possible to give HUD—and the Office of Economic Opportunity (OEO)—additional powers and resources, at least for a short time.

THE MYTH OF THE NEW TOWN

Perhaps the most enduring myth has developed around the new town, the independent and clearly bounded new community with its own government, public facilities, and sources of employment. This myth holds that, by building new towns, America can solve a number of its urban problems, establish better public services, create new forms of class and racial integration that do not now exist in its cities and suburbs, and implement other innovations.

This is, however, a dangerous myth, for the new towns that have been built so far in America are new in only a few ways. Starting

with Radburn, they have accomplished some innovation in site-planni
and in public services, but most of them have been only slightly supe
suburbs for the upper-middle and middle classes. Economically,
socially, and politically, they are just old communities on newly
residential land.

Their lack of novelty stems from several causes. First, new
towns are not built on politically, economically, or socially new
ground. Even previously empty land is already someone's political
turf, controlled by power structures and by state and local regulatior
that define in advance the limits of political innovation.

Second, new towns are not economically novel; even with the
advent of government subsidies, they are still largely dependent on
existing mechanisms for the financing and construction of housing,
and innovation is limited by the careful conservatism of the funding
agencies. The clearest example is Reston, Virginia, where innovatic
came to a virtual halt when Gulf Oil took over the town from Robert
Simon.

Third, unless new towns are built in a seller's market, they
must adapt themselves to the expected demands of their potential
buyers, and these demands rarely include innovation. The people wh
buy homes in new towns are not very different from those who buy ir
ordinary suburban tracts; a few are pioneers who come to make a
new life or a new community in the new town, but most come becaus
they like the house, and they will like the house only if it is not
radically different from what other builders offer. The market failu
of much of Simon's architectural innovation in Reston is again an
example.

Moreover, new-town purchasers bring with them their old cul
and their ideas about what kinds of civic, social, religious, and othe
organizations are desirable. Sometimes these old ideas do not worl
so new ones are invented on the spot; for the most part, though, the
old ideas do work—and precisely because the new town is not social
novel—so that the new-towners often reestablish the kind of commu
found in conventional suburbs and small cities.

Consequently the belief that a new town is automatically innov
tive leads only to self-deception. This is not to say that innovation
is impossible; rather, rational planning must develop policies that
will actually bring it about.

The remainder of this study deals with the possibilities of one
kind of new-town innovation—class and racial integration—and sugge
some policies that could achieve it. The analysis is restricted to n
towns beyond the city limits, although some—but by no means all—
of its conclusions apply to new-towns-intown as well.

THE POSSIBILITIES OF INTEGRATION IN NEW TOWNS

Class and racial integration have long been advocated by citizens, and planners and other experts, and are frequently stated to be the law of the land in official government policy statements, legislative preambles, and of course U.S. Supreme Court decisions. Nevertheless almost all American communities, particularly those beyond the city limits, continue to be segregated by class and race, and governmental attempts to eliminate such segregation, whether through school integration, busing, or outright residential integration, have almost always been met with bitter political opposition from present residents. Although the failure of racial integration has been most publicized, the failure of class integration is equally pervasive; but only when affluent black homeowners oppose a black housing project in their neighborhood does the opposition to class integration become newsworthy.

Consequently this study is grounded on the realistic—if normatively unfortunate—assumption that class and racial integration will be extremely difficult to achieve in new towns—and for the same reasons as in established towns. Homebuyers (and even renters) are generally reluctant to move into an integrated community, for when they buy a house, they also buy an investment and a sign of their familial status; they want to assure the stability of the future status and property value of their house. As a result, people of higher status and lighter skin (hereafter to be called majority people or residents) are often unwilling to purchase houses in a community in which they will—or expect to—find many people of lower status and darker skin (hereafter to be called minority people or residents.) In addition, home purchasers seem to want compatible neighbors— for three important and persuasive reasons. First, they want to live among people with similar interests, so that they can find friends nearby. Second, even if they do not want to choose their friends from among neighbors, they want "friendly neighbors" so that everyday life on the block is harmonious. Third, they do not want neighbors with a vastly different life style, because, in order to live with such neighbors, they would have to make compromises in their own life styles, and this could force them to give up, or at least rethink, their fundamental cultural values. For example, when permissive parents find themselves living next to disciplinarians, conflict is likely to result the moment the two sets of children play together and misbehave. The disciplinarian parents will be upset if the other children are not sufficiently punished; the permissive ones will be upset if the disciplinarians try to punish the children in their way.

Many other aspects of life style can result in conflict, which is why homebuyers seek not only homogeneity but enough privacy so

that they can isolate themselves from lifestyle differences with confl
potential. Operationally the desire for friends, friendly neighbors,
and life-style compatibility means that homebuyers look for people
of roughly similar socioeconomic level and education. Parents,
particularly of younger children, also want playmates for them, as
well as other parents with whom they can discuss common childrearing problems, so that indirectly they also desire a considerable
degree of age-homogeneity. Finally, most white homebuyers want
racial homogeneity, although often they are less afraid of color difference per se than of the possibility that neighbors of other color
will also be of different socioeconomic level. In other words, white
are fearful about black neighbors because they believe that, because
many blacks are poor, their black neighbors would practice life styl
associated with poverty and the slums.

All of these preferences—as well as those of lower-status peo
who are asked to live with higher-status ones—combine to form a
demand for homogeneity, although it must be emphasized that no on
yet knows how much homogeneity people actually want, particularly
with respect to class; that is, how similar neighbors must be in inc
occupational status, and education.

Purchasers in a new town (or suburb) may, however, be sligh
more receptive to some kinds of heterogeneity. When people buy in
an established community, they have, by their purchasing decision,
also decided to adapt themselves to the social, economic, and politi
characteristics of that community, if only because they cannot chan
them. When they come into a new town, however, there is as yet
nothing to which to adapt. Because everyone is a stranger, and the
new town has no preexisting status-image other than that which can
be projected from the prices of the houses, it is sometimes possibl
to go beyond the typical kinds and ranges of homogeneity.

Also, moving into a new town or suburb is, at least for a shor
time, an exhilirating experience. As a result some people come wi
the intention of giving up old habits, which makes them more willin
to try to establish social ties with neighbors of other ages, classes
and sometimes even racial groups. Occasionally the initial integra
persists, but more often conflicts arise between heterogeneous nei
bors, and, after a couple of years, most people tend to concentrate
their friendship and neighboring relations with homogeneous others
Conversely, yet other new-towners or new suburbanites are fearful
of being surrounded by strangers, and thus prefer from the start th
their neighbors be as much like themselves as possible.

People's receptivity to integration is also affected by the soc
intensity of that integration, and by whether they are required to
associate involuntarily with people from whom they would prefer t
remain distant. Consequently it is necessary to distinguish betwee

140

two kinds of integration: potential (or physical) and actual (or social). Potential integration exists when heterogeneous people only occupy adjacent physical space; actual integration exists if such people also interact socially, particularly in the informal relationships found in clubs and coffee klatches, and through neighborliness and friendships. My observations suggest that homebuyers are less likely to move voluntarily into communities that require actual integration, even if only unintentionally, but that they may be more willing to live with heterogeneous people if they are free to abstain from intensive social relations with them.

Also, when people move into a new town, they do not move into the new town as a whole, but into a particular house, block, and neighborhood; they are more reluctant about integration on the block and in the neighborhood than in the community as a whole. This apparent fact suggests a distinction between two very different kinds of integration policy: micro-integration and macro-integration. By micro-integration I mean integration of the block or neighborhood; by macro-integration I mean integration of the community but not of its blocks or neighborhoods.

Micro-integration carries with it the possibility of actual integration; it means that people of different class and race will be sharing those physical spaces in which potential integration could become actual integration. Micro-integration does not automatically require actual integration, however, for even nextdoor neighbors can avoid social intercourse. Nevertheless such avoidance is not easy, and, more important, it is not pleasant, for most people want to be able to be friendly with their neighbors if at all possible.

Macro-integration puts less pressure on people to engage in actual integration, without, however, precluding it. Instead they have the opportunity to engage in social relations with heterogeneous community members on a voluntary basis; the spatial separation from heterogeneous others gives them a choice.

The distinction between micro- and macro-integration is not just analytic; it is made by homebuyers themselves, for they are primarily interested in a minimum of micro-integration. Indeed, if their blocks or neighborhoods are relatively homogeneous, they may be willing to accept—or even support—macro-integration, as long as the people of lower-status or darker skin remain a numerical minority in the community, do not dominate the community's public facilities, and do not obtain political control of its public agencies. Even a degree of micro-integration may be achievable; some minority residents may be accepted on the block or in the neighborhood if their number remains small, and integrated neighborhoods may be acceptable as long as individual blocks are segregated and separated by social or physical barriers—of yet unknown characteristics and "height"— from blocks with minority groups.

141

Unfortunately too little is known about attitudes toward integration and about behavior in integrated situations to permit firm conclusions about how much micro-integration—and of what kinds—is possible.

Racial micro-integration is rare, except temporarily when communities are in racial transition and until the "tipping point" is reached, and it is rare in most new towns because it has not often been tried, except on a token basis. Still, it exists in new towns such as Columbia, Reston, and the Levitt-built Willingboro, but partly because the blacks who moved into these towns were of high status. (Willingboro, however, had difficulty in attracting white buyers for some years after it was integrated by court order.)

Racial micro-integration is most feasible when there are no significant class differences between the races, or when the minority racial groups are of higher status than the whites. However it is probably most feasible in upper-middle class areas, not so much because of any special virtues of that class, but because affluent people seem secure enough about themselves and their status position to be able to live with racial minorities. When they are not secure— e.g., when they are newly arrived to upper-middle-class status—they are less likely to accept racial micro-integration. This lack of security, I would hypothesize, is greater as one goes down the socio-economic hierarchy, which is why racial micro-integration has been much rarer among lower-middle and working-class people. Conversely such integration exists in some poor and moderate-income neighbor-hoods—for example, slums, public housing, and in subsidized projects [e.g., "221 (d)(3)" and "236" housing]—but largely because of lack of choice on the part of their residents, who are captives in a complete seller's market. Having no place else to go, these residents accept micro-integration, and some of them establish intensive interracial social relationships. Still, if and when white or black residents are able to move elsewhere, such projects often become segregated.

Class micro-integration is somewhat more frequent, but only where class differences are limited. Willingboro, for example, like the earlier Levittowns, was initially class micro-integrated and families in the upper-middle, lower-middle, and upper-working classes lived as neighbors on almost every block. (There were no rich, lower-working-class, or poor people in the new town.) Over time, however, many upper-middle-class families moved away, as they did in other Levittowns. Consequently micro-integration appears to be most feasible among "adjacent" classes, so that, for example, upper-middle- and middle-class people can live together, although upper-middle- and working-class ones probably cannot. The amount of security-in-status is also important here, and I suspect that the micro-integration of working class and poor people would not be feasible because the former are—and have traditionally been—

142

extremely fearful of possible downward mobility. The principle of "adjacency" seems also to apply to racial micro-integration, for whites are willing to live with Asians more readily than with blacks, and they accept light-skinned black neighbors better than dark-skinned ones.

Actually, whatever their preferences, prospective homebuyers really have little opportunity to express them; they can only decide to buy or not to buy, and much of the decision about the extent of class and racial integration in a new town falls back on the developer.

In theory the developer is free to make that decision as he sees fit, but in practice he is restricted by a number of considerations. Current HUD guidelines and other federal regulations and laws do not, of course, permit him to practice overt racial discrimination. Although local communities can put all kinds of covert obstacles in his way, the developer who buys an entire township or a large part of a county is somewhat freer from such obstacles.

Class integration faces similar obstacles, particularly from preexisting zoning ordinances requiring large lots. Also, the developer who wants to attract poor people to his new town cannot do so unless he can obtain government subsidies for low-income housing, or can skew house prices so that more affluent buyers subsidize less affluent ones. When the developer is not restricted by zoning ordinances, however, he can determine the extent of class integration above the low-income level by the price of the housing he builds.

Assuming that he wants to maximize racial as well as class integration, he is, however, at the mercy of the market, for unless he is operating in a strong seller's market, a high degree of class or racial integration could scare away buyers whose purchase decisions he needs. Conversely, if he can build at very competitive prices and offer purchasers a bargain they cannot afford to turn down, even in a buyer's market, purchasers who prefer a great deal of class and racial homogeneity may buy anyway. And if he is in a buyer's market and cannot underprice his competition, and if many potential buyers want homogeneity, he must bend to their preference. Since a developer does not meet the people in his market as a group, he cannot know in advance how they will react. The success of Columbia and Reston as racially integrated new towns and of Columbia and the Levittowns as class-integrated new towns illustrates that, under relatively favorable market and other conditions, the substantial town developer can bring about more integration than is possible in smaller subdivisions.

In part the developer's options are a function of timing. If a large number of the initial residents are of low status or darker skin, then the new town is quickly given a definite status or racial image, and this may discourage buyers of higher status who dislike that image.

On the other hand, if the developer starts out with higher-status residents and can create an accordingly high-status image for the town, he may find it easier to subsequently bring in minority people. In the latter situation, though, initial residents may attempt to discourage him from "lowering" the town's status; this happened in Willingboro when Levitt first tried to build apartments and rowhouses although a few years later the opposition from initial residents had died down sufficiently to permit the necessary zoning change to be passed. In such situations the amount of democracy in the new town is crucial; if the residents lack the necessary political authority or power, they cannot interfere in the developer's plans. Of course, if they are secure enough in their own status and believe that their own property values will not be harmed, they may feel no need to fight a developer who wants to bring in purchasers of lower status.

Integration: The Minority Perspective

So far, my analysis has proceeded from the perspective of the majority population, discussing its readiness for class and racial integration. The possibilities of integration must also be considered from another perspective as well—that of minority people. Although discussions of new-town planning generally take only the first perspective, assuming that new towns are so desirable that minority people will automatically come to them and live where the majority population wants them to live, this assumption is by no means warranted, particularly in an era when some blacks have sought to achieve racial equality through voluntary self-segregation.

Nevertheless opinion polls about residential preferences among blacks indicate that the Suburban Dream is as much a part of their culture as of all other Americans, and that they too can be considered potential purchasers in new towns. The polls also suggest that, while blacks want to have the same right to choose their place of residence as whites, some blacks will prefer to choose to live under integrated conditions, others under self-segregated conditions.

Probably much the same statement can be made about working-class buyers, white or black. Assuming that they can afford to live in a new town, which is not always the case, some will want to live with lower-middle-class neighbors, but others will undoubtedly prefer class homogeneity. Just as higher-status people feel they are required to pay social costs by living near lower-status neighbors, lower-status people feel the same about living on a high-status block, particularly when they are a minority. Their status increases, to be sure, but often only at a price: for example, having to give up living patterns of which their more affluent neighbors disapprove; having to spend more money to keep up with the prevailing standard of house and yard care on the block. This is not to mention providing their children with the same toys as their more affluent neighbors, and running the danger of being socially isolated because they cannot find friends or compatible neighbors. Consequently it is likely that many working-class people will also want to live among "their own."

The ability and willingness of the poor to move into new towns is more doubtful, even if they could obtain housing they can afford to buy (and maintain) or rent. Many would want to escape the slums, but they could come only if jobs were available for them. Since new towns have for the most part failed to attract industry, particularly that employing unskilled and semiskilled people, and since the location of new towns makes them fairly inaccessible to other parts of the metropolitan labor market, it may be difficult to attract poor people to the new towns without special policies. (These are discussed below.)

The poor would also suffer, even more than working-class people, from the previously mentioned social and financial costs of integration; only the hardiest would want to move into a community where they are a numerical minority living amidst a hostile majority. Moreover they need all kinds of supportive facilities that are rarely found in new towns—for example, secondhand stores, public transit, liberal welfare agencies, and walk-in clinics for medical help. In addition they need the informal support provided by relatives, friends, and neighbors in urban low-income areas, and this too is hard to provide in a predominately middle-class new town. And, needless to say, all of these problems are far more serious for poor black people than for poor white ones.

POLICIES FOR CLASS AND RACIAL INTEGRATION

The preceding analysis has attempted to show that class and racial integration cannot be expected to develop automatically in new towns, and that, insofar as new towns are only old communities on new sites, they have much the same class and racial hierarchies as established communities. Thus the only way to create integrated new towns is to develop policies that make integration possible. The rest of this study will be devoted to such policies, first for macro-integration and then for micro-integration.

The Goals of Integration

Before describing these policies it is necessary to devote some attention to the goals of integration, for not all such goals are equally desirable. Planners have generally favored class and racial integration to create a balanced community, which duplicates the prevailing demographic mix in the metropolitan area. Nevertheless I do not consider balance to be a viable goal for current new-town planning. Communities serve many different functions, and different people choose among these communities in part because of these differences. For example, new towns—and suburbs—generally attract the young rather than the middle-aged and old. They attract families rather than single people (even though housing for "singles" is now to be found in suburbia). They also attract people of ethnic origins and those recently arrived in the middle class who are fearful or reluctant about moving into the traditional WASP-dominated older middle-class suburb or small town. Conversely, working-class and poor people with little job security often prefer to live within easy access of all parts of the metropolitan area labor market, which is still best available (though less and less so) near the center of the city.

Because people try to select the communities that fit their needs, it seems wrong or at least irrelevant to aim toward a balance that would make every community a mirror image of every other, and to try to duplicate the population mix of a 200-year-old city of half a million in a brand new town of 50,000. Instead, integration should be guided by other goals. With respect to macro-integration, one such goal is that every community must employ some low-income people and that they should be able to live in the community in which they work.

A second goal is that every community should house some people of lower income, so that they can benefit from the services funded by high-income taxpayers. (In this case, however, the proportion of the poor should be low, so that they will derive maximal benefits, per capita, from the high public expenditures of a rich community.) This argument loses some of its validity, however, when a higher portion of local expenditures comes from state and federal funds, particularly if funding is progressive and compensatory, so that poor communities get more than richer ones.

A third goal for macro-integration is the improvement of the socioeconomic status of the poor. Since more of the good jobs in our economy are now located beyond the city limits, it is urgently necessary that more poor people be enabled to live there.

A fourth goal is for freedom of residential choice, enabling everyone to live in the community of his choice. This goal is particularly important for racial minorities, and racial macro-integration can be justified on this count alone.

Micro-integration has generally been sought to create balance or diversity on the block, to abolish class and racial inequalities in community life, to give children the educational benefit of encountering others of different status and skin color so as to prepare them for such encounters in adulthood, and to extend to lower-status people the social and cultural benefits—such as the opportunity for self-improvement and upward mobility—of mixing with higher-status neighbors.

While many of these goals are desirable, it is doubtful whether micro-integration can achieve them. It would, of course, make for balance or diversity on the block, but, as I noted earlier, it would be at fairly high social and financial costs to both majority and minority people. Micro-integration, though, cannot eliminate class and racial inequalities, because they are caused by the national economic and social structure, which pervades a new town as completely as an old one. As a result the educational lesson children learn from micro-integration is that to be rich and white is to be better than being poor and black, and micro-integration alone teaches them only how to live in an unequal society.

Whether lower-status people obtain social and cultural benefits by living with higher-status neighbors is hard to say, although the former would certainly resent—and rightly so—the idea that they should live with their so-called betters in order to improve their ways of living. The Coleman Report showed that poorer children performed better in schools in which the majority of students were of higher status, but it is not clear whether this result stemmed from inter-class contact or from self-selection; i.e., that upwardly mobile poor parents sent their children to higher-status schools. I suspect that self-selection is a more potent causal factor than inter-class contact, but the Coleman data justify micro-integration even if it is effective only for the upwardly mobile—provided, however, the nonmobile do not suffer by being rejected or stigmatized by their high-status peers.

Micro-integration may be effective in schools because it is relatively compulsory; students have to mix in the classroom, except when the school minimizes micro-integration through tracking and other devices. On the block or in the neighborhood, however, mixing is voluntary, and thus actual integration is not likely to take place very often, except among small children who are blind to class and racial differences, which is why parents often try to prevent them from having contact with playmates of different status or color. Among adults, inter-class or interracial contact is likely to be highly superficial and thus of minute benefit—and this benefit is nullified if lower-status people must pay financial and social costs for living next door to more affluent people.

That micro-integration may not achieve the goals for which it is intended is of course no argument against the goals themselves, and micro-integration is desirable simply on democratic grounds, for, in a democratic society, people should be free to live where they choose and class or racial characteristics should not force them into socially inferior neighborhoods or blocks. Even so a micro-integration policy will produce only potential integration, and the value of this benefit has to be measured against the resulting costs for minority people and the opposition to micro-integration among majority (and minority) people, which could endanger the feasibility of a new-town proposal. When across-the-board micro-integration for the whole community is not feasible, the most viable compromise is to make it partial and voluntary, providing it only in some parts of the community for those people who want it. Actual micro-integration is possible only when the heterogeneities that now preclude social mixing are eliminated through egalitarian, economic, and political policies that reduce income and class differences, and through anti-discrimination policies of a kind that make color an irrelevant factor in social life.

Policies for Macro-Integration

Effective macro-integration requires at least the following policies:

1. Seller's Market. In order to assure a macro-integrated new town, the developer should choose to build in a seller's market, where housing is scarce, so that majority purchasers will come even if the town is macro-integrated.

2. Underpriced Housing. If the developer must operate in a buyer's market, he has to provide housing that is so attractively priced that majority buyers will come even if the community is macro-integrated.

3. Attractive Community Amenities. If the developer cannot provide better housing at a lower price than his competitors, he may be able to attract majority buyers to a macro-integrated town by offering amenities and facilities that the competition cannot offer. This is easier said than done, for we know relatively little about which amenities are sufficiently attractive to homebuyers to affect their purchasing decision, and even less about which amenities could offset negative feelings about integration. We know which amenities are preferred by planners and architects, but we also know that home buyers do not always share these preferences. Probably the most attractive such amenity is low taxes.

4. Resident Selection. In order to attract majority people to an integrated community, the following resident selection policies are necessary:

a) The developer must provide full information about the nature of the town's integration so that he will attract buyers who favor living in an integrated community, and discourage those strongly opposed

148

to it even when he can provide the benefits described in points 2 and 3 above.

b) Another approach to reducing hostility to integration is possible, however, by trying to attract residents who are more interested in shelter than in status and property-value considerations. Such interests are sometimes—but by no means always—found among single persons, childless couples, and transient or short-term residents. They are also sometimes found among renters; rental housing should therefore be made available.

5. Property Value Insurance. One possible method of reducing the fears about integrated living is to provide free insurance that will guarantee the purchaser that he will suffer no loss in resale value due to the integrated nature of the community. Insurance experts can determine how such a policy should be written, but one of its major purposes is a symbolic guarantee to purchasers who are irrationally fearful about property-value declines linked to integration.

6. Selection of Minority Residents. The success of integration is probably increased if minority residents visibly contradict the stereotypes that majority residents hold of them. This requires the following specific policies:

a) Minority Percentage. Minority residents will have to be a fraction of the total population, although further research is needed to determine what fraction is tolerable for the majority residents, where the tipping point lies at which they begin to be more anxious about living in an integrated community and whether racial quotas are politically acceptable to darker-skinned residents or to black, Puerto Rican, and chicano political organizations in the area.

b) Screening for Problem Families. Families with emotional and social problems that are visible to their neighbors should be discouraged from coming to the new town. This is particularly true of those problems conventionally associated with lower status and darker skin.

e) Selection of High Status Dark-Skinned Residents. Because racial integration seems to be more feasible when there are no class differences between racial groups, the developer should seek especially to attract high-status people of darker skin, and make sure that a large proportion of the lower-status residents are white.

7. Timing. As noted earlier, integration is facilitated if the community is initially settled with majority people, so that it develops a secure high-status image before minority residents are allowed to move in.

8. Powerlessness of Residents. The developer should make sure that residents cannot obtain power to affect the population mix, so that initial residents cannot force a rezoning of the community to keep out later arrivals of minority status.

9. Physical Planning. Macro-integration can be achieved by establishing separate neighborhoods and/or blocks for minority people. Further research in existing integrated communities is needed to determine if segregation by neighborhoods or only by blocks is necessary to affect the willingness of majority and minority purchasers to move in. If class or racial homogeneity of blocks is sufficient, so that blocks vary by class or race but neighborhoods are integrated, then individual blocks would probably have to be separated by physical and/or social barriers to allay the status and property-value fears associated with integration.

10. Minority Subcommunities. Although the proportion of minority residents must be low enough to attract majority purchasers (see point 6(a) above), it must also be high enough to attract minority ones, to let them know they will not be alone, and to enable them to create social subcommunities of their own if they encounter hostility from the majority newtowners. These subcommunities will of course be created almost automatically if segregated neighborhoods or blocks are developed; nevertheless subcommunities must be large enough to enable minority people to establish the formal and informal agencies that provide social and emotional support.

11. Political Organization. In instances where minority residents are numerical minorities, they will generally be powerless to affect community decisions, if the new-town polity is organized along conventional lines of representative democracy and majority rule. Consequently the new-town polity must be structured not only to guarantee minority rights but also to provide minorities with some political power to control their decisions. If neighborhoods are segregated, then political decentralization can provide such control, except that decentralization also disperses, and thus reduces, the total power of an individual minority group to affect centrally-made decisions—e.g., on the municipality's budget. Since central decisions tend to be more important than neighborhood decisions, an optimal balance must be struck between decentralization and centralization so as not to make minorities powerless.

12. Attraction of Industry. Because low-status people will not come to a new town unless jobs are available, the developer must be able to attract industry, and federal new-town legislation should include some provisions to help bring in industry—for example by providing special incentives for locating in an integrated new town. Moreover the industry to be attracted must either offer jobs for unskilled and semiskilled persons or offer job training so that poor newtowners will be able to obtain skilled jobs. Federal legislation to provide additional incentives to firms that will carry out such training is therefore necessary.

13. Facilities for Lower-Status Residents. New towns that want to attract lower-status residents will need to provide the necessary community facilities. For example, the new town must have a low-cost public-transit system for poor car-less residents (although it may be cheaper and more desirable to give them free cars or below-market loans to purchase cars through special federal legislation). Similarly the new town must establish low-cost medical facilities, including an outpatient clinic and inexpensive medical insurance again, though, it may be more desirable to give poor newtowners special medical subsidies so as not to create a dual medical market that may only stigmatize them). Unless federal legislation to provide a national minimum income grant is created, a welfare agency will also be necessary; most important, perhaps, low-priced shopping facilities must be available.

Secondhand stores may be difficult to establish in new towns; hence the developer must either plan for a low-price shopping center or, preferably, accept only those food, department, and other stores that promise to include low-price items among the goods they sell. Credit unions or other agencies that can offer low-cost loans will also need to be planned.

14. Direct Subsidies for Low-Income Residents. Since lower-income people will face other financial difficulties in living in a predominately middle- or upper-middle-class new town, direct subsidies may also be necessary. For example poor newtowners may need financial help to buy new furniture, maintain their homes and pay for transportation and medical care, etc., if these are not provided at subsidized prices.

15. Indirect Subsidies. Unless the subsidies mentioned in points 13 and 14 can be funded through federal new-town legislation, perhaps the best and least stigmatizing method of funding them is indirectly, through a progressive local tax system that requires the more affluent to subsidize the less affluent. For example local taxation should be based on a graduated income tax if at all possible; if property taxes need to be levied, they should also be graduated. Another way of providing indirect subsidies is to build them into the house price—again, in graduated fashion, so that affluent purchasers pay a larger share of at least the capital costs of community facilities in the house price. This is possible, however, only if the developer is able to build housing at below prevailing costs so that his prices can remain competitive.

Policies for Potential Micro-Integration

The fifteen policies I have just described for macro-integration would also be necessary to establish a potentially micro-integrated

151

new town. In addition, though, the following policies would be necessary:

1. Extremely Favorable Market and Pricing Conditions. Micro-integration can probably work only if the new-town developer is workir in an extreme seller's market, and can also provide such excellent housing at such a low price, and with such attractive community ameni ties, that majority purchasers cannot afford to stay away and will con- sider micro-integration a fair cost in return. If, for example, a developer could offer $50,000-houses for $20,000, even people bitterly opposed to micro-integration would probably purchase in the new town although afterwards they would make life difficult for their minority neighbors.

2. Physical Planning. Potential micro-integration is probably most feasible if involuntary contact between residents of different classes and races can be minimized. This is possible in high-rise apartment buildings, where such contact is necessary only near the elevator and in laundry rooms, and in low-rise housing of extremely low density, where there is sufficient land between houses so as to reduce involuntary contact. If low-density development is impossible, lots should probably be laid out with large frontages and houses so sited that the space between houses is maximized; cluster develop- ments, cul-de-sacs, and other site planning solutions that put houses close together should be avoided.

3. Resident Selection and Location. Micro-integration can succeed only if there is racial mixing without class mixing, or vice versa. Mixing both the races and the classes is not likely to be acceptable either to majority or minority residents; upper-middle- class whites would not live with poor blacks; upper-middle-class blacks would not live with poor blacks—or poor whites.

Locationally micro-integration must be pervasive; class or racial integration must exist on every block. The fraction of minority residents on any one block would have to be kept low; a single token family would most suit majority neighbors, but this would isolate the token family unmercifully. The exact size of the fraction requires further research, but the longer the blocks, the more minority resi- dents can be micro-integrated. In addition minority residents should be given lots—for example—corner lots, that minimize involuntary contact with neighbors. This is easy to implement, for these are often the most desirable lots, and if minority residents are given the first choice of lots, they will naturally pick these. Moreover, if majority residents are told which lots have been chosen by minority residents, those most agreeable to having minority neighbors will then be more likely to pick lots adjacent to them.

4. Supportive Policies for Minority Residents. Because minor residents would face considerable hostility and isolation under potent

152

micro-integration, there is even greater need for the supportive facilities and subsidies—and at higher levels—described under macro-integration policies, particularly points 11 and 13 to 15. It is especially important to help minority residents to establish political, social, and other organizations in which they can come together—even under segregated conditions—to defend themselves against isolation from majority residents and to counteract any hostility directed toward them by the latter.

Policies for Actual Micro-Integration

As noted previously, micro-integrated planning would produce only potential integration, and only a small number of people would engage in the social relationships that I have described as actual integration. In order to bring about actual integration among a much larger number of people, policies would be required to eliminate all those differences between residents encouraging segregation and self-segregation. This can be done only by establishing an egalitarian community, which provides every newtowner with a house of the same quality and price, regardless of his prior income, and which creates class homogeneity after people move in by giving everyone just about the same income and jobs of roughly equal levels of skill and status. Moreover the egalitarian new town would have to be virtually isolated from the rest of American society, so that the latter's inequalities could not gain foothold in the community. These policies would not be totally effective, for they could not erase prior differences in education and life style among people, but they would create a community with as much actual class integration as possible. Color differences, with all their inegalitarian consequences, can obviously not be eliminated, but if the community were egalitarian in class, those elements of racial discrimination based on class-fear (that is, the lower-class behavior now associated with racial minorities) would begin to disappear, and, over time, color would no longer be a factor in social life.

CONCLUSIONS: TOWARD A FEASIBLE
NEW-TOWN POLICY

In the preceding sections of this study I have tried to describe the possibilities—and difficulties—of class and racial integration, and have suggested policies for creating integrated new towns. So far, the analysis has emphasized rationality—searching for any and all policies that would bring about more integration in the abstract. Now I will attempt to combine rationality with feasibility in order to outline a viable new-towns policy. Such an analysis suggests the following conclusions:

1. Macro-integration is clearly more feasible than micro-integration, and although it would require new federal legislation and new forms of subsidies, it is not out of the question if the federal government—and the public—are determined to build macro-integrated new towns.

2. Potential micro-integration can work if only adjacent classes are integrated, and if racial integration is limited to middle- and upper-middle-class people. Actual micro-integration is out of the question in a society with the kinds of class and racial inequalities that still exist in America.

3. A feasible new-towns policy that achieves the goals that I consider most desirable would have the following components:

a) The most important goal for new-town development is not increased integration, but the opportunity for large numbers of poor and working-class people to gain access to good jobs and incomes, and in the process to good housing and communities as well. Considering the difficulties of creating micro-integrated new towns in which poor people would live next door to middle- and upper-middle-class people, and believing that access to good jobs is more important than micro-integration, I favor strategies and federal policies of community and industrial development that would result in macro-integrated new towns with a large number of poor and working-class residents.

Such new towns would probably need to have class-segregated neighborhoods, or at least blocks, and, if poor blacks are enabled to move in (as they should be), racially segregated ones as well. Of course, if the jobs created by industrial development paid sufficiently high wages, or if sizable income and housing subsidies were available, then the low-income people moving into the new town would no longer be of low income once they arrive and could obtain middle-class housing. Then many could live under conditions of micro-integration with their middle-class neighbors. Since the wages or subsidies that would raise poor people to middle-income status would need to be quite high, they are probably too expensive to be feasible, at least now.

b) Consequently federal new-town legislation that involves subsidies ought to be limited to macro-integrated (and, where possible, micro-integrated) new towns that enable the largest possible fraction of poor and working-class people to obtain good jobs in them and to be able to afford to live there alongside more affluent buyers (and renters). Federal assistance for the development of other new towns (those solely for middle- and upper-middle-class residents) is also desirable as long as it does not include any subsidies, for sufficient

154

housing subsidies exist already for the affluent to enable private enterprise to build new towns for them, and as long as providing such assistance does not in any way impede the development of new towns that provide access to low-income people. Exceptions to this policy should be made only for the purpose of enhancing racial micro-integration; that is, if federal subsidies are necessary to enable affluent blacks to live next door to affluent whites in such towns, but even such subsidies are of lower priority than those that will provide new-town access to the poor.

4. Current political conditions suggest that new towns built with federal subsidies probably cannot plan for class or racial ghettos, but must be planned on a micro-integrated basis. This is likely to have at least two clear consequences. One is that few developers will be willing to build housing that poor whites or blacks can afford; the other is that even if local market conditions enabled a developer to build a community that would initially mix rich and poor, white and black, some portions of the community would eventually be segregated, both by class and by race, and many majority residents would move to other parts of the new town—or out of the new town altogether. The first consequence is of course undesirable; that is much less so for the second one, though, for even if they are eventually more segregated than at the start, the new towns would still be providing a place for low-income people.

Nevertheless the first consequence is more likely to happen, and most new towns will not include many poor whites or blacks. Most likely these people will be able to gain access to the good jobs in the suburbs only by moving into present middle- and working-class suburban areas, and transforming them into low-income class and racial ghettos. I would consider this consequence desirable, however, for it does create access to better jobs for the poor. Whatever federal aid is politically feasible to enhance such access is justified.

5. My emphasis on providing the poor with access to jobs, combined with the difficulty of building integrated new towns, may suggest another policy alternative—new towns made up entirely of poor people. Even if employers would come to such a town, which must be considered doubtful, I think this alternative is undesirable, since such new towns would become unintended prisons of the poor, isolating them politically and socially from urban low-income areas and also from middle-class America.

6. Any policy calling for a large number of poor people to move into new towns, including the one I have proposed, requires large subsidies for them. This raises the question of whether the subsidies are worth the benefits, and whether they could not be better spent elsewhere. For example, a large item in the subsidy package is the provision of brand-new housing for poor people. If subsidies are

limited, the planner must confront the question of whether it is better to spend them on new housing for the poor in new towns or for other policies in the city—such as, job creation, income grants, or the rehabilitation of old housing. Only a comprehensive benefit-cost analysis can answer this question, but it must be answered before new legislation can be proposed that would create subsidies for poor people in new towns.

7. If the federal government and public opinion were ready to approve the policies and subsidies I have suggested for new towns, they would probably be ready as well to approve similar ones for the cities, in which case the planner would also have to ask whether the higher costs of new towns are worth the extra benefits. Of course it is possible that, because of the potency of the myth of the new, the federal government is willing and able to grant subsidies for new-town development—particularly such development that provides the poor with good jobs—that it would not grant for the poor in the cities. In this case the benefits could well be worth the extra financial subsidies incurred in building new housing for the poor.

Nevertheless it is hard to imagine that the myth of the new is politically so potent that the federal government would be sufficiently generous with subsidies to give poor people a better opportunity in new towns than in cities, particularly since the people's political strength—and thus their influence on federal policy—is greater in the cities than anywhere else. Consequently I suspect that the new towns of the future will not be vastly different from those already built or on the drawing boards, in that they will be largely unintegrated suburban communities of higher quality than present suburbs, but not mechanisms for greater social change or more class and racial integration—which is what new-town advocates would like them to be.

APPENDIXES

Appendix I: A Note on New-Towns-Intown

New-towns-intown differ in two major respects from new towns beyond the city limits: they are not politically independent communiti and they are more integrated into the urban economy, even if they attract their own sources of employment. In most other respects new-towns-intown are not very different from other new towns, however, and most observations and policies regarding class and racial integration apply to them as well.

Because new-towns-intown are not politically (or socially) independent of the city, they will be strongly affected by the political cross-pressures and social climates of the cities in which they are built. This has both advantages and disadvantages. In a politically liberal city, opposition to an integrated new-town-intown may be less severe than in a rural area; in a conservative city, though, opposition may be greater, particularly if the class and racial makeup of the new town is very different from that of adjacent communities and neighborhoods, and if the latter have sufficient political power to effectively oppose the new town. Conversely, in a liberal city, especially one with a severe housing shortage, there may be less reluctance on the part of majority people to move into a micro-integrated new town, for they will include a higher proportion of urban dwellers already used to micro-integration than in a new town beyond the city limits.

Among the great advantages of the new-town-intown are its relative closeness to the rest of the city, and its access to the urban area labor market and to urban facilities and institutions. This is particularly helpful if the new-town-intown is planned to include a significant number of poor people. Moreover such a town will be able to establish supporting agencies for the poor, such as welfare offices, clinics, and the like; to extend public transit; and perhaps even to establish branches of municipal government that could provide employment. In fact, given the difficulties in settling poor people in a micro-integrated new town beyond the city limits, the new-town-intown may be the most feasible new town for the urban poor, providing that other people and some industry are also willing to move in. Consequently federal new-town legislation should emphasize the development of new-towns-intown if they can provide jobs for the poor.

Appendix II: A Note on Age Integration

This study has not discussed integration of age groups in new towns, largely because I think it is less important than class and racial integration. Also, despite the rhetoric about the desirability of age balance and the virtues of the three-generation family, all the available evidence indicates that in a postindustrial society, cultural and other differences between age-groups are widening; consequently such groups have little interest in living together. To be sure, some young people like having old neighbors around, particularly as baby-sitters, and some old people enjoy being around younger people in order to enjoy their youth and vitality, if only vicariously; nevertheless most young people do not want continued contact with old people, and the old would be isolated if they lived under micro-integrated conditions. This, though, does not rule out experiments with both micro-integration and macro-integration—neighborhoods or blocks for the elderly.

Still, the most important problem of age integration is intra-familial—how to create new towns in which children and particularly adolescents are not bored to death or harassed by adults because of the wide and growing cultural differences between the generations. The adolescents' problem in new towns is that they must live under compulsory micro-integrated conditions with adults, and that they have no viable functions in new towns other than as students and as members of an involuntary leisure class (although this lack of viable functions exists in cities and suburbs as well). Suggesting policies for improving the lives of adolescents in new towns is beyond the scope of this study, but such policies would include providing job opportunities for them in school and after school, and experimenting with some forms of residential segregation for them, particularly the older ones, resembling the segregation that now exists in universities, "singles" projects, and the so-called youth quarters that are springing up in various cities, especially near university campus

10

NEW-TOWNS-INTOWN
IN A NATIONAL
NEW-COMMUNITIES
PROGRAM
Harvey S. Perloff

Given the predominant attitudes in the United States today—largely those of resistance to racial and class mixing—a major movement of new-community building could easily become the 1970s counterpart of the FHA-encouraged segregated suburban building of the post-World War II years. A further polarization of our society would be a high price to pay for the improvement in life styles that new communities could conceivably bring about for their residents. It is possible that those new communities that have been reliant upon federal government subsidies could be forced to provide a certain amount of racial and income-class mixing as the price for the subsidies, but a little arithmetic—combined with the logic of modern U.S. politics—suggests that the number of minority and poor families that are likely to gain in this way would be quite small.

We need a strategy that can balance improvements in the lives of minority and lower-income groups with the anticipated improvements in the lives of middle-class families that the new communities are expected to bring about. The new-town-intown concept, already part of the federal government's new-communities program, provides a valuable counterpart to new-community building in outlying areas. Those who are embarrassed by this kind of open quid pro quo strategy should remember that the most probable alternative under current social and political conditions is a gradual or even rapid abandonment

I want to express my thanks to David Vetter for his valuable assistance in the preparation of this study. I am also grateful to a number of colleagues, associated with me in a new-towns-intown project in the School of Architecture and Urban Planning of the University of California at Los Angeles, for helping me develop some of the concepts included herein.

of the inner city and its troubled (and troublesome) residents, while attention is shifted to so-called areas of future growth. Abandonment of the inner city by both private and public interests is already under way in various communities across the country, and the consequences are to make the human environment for many minority and lower-income families a thing of ugliness and terror.

Concern for both equity (or simple human decency) and quality of life requires more than merely highlighting the potential value of a major new-communities building program in the United States. It requires careful attention as to who is to be helped by such a program. Nor is it enough vaguely to suggest that "some" of the federal subsidy be directed to helping minority and lower-income families achieve a better living environment. Justice demands that the largest share of the federal government subsidy be directed to the revitalization of inner-city areas where the most undersatisfied human needs as well as the greatest danger to regional viability are to be found. Thus it seems to me that major emphasis on new-towns-intown within a federally subsidized new-communities building program makes both moral and political sense. Specifically the case for emphasis on intown-new-towns can be made on the basis of an analysis of the major goals generally associated with development of new towns. I take these goals to be (1) "healthier" national urban growth, (2) opportuniti for innovation, (3) better opportunities for individual development and community development, (4) better opportunities for political partici-pation, and (5) new and better opportunities for racial and income mixing.

Before launching into these, there is need for an explanation of the new-town-intown concept. It is well to note immediately that it is not a well-developed concept. Largely, it is today an empty box waiting to be filled. The Housing and Urban Development Act of 1970 which first introduced the concept into federal legislation, does not give much of a lead as to what it is all about; nor do the early efforts to launch developments in central cities called new-towns-intown, such as the Fort Lincoln project in Washington, D.C. In fact—and unfortunately—the concept does not have much more content than when I first introduced it as a strategy for the development of the area surrounding the University of Chicago in the early 1950s, or when I proposed it as the base for a national program in an article in the Journal of the American Institute of Planners in 1966.[1] All I can do, then, is to spell out what the hope is.

The new-town-intown concept, as I see it, aims at substantial and continuing inner-city modernization and revitalization by bringing together in a single programmatic approach a variety of human-assistance and urban-development components of a character, scale, and combination that would maximize the chances for greatly improving the quality of environment and quality of life of inner-city residents. This definition itself needs explanation. Through the many urban programs that have been tried, we have learned some useful things about the social, economic, and physical development of the inner city. This knowledge has not come easily or cheaply. We have learned from our mistakes—mistakes that have been costly in both human and economic terms. Basically the new-town-intown concept channels what we have learned into programmatic ideas (with, it is to be hoped, inherent logic) aimed at improving the quality of life of people in the inner city. It differs from existing urban programs in important ways.

OBJECTIVES OF A NEW-TOWN-INTOWN PROGRAM

Many of the existing governmental urban programs, we have learned from experience, suffer from certain common ills. They are more place- or territory-oriented than people-oriented; they tend to deal more with outer symptoms than with underlying causes; they tend to be largely static in nature rather than dynamic (that is, they do not deal with fundamental urban development processes); and their human objectives are far from clear. The provisions for new-towns-intown in the federal government's 1970 new-communities act do not indicate at all clearly what the objectives of such a program are to be, nor how the other common ills of the existing inner-city programs are to be avoided.

It seems to me that, against the background of conditions in American cities today, new-towns-intown should aim at achieving two interrelated objectives.

The first objective should be to enhance opportunities for the disadvantaged people of the inner city to live better lives. This has been an objective of several federal government programs, including the public housing and Model Cities programs, but the approach and scale of these have been inadequate. The term "disadvantaged people" is taken to encompass individuals and families from minority groups and/or having incomes below the poverty level. This is not a particularly felicitous term, but there is no fully satisfactory way to identify people whose living and environmental choices are far more limited than those of the majority. The disadvantaged in the inner city are taken as the "target population," rather than all "disadvantaged" wherever they may be located, because a new-town-intown program can provide special (and additional) place-oriented improvement opportunities not provided by nonplace programs (such as minimum income, rent subsidies, and education supports). In other words it is assumed that the new-town-intown program will build on the

161

nonplace programs and open new possibilities beyond. Also, the inner-city areas, because of the territorial concentration of poverty and minority groups, have substantial political clout of the kind needed to carry out development programs. At the same time this concentration provides a good base for popular participation; that is, a base for involving poor and minority persons in the planning and execution of plans. It is hard to organize this kind of participation if the populations are scattered.

Enhancement of "opportunities . . . to live better lives" can be taken to require the following:

1. More and better jobs (and therefore higher incomes), as well as training for these jobs; more broadly conceived this means econom development.

2. Improved public and private services, and more personal security.

3. Improved housing (higher quality, more varied choices, more accessibility to jobs and other activities, or lower prices).

4. Improved environment (i.e., better neighborhood conditions).

While each of these supports the others in various ways, and ideally all should be included, it is essential that there be a priority ordering—given the inevitable limitation on resources—with the greatest effort directed to the higher-priority items. It seems to me that economic development should receive the greatest attention and serve as the main base for the other elements. If programs are too ambitious and try to be comprehensive from the beginning, they may well suffer the fate of most other federal urban programs that have been too ambitious in terms of the funds made available. This is not to imply that the planning should not be very broad from the beginning; rather it is to stress the necessity for building one program element on another so that important, even if modest, gains can be realized if program funds fall short of those needed for large efforts. Our experience with housing and urban-development programs over the last three decades demonstrates the importance of the so-called building-block strategy. Funds have just not been available to carry through the kinds of comprehensive programs initially planned. The Model Cities program is an excellent example of what can happen. As Kaitz and Hyman put it, "The design of Model Cities is grand, the objectives laudable, and the resources negligible."[2] The operational strategy for new-towns-intown should permit meaningful (and greatly multiplied) returns from whatever resources are devoted to this program.

In addition to "enhancing opportunities . . . to live better lives," as the second objective new-towns-intown programs should aim to strengthen the processes of central-city modernization and revitaliza tion. The latter term is not used to suggest the reestablishment of

162

old central-city functions, but rather the establishment of new functions and activities appropriate to central locations.

We have remarkably little understanding of what is involved in maintaining the efficient functioning of core-city areas and their continued vitality. Our urban-renewal experience suggests that it probably does not involve reestablishing the commercial dominance of the downtown area or substituting isolated new middle-class neighborhoods for former slum neighborhoods, scattering the former slum dwellers to wherever housing can be found for them. Nor does it seem to demand the construction of inner-city superhighways or freeways to bring hordes of subarbanites to jobs in the city for a few hours a day. For in this process lies the continuing decline of even larger areas than can possibly be "cleared" by urban renewal and an undermining of the sound functioning of the central city. It is far less clear as to what is essential to central-city modernization. I would suggest that at a minimum it calls for strengthening—in economic, political, and human terms—the inner-city communities where the disadvantaged families live.

In the past the city in the United States has always functioned as a "human upgrading factory," preparing workers for the jobs that needed doing and preparing families for effective urban living. It was the place where the new entrepreneurs and the new ideas could be launched. In the process, capital as well as human skills would be put to work, and continuing change (or modernization) would result. The opposite is the case when the city becomes simply a dumping ground and the place from which capital and skills flee.

"Revitalization" in such human terms is clearly compatible with the first proposed objective (i.e., providing better living opportunities for disadvantaged families). Such a modernization and revitalization objective is a key reason for bringing the inherent vitality of new towns to the inner city. The inner city more than any other place needs the powerful leverage that coordinated overall planning and development can bring. In the case of the inner city, this means specifically (1) reversing the outflow of capital, and (2) creating a linked set of "resource-and-opportunity" developmental areas throughout the metropolitan region to support the core new-town-intown. Both of these require explanation.

Most of our present intown programs founder on the rock of capital disinvestment in inner-city areas. In the face of expanding housing needs, many existing housing units in our downtown areas are either being abandoned or are not being properly maintained. As Sternlieb points out: "Abandonment is a process, a reflection of a much deeper seated and extensive phenomenon—the disinvestment of private capital in the cores of our cities."[3]

An important aim of new-towns-intown would be to stem this flight of capital. What happens now is that institutional lenders abandon the inner city due to fear of neighborhood decline. Unfortunately institutional lenders acting individually to protect themselves from neighborhood decay often accelerate the very blight they fear. At the first sign of deterioration the lender will often refuse to make loans in the neighborhood. This in itself causes neighborhood decline. And such decline is reinforced by the fear of businessmen to build commercial and industrial establishments in "declining" areas. Thus the vitality that new economic activities tend to bring is lost.

A new-town-intown effort would seek to halt neighborhood decline and to organize lenders so that they could act collectively to provide the steady flow of capital so vital to neighborhood maintenance and improvement. It would proceed on the notion that just as decline and disinvestment make up a process building on itself, so does investment and improvement. Whether, and to what extent, higher-income persons and particularly higher-income whites have to be attracted back to the city for this investment-and-improvement process to take hold firmly will probably not be known until a number of new-towns-intown have been under way for some time. Under a substantial new-towns-intown program, there are strong reasons to assume that, at a very minimum, the spread of blight can be halted, entrepreneurship encouraged, and activities that normally function most effectively in the core-city areas encouraged to return to the central city or to set up shop there anew. There are strong favorable forces to be built on, including the slowdown in in-migration from the poor rural areas and the continuing increases in nonwhite family incomes.

Stemming the flight of capital is by itself clearly not enough. A strong forward thrust must be initiated. The latter calls for an area-wide developmental approach. As I see it, what is needed is not too far removed from what is involved in broad-scale regional development programs both here and overseas. In both cases a key objective is to find the most critical leverage points for change in desired direction, looking to such things as investment in human upgrading, finding of new and expanding economic opportunities, and the construction and improvement of infrastructure that would provide a base and framework for public and private efforts—and all of this within a territory specifically designated to encompass opportunity and not the problems alone. This is true for the present-day America city as much as for Appalachia or other so-called problem regions. Opportunity has to be found and "leveraged," whether in growth centers or in the encouragement of activities that promise good returns.

The Model Cities experience provides some suggestive lessons. The legislation requires that Model Cities areas encompass the worst slums and problem areas, the city counterpart of the unhappy "worst first" strategy of the Economic Development Administration of the U.S. Department of Commerce in rural and small-town areas. The way the Model Cities program was designed made it impossible to do the kind of planning originally advocated: "Planning difficulties arose out of the relation of the target neighborhood to the rest of the city, especially since the ghetto was the most dependent and least viable part of any city's economic and social structure. On the other hand, the dilution of effort with larger boundaries would be fatal to the program given the modest level of funding. . . ."4

The ghetto may be the least viable part of the city economically, but it does not follow that larger boundaries would dilute the resources available. In fact, by increasing the size of the target area, the total amount of resources may be increased. By encompassing economically and socially stronger areas and providing more leverage for investment, more private capital may be attracted, so that every dollar of federal funding could conceivably attract additional flows of funds into the target area. Under the present nondevelopmental approach, almost all of the funding must come from the federal government and can easily be absorbed into programs with only a temporary impact. It is typical of the present approach that only by accident would the urban economic development program sponsored by the Economic Development Administration coincide with a Model Cities program. Nor do Model Cities programs have any special priority with regard to federally sponsored manpower-training programs or any other programs that could conceivably increase the economic or social viability of the target area.

A particularly important consideration of an inner-city program (as of other developmental programs) is its multiplier impact. Spending in any part of the urban system normally generates spending in other parts of the system. The amount of additional spending generated by each dollar spent is called the multiplier. A key indicator of the success of a new-town-intown program is the amount of public and private investment induced by the initial government expenditures. One often-ignored characteristic of the multiplier is that it works both ways. A given decrease in spending will also be multiplied to accelerate the decline of an area (as already noted). The size of the multiplier will depend to an important extent on the ways in which the government investments are linked to the private sector. For example functional deficiencies within the inner city may make it quite unprofitable for existing firms to expand or new firms to move in. There may be inadequate transportation, parking, or personal security, and it may be difficult to secure land. Thus there is a strong forward linkage between the strengthening of the infrastructure of the inner city and other investments in the private sector. These developmental considerations must be among the dominant ones in defining the size and scope of new-town-intown programs.

TERRITORIAL EXTENT

A key aspect of the new-town-intown concept is to view physical development as a "tool" for achieving human objectives. Thus the territorial extent of a new-town-intown is not to be determined by the physical condition of structures (as in urban renewal). Nor is it to be determined by extremely bad social conditions within a given neighborhood (as in the Model Cities program). Rather it is to be determined on the basis of future community viability. The boundaries of urban-renewal projects have been set by the extent of physical "blight"—blight defined strictly in terms of the condition of physical structures. In the Model Cities program the definition of blight was broadened to include social factors; however, not only were the boundaries of the target area restricted to a single residential neighborhood, but also the choice of area was to be dominated by how bad social conditions were. At least a major part of the neighborhood had to be "hard-core slum in which low-income families are concentrated."[5]

The territorial extent of a new-town-intown project would have to be determined, case by case, by certain principles aiming at long-term community viability and the ability of a developmental agency to "turn things around" so that a strong sense of improvement can be generated and sustained throughout the area. I appreciate how difficult it will be to designate areas on such broad principles with any sense of assurance. At the very least this approach would let down territorial barriers that now condemn most in-city projects to failure.

Probably three factors will have to be brought into play in the designation of territorial extent of a new-town-intown program: (1) large scale, (2) the configuration of certain key physical and nonphysical features, and (3) noncontiguous character. These are all interrelated. It can be expected that in most cities there would be at least one core or "primary" new-town-intown in the inner city covering a substantial territory—that is, at town scale—as an important element in achieving the major objectives of a new-town-intown program. It would encompass a territory much larger than either the typical urban-renewal project or Model Cities neighborhood. It would include commercial, industrial, and recreational areas as well as residential areas, stable neighborhoods as well as declining and slum neighborhoods. Territorial designation would be based on (1) the extent of the public-service delivery systems and the location of public facilities, (2) present and future economic possibilities, (3) the configuration of transportation networks, and (4) and the extent of community awareness and community institutions.

It seems unlikely in most large cities that one such concentrated new-town-intown will be able to go a long way by itself in achieving the major objectives. It is more likely that the optimal arrangement will need to involve, in addition to the core area, several different territories designated within a new-town-intown program as linked resource-and-opportunity developmental areas throughout the metropolitan region. These would be areas in which particularly attractive employment opportunities could be developed (say, an underdeveloped port area or an open area near the core new-town-intown where an industrial estate could be established). It may also involve an open area outside the builtup metropolitan zone that could be developed as a "paired" outlying new town with strong links to the intown new town.[6] Such areas could be referred to as resource-and-opportunity areas, to suggest that they are included in the new-towns-intown program because they provide new opportunities for the inner-city target population—mainly new opportunities for jobs, improved services, and housing.

The important point to appreciate, it seems to me, is that inner-city areas should not be developed in isolation—i.e., aside from the larger regional considerations. Clearly, as Vietorisz and Harrison argue so convincingly in their thoughtful study of the economic development of Harlem, "The major symptom of underlying economic and social distress—pervasive employment and income deficits—could not be dealt with exclusively within the confines of the ghetto."[7]

Relating inner-city development to broad regional considerations imposes three requirements that largely have been lacking in previous inner-city programs.[8] In fact the ultimate success of a new-town-intown program, given its human-welfare and quality-of-life objectives, would depend on how thoroughly these requirements can be met.

One requirement is to make it much easier than at present for ghetto residents to get to jobs in every part of the region. For the lesser-skilled workers, who tend also to be those who shift jobs most frequently, an inner-city location close to transportation hubs is a decided advantage. But it takes effort to fully exploit this advantage. There is need for the development of means by which inner-city workers can get to jobs throughout the region with greater ease and at lower cost than in the past. Training for jobs wherever they may be located is an even more important need.

A second requirement is to encourage the new-town-intown local economy to become essentially a human-development and human-convenience economy. The aim would not be, as it supposedly is in large outlying new towns, to create enough jobs for most of the local residents. Economic development in inner-city areas has to have several different elements.

There could be, and should be, a major effort to exploit all of the economic advantages that an inner-city area may have because of both its location within the region and its special labor supply. Thus industrial land could be made available at various high-accessibility points, but not necessarily within the ghetto or slum itself. These sites would have to be competitive with other sites in the metropolitan economy, as well as accessible to the work force in the new-town-intown "core" area. Some subsidy may be required to make these sites fully competitive, but at the edges of the area such subsidy would probably not be as high as that required to locate and maintain industry in the heart of the ghetto. Such subsidy for land cost write-down would surely be more justifiable than the write-down in the typical urban-renewal project in the past, which removed slum dwellers in favor of middle-class residents.

In addition to new economic activities for the more-or-less established labor force in the inner-city areas, there may be need for what Vietorisz and Harrison call "greenhouse industries"—i.e., heavily subsidized industries intended primarily to raise the caliber of the work force in the ghetto. This is an admittedly tricky business, and it could be argued that it is better to subsidize established business to take on the job of raising the caliber of the work force than to bring in special industries for this purpose. Subsidization of already established business for training purposes could well be the backbone of a manpower-upgrading program. Experience with all sorts of "upgrading" programs, however, suggests the importance of nearby location in the case of some of the workers—in fact of those who need the most assistance. The geographic range of their movements tends to be restricted, and nearness is a helpful factor. The subsidization of such industries would be an interim step certainly not a final solution, in the integration of minority and untrained workers into the regional economy.

A third requirement relates to the character of the surrounding environment. Economic upgrading and economic integration of ghetto workers into the mainstream undoubtedly depend—to an unknown but surely significant degree—on self-image, and this in turn is intimately related to the quality of the environment and the quality of life that an individual experiences. Vietorisz and Harrison put it well when they point to the idiocy of a situation in which a worker is "exiled every night to a rat-infested, overcrowded, personally hazardous, and miserably serviced environment while being expected to deliver a high degree of productivity on the job."[9]

We now know—particularly after our experience with public housing and the findings of the Coleman Report—that physical improvement, and even spanking newness, can make little difference in the life and performance of disadvantaged persons when other socially helpful conditions are not also available. But surely we also know that a degrading and insecure environment and way of life make it inordinately hard for individuals to pull themselves up by their bootstraps.

Beyond the question of self-image there is the more direct matter of the close relationship between environmental adequacy and ability to achieve economic and social betterment goals. Even minimal economic improvement goals require a relatively efficient and safe environment, while social improvement goals call for substantial improvement in public facilities and services. I read past experience to say, not that physical improvement is unimportant, but that either the forces of decline—human and physical—are stopped and turned around, with forces for improvement encouraged along a broad spectrum, or else human progress will be painfully slow in the ghetto.

CENTRALIZED MANAGEMENT

One of the key features of a new-town-intown should be the centralized management of all federal and state assistance monies and related activities for the given area, as well as certain of the municipal government's funds, through a strong development corporation. It seems to me, therefore, that all of the following should be managed through the development corporation:
1. economic-development activities and funds;
2. manpower-training activities and funds;
3. special education-planning and experimentation grants;
4. special health-planning and experimentation grants;
5. all housing assistance;
6. facilities grants;
7. urban renewal (of a new type, geared to the specific objectives of new-towns-intown);
8. other human resources funds (including poverty, Model Cities, and similar funds where available); and
9. funds specifically made available for new-towns-intown and related activities.

If the corporation is to manage such funds and related activities, it would have to be public in nature or of a mixed public-and-private variety. In addition to having control of such funds, it would be necessary for the corporation to have powers of eminent domain, as well as related powers needed for land development and rehabilitation.

What this says in effect is that the intown modernization and revitalization job can be carried out only if there is a developmental unit strong enough and well enough funded to do it. Can such development corporations be established under present conditions characterized by extreme fragmentation of governmental activities and little tradition in public-private administrative cooperation? My guess is that such corporations will be established only if the federal government ties its financial assistance to given areas to the requirement that such corporations be established. This is a logical enough requirement, since the chances for successful inner-city improvement on town scale are slim without such a strong agency to manage it.

While such an agency with public powers may be needed to direct the public-oriented activities, it does not follow that it must necessarily carry out the developmental (building and rehabilitation) tasks itself—although it may choose to do so. It may well turn over these developmental tasks to a private developer under contract, or to a number of private developers. This may be needed to mobilize both the necessary funds and the necessary skills for large-scale development. In fact the few new-town-intown projects already underway are being carried out by private developers (working closely with urban renewal and housing agencies). What are lacking now are institutions capable of coordinating and channeling the public funds and activities so that the projects can achieve the kinds of objectives discussed above.

If inner-city residents are to gain from new-town-intown projects, it is also essential that development corporations be controlled by such residents—that is, by the target population whose welfare is the raison d'etre of the corporation. The problems of achieving such resident control while maintaining effective centralized management of a complex program should not be underestimated. No formula has yet been discovered to achieve this dual objective, but we do have some useful experience to go on.[10] I interpret this experience to suggest that the following deserve special attention:

1. Major emphasis should be placed on a sound system of representation, with a reasonable balance between resident and nonresident members of the board of the corporation, and with the residents members elected in such a way that the community feels it is effectively represented.

2. Opportunities should be provided to enable community members and minority entrepreneurs and minority organizations to acquire equity holdings in the corporation and its developmental arms, so that the community feels it has a stake in the enterprise on this score as well. This type of equity arrangement has already been worked out in the Fort Lincoln new-town-intown being developed

through a private development corporation. It should be even simpler in the case of projects directed by public or mixed public-and-private corporations.

ADJUSTMENT TO INNER-CITY POPULATIONS

There is yet another characteristic of new-towns-intown, at least as I conceive them. Such towns are intended to serve a highly varied and highly mobile intown population. In the past, urban-development programs have either largely disregarded inner-city residents (as in urban renewal) or treated them simply as "problem families" or problem situations (as in the public housing and Model Cities program). But if we view the inner city broadly, and not just in terms of the poorest, most run-down and crime-ridden sections, certain formerly invisible people become visible, and certain needs not normally associated with the inner city appear. The needs of the following groups should be considered:

1. Families currently in a lower-income status, often recent in-migrants, who are upwardly mobile and are concerned about education and job opportunities for themselves and even more for their children.

2. Individuals and families in the lower-income class who have limited income because of physical disability, age, or the like, who are much concerned about the quality of certain public services and recreation facilities. They also greatly value nearby opportunities for earning extra income.

3. Middle-class minority families who prefer to live with their own racial and ethnic group, but want better housing, better shopping, and better public services (particularly better schooling), as well as greater personal safety.

4. White and minority families who like being in a highly urbanized environment, where "the action is," but who also want better housing (or lower-cost housing), better services, and a safer and more attractive environment.

An intown program must be fully sensitive to these varying needs and situations. Thus a new-town-intown program should not be viewed as some sort of upgrading abstraction, as was generally true for urban renewal in the past, but rather as a program seeking to understand and to meet the needs and aspirations of specified groups of people with specific characteristics. Again, this highlights the requirement for the kind and scale of planning, building, and rehabil-itation typical of a town rather than a neighborhood, and covering not only housing, localized services, and shopping but the full spectrum of human concerns viewed at the town scale—including particularly jobs and income, personal safety, and different kinds of services and facilities for a wide variety of population groups.

A new-town-intown would seek to incorporate the concept of broad-scale planning and carefully planned building sequences (here also, rebuilding and rehabilitation) central to most thinking about new-community development. But other features would be very different. Thus the planning in a new-town-intown would be for and with population groups already in the area, not for a future population with characteristics dictated largely by market considerations. Jobs would be given top priority so that workplaces would be located in whatever part of the community to which they could be attracted, consistent with overall town efficiency. A so-called Lighted Center would be a dominant feature of a new-town-intown to achieve a number of objectives—such as to enlarge the scope for jobs and income, bring excitement and urbanity to the inner city (as well as spenders), and enhance personal safety.[11] Physical features in general would be incorporated in a new-town-intown to achieve specific developmental objectives, aiming for the greatest returns in human terms for a given expenditure, rather than to achieve a predetermined aesthetic and tone, as in most thinking about outlying new towns.

ACHIEVING NEW-COMMUNITY GOALS

As suggested at the beginning of this study, it seems to me that new-towns-intown can contribute significantly to the objectives or gains that are normally associated with new-community development. In fact it can be argued that, for most of the objectives, new-towns-intown can make an even larger contribution than outlying new communities. It is worth examining some of the gains associated with new communities in general.

Healthier National Urban Growth

The widespread concern over the unhealthy growth of the present giant metropolises is closely associated with the endless urban scatteration and the growth of so-called slurbs. But the latter are themselves closely related to the decline in the attractiveness of the central city. Clearly the pressures on the outlying areas will be reduced by greatly increasing the attractiveness of the core city through new-town-intown programs. More generally, it seems to me that healthy urban growth implies a wide choice among many satisfying forms of urban living. Today one of the most important of these choices is being denied to many people—that of living well and safely in the core city. Finally, and most importantly, healthy national urban growth should imply that various racial and income groups gain fairly from the unique opportunities that urban life provides. This can be achieved only if the inner-city populations are helped to achieve better lives and environments.

Opportunities for Innovation

The major urban problems, at least in the United States, are associated with the difficulties arising in the human, social, political, and economic realms (and probably in that order). This is evident in any list of the top-priority problems of American urban communities— a list that must include the relatively poor educational performance of many minority children, the extent to which crime and self-destructive abuses (such as drug abuse) are associated with poverty clustering, the financial difficulties of central cities and suburban areas, and the governmental problems of dealing with region-wide matters. Clearly here are the areas where innovation is most urgently needed, not in the areas usually mentioned in connection with experimentation in new-communities development—the delivery of garbage, water, and sewerage services or in transportation and communications, or even the provision of health, education, and recreation services. Moreover probably little that is innovated in an isolated, brand-new community can be carried over even to most of the established suburban communities, much less to the central city.

Much that is innovative in human, socioeconomic, and political terms could conceivably be tried in outlying new towns, but the probabilities are against it. There are no really significant pressures to take the kind of risks that are involved in genuine nontechnical innovation. The average builder feels that it is tough enough to sell and rent housing and industrial land without worrying about en-couraging social experiments. And anyway, people are not interested in innovation when they are not in trouble. Mostly they want a nice simple, clean life—without the old urban problems.

The creation of new-towns-intown, by contrast, demands innovation in these very areas. People associated with a new-town-intown development will have very strong incentives to innovate, since they know that the old methods do not work; new methods are the key to success.

In an outlying new town the developer can make anything look like innovation by simply doing traditional things well, particularly since he has the advantage of not being forced to cope with the really difficult urban problems; he can keep most of them out by a careful choice of business units and selective choice of buyers and renters. The new-town-intown developer is in the opposite camp; his task is to cope directly with the major urban problems. Here, making even simple things work calls for genuine innovation. For example, the use of a basic organizational tool such as a strong development corporation with substantial power for coordinated action—certainly no big deal in the construction of an outlying new town—would be a major innovation in the central city. In the same light, racial, ethnic, and income mixing in outlying new communities will surely involve nothing more startling than figuring out the largest number of minority and poor families that will be acceptable to the predominant middle-class residents. In the inner city, however, the issue of mixing is quite another matter, and it involves such complex questions as the possible loss of minority-group political control and the kinds of incentives that can induce white middle-class families to return to the inner city.

More Opportunities for Individual and
Community Development

Although it tends to be discussed more seriously overseas than in the United States, even here progressively inclined people think of this goal as one of the more appealing of a new-town program.

While human development as such is of importance to all groups in all strata of society, the major human-development problems in the United States are strongly class-oriented. The middle-class individual already has many advantages and options. The most severe difficulties arise in the case of the poor and minority populations. These are stated powerfully in the findings of the Coleman Report, which highlights the difficulty in overcoming through educational inputs the educational disadvantages imposed on children growing up in poverty surroundings. These findings pose what I take to be one of our most critical challenges. Mixing of social groups evidently helps to some extent, but surely it is at least as important to try to turn the family and community surroundings of the poor, minority child into less of a personal-development disadvantage. Outlying new towns could certainly contribute to such an effort, and socially helpful environments could be created, but here we have to face the conflict between such a goal and the fact that private new-town developers find it economically attractive to "sell" escape and safety to white middle-class families. Also, numbers are important. I suspect that during the next two decades at least, we can do very much more in the central city for the disadvantaged children taken as a whole than in outlying new towns. In the latter the rate of absorption of poor, minority families into middle-class communities must be relied upon, and, for the reason stated above, this is likely to be limited. Almost by definition the new-town-intown effort makes the creation of more helpful environments for poor, minority children a central goal, and it must do this for all such children living within its territorial boundary.

Community development is closely associated with individual development as a new-town objective, particularly in the sense that one of the major goals of community development is to provide new sources of support for the individual and new strengths for self-development. Clearly the question of individual and group self-image is important here. So is the possibility of finding community means for overcoming certain of the developmental limitations growing out of disadvantaged home lives. Also, as is discussed in the next section, the development of new and greater minority leverage in urban politics can be a significant force in eliminating some of the personally destructive features associated with a sense of utter powerlessness. Community development in a new-town-intown, unlike the situation one expects to find in an outlying new community, is not a matter of absorbing new neighbors and colleagues into established white-middle class institutions and community arrangements. Rather it is a matter of developing stronger and more viable communities with their own character, institutions, and arrangements—some where nonwhite families are in the majority, alongside others that are blended, with nonwhites making up a substantial—rather than an un-important—minority. While the existing suburbs and already built new towns provide ample opportunity for testing the effects on individual development of absorption of poor and minority families into white middle-class communities, only a concentration of major effort in the central city can begin to test the possibilities of building on minority cultures and/or a strongly blended situation.

More Opportunities for Political Participation

As Robert Wood has suggested, the present white middle-class suburban community is a model of active political participation.12 Of course such participation is often directed at promoting the isolationist feelings of the white middle class, as witness the active support of exclusionary zoning. Surely the major problem in the realm of political participation arises from the present powerlessness of poor and minority groups and the lack of a regional politics—that is, a politics that can support needed region-wide planning and region-wide service activities. On the first of these, there is no question as to the advantages of new-town-intown development. On the issue of regional politics, I am afraid that neither intown nor outlying new towns will contribute much, if anything.

Providing More Opportunities for Racial and Income Mixing

Events of the past decade have provided important new insights to the issue of "integration" and have posed new questions.[13] Earlier it was easy to assume that the answer lay entirely in the mixing of racial and income groups. The problem was one of opening up formerly segregated areas to minority groups. It was a matter of providing free choice for everyone.

I still think that it is indecent and socially harmful to exclude individuals and families from any spot in the country because of race (or religion, or national origin, or whatever). But I now appreciate that this is a necessary but not sufficient condition to achieve anything resembling an equitable and socially healthy situation. The latter requires more choices for nonwhites than simply the choice of either being a minority member in a relatively pleasant but white-dominated community or a resident of a hand-me-down area already totally nonwhite or always threatening to become so. The problem would not be so difficult if nonwhite incomes were more-or-less comparable to those of white families. Then the equity issue would depend on genuine enforcement of antidiscrimination laws on the racial side, and greater income distribution efforts on the income side. These three—rapid equalization of nonwhite and white income, genuine enforcement of antidiscrimination laws (and stronger laws), and a rapid narrowing of the income gap between rich and poor—seem to me to deserve the highest priority in any national political agenda.

While at a lower priority than the above, new-towns-intown can make a significant contribution to the equity goal. Some of their advantages have already been identified. They would enable minority members (those who so preferred) to live in all-black or other minority communities while enjoying a good level of public services and an improving rather than a declining environment. Alternately they could live in stable communities in which they are a substantial minority or a small minority, again depending on choice and income. This assumes, and it is an important assumption, that substantial and imaginative investment in the inner city—based on the many attractions that a new-town-intown can contribute to urban living—will provide a strong element of stability to all-minority and to already mixed neighborhoods, and will serve to attract white families back to the city. Outlying new communities as such simply cannot make this kind of contribution to the welfare of nonwhite and poorer families.

176

The important thing they can do is to provide housing for minority and poorer families close to major new employment centers. (Unless the centers are large, such families may soon find themselves stranded when the employment situation changes, since being on the margin of the job market they tend to have to change jobs fairly frequently.)

CONCLUDING NOTE

What is suggested here, then, is the logic of directing the great bulk of federal subsidy for new-town development to the central city, since development of the inner city along new-town lines is the key to achieving the major objectives associated with new-community building. I am convinced that the decision by the federal government to do so or not to do so will have a great deal to do with whether the polarization of our society will be increased or diminished within the next decade or two.

NOTES

1. Harvey S. Perloff, "New Towns Intown," Journal of the American Institute of Planners, Vol. XXXII (May 1966) pp. 155-62.
2. Edwin M. Kaitz and Herbert Harvey Hyman, Urban Planning for Social Welfare: A Model Cities Approach (Washington: Praeger Publishers 1970), p. 36. For a short history of the development of the Model Cities concept and an evaluation of the program to 1970, see Judson Lehman James, "Evaluation Report on the Model Cities Program," in Papers submitted to Subcommittee on Housing Panels, Committee on Banking and Currency, U.S. House of Representatives, 92d Congress, 1st Session, June 1971. For an evaluation and history of efforts to plan for Model Cities see The Model Cities Program: A Comparative Analysis of The Planning Process in Eleven Cities, U.S. Department of Housing and Urban Development (Washington, D.C., 1970).
3. George Sternlieb, "Abandonment and Rehabilitation: What is to be Done," in Papers submitted to Subcommittee on Housing Panels, Committee on Banking and Currency, U.S. House of Representatives, 92d Congress, 1st Session, June 1971, p. 315.
4. Judson Lehman James, op. cit., pp. 847-48.
5. Improving the Quality of Urban Life: A Program Guide to Model Neighborhoods in Demonstration Cities, U.S. Department of Housing and Urban Development (Washington, D.C., 1967), pp. 6-7.

6. For a specific proposal for the building of paired new towns in both inner-city and outlying areas, see Metropolitan Fund, Inc., Regional New-Town Design: A Paired Community for Southeast Michigan (Detroit: Metropolitan Fund, February 1971).

7. Thomas Vietorisz and Bennett Harrison, The Economic Development of Harlem (New York: Praeger Publishers, 1970).

8. These are aside from the requirement of enabling minority workers to find housing near jobs in the suburbs and other outlying areas. See Harvey S. Perloff, "What Economic Future for the Inner City Ghetto?" presented to the Committee on Science and Astronautics, U.S. House of Representatives, 91st Congress, 1st Session, February 5, 1969.

9. Vietorisz and Harrison, op. cit., p. 59.

10. For a discussion of this problem, see Charles E. Olken, "Economic Development in the Model Cities Program," Law and Contemporary Problems, Vol. XXXVI (Spring 1972), pp. 205-26. Methods through which development corporations are currently controlled are discussed in CDC's: New Hope for the Inner City, Report of the Twentieth Century Fund Task Force on Community Development Corporations (New York: The Twentieth Century Fund, 1971), with background paper by Geoffrey Faux.

11. The Lighted Center idea is discussed in Perloff, "New Towns Intown," op. cit., with design suggestions by Bertrand Goldberg and the Harper Court Lighted Center in Chicago Discussed by Bruce Sagan.

12. Robert C. Wood, Suburbia (Boston: Houghton Mifflin, 1959).

13. Anthony Downs, Urban Problems and Prospects, (Chicago: Markham, 1970), pp. 27-74. Note particularly his discussion of the integrated-core strategy in his "Alternative Futures for the Ghetto."

11

THE REALITIES
OF INTEGRATION
IN NEW AND OLD TOWNS
Neil C. Sandberg

Can meaningful social class and racial integration be achieved in new towns and new-towns-intown, as people regroup themselves in these new environments?

Recent trends in the United States point to increasing opposition to integration, of both the socioeconomic and racial varieties.[1] Among other indicators, this is evidenced by a substantial resistance to busing for school desegregation as well as to such programs as low-income scattersite housing. In addition, government housing policies have for many years encouraged segregation by facilitating white home ownership in the suburbs and public housing for blacks in the inner cities.

The separation of the races is further encouraged by the fear of crime and the general tendency to associate it with race.[2] This is also supported by the emergence of new social movements stemming from an ideology of separation, as disadvantaged minorities utilize new forms of social, economic, and political organization in order to gain a greater share of the goods and services of society and to influence the decisions that affect their lives.

In this context a growing climate of suspicion and fear has developed, manifested by a polarization of attitudes and a sharp increase in intergroup conflict. It seems apparent that for many people the belief in an open, integrated society based on the concept of equal opportunity for the individual is giving way to one of group interest and the utilization of power to assure group achievement.[3]

As more blacks and whites accept the notion that integration will not work and the belief grows that the social and psychological security of the individual is directly related to the support he gains from his own group, a number of important questions are being raised, including: Is integration necessary? Can we afford it? Isn't the alleviation of poverty the higher priority?

The questions could well be answered with still other questions in seeking to determine what kind of society this should be in the future: Can a democratic country afford to abandon integration as a major goal? Will current and projected government and private interventions lead to the institutionalization of segregation and the freezing of patterns, so that they result in an "apartheid society"?

These simple questions may lead some socially concerned individuals to simplistic answers, which often tend to express their values and points of view rather than the realities of life. And yet it seems there is an inherent truth in the recognition that policies and programs that accelerate patterns of racial separation will be bad for America, bad for both the minorities and the majority.[4]

Having said this, another belief can be stressed—and that is the view that individuals of diverse racial, ethnic, religious, and cultural groupings have a right to live apart from others if they choose to. And while integration and separatism may seem like conflicting values—and at times they are—they represent the critical ingredients of cultural pluralism, a concept that continues to be operative in American life. This notion allows for primary-group associations of friends, family, and other in-group structures, while at the same time permitting mobility in the secondary-group environment—the larger social, economic, and political milieu.[5]

Current research findings suggest that various racial and ethnic subgroups still find meaning within their own communities. In their recently revised preface to Beyond the Melting Pot, Glazer and Moynihan indicate more strongly than before that the anticipated demise of ethnicity may have been a premature judgment.[6] Other research on the assimilation of white ethnics, which points to a decrease in ethnic identification over the generations and in relation to upward class mobility, also confirms a substantial residue of ethnic vitality into the fourth generation.[7]

It appears, therefore, that integration and separatism are meaningful values, and that they are not necessarily mutually exclusive. The experience of the past, as well as present, demographi movements, points to a visible, although relatively limited, degree of integration, usually where there is social class homogeneity. At the same time one can observe the ongoing existence of racial and ethnic enclaves in the core areas of the cities and in working-class neighborhoods, many of them occupied voluntarily by those who have the capacity for outward mobility but choose not to use it.[8] This is not to suggest, of course, that the racial minorities have substantial freedom of movement, for, as a result of their generally disadvantage condition and the prejudices imposed by the larger society, many of those who would opt for an integrated environment may not be free to do so.

THE POSSIBILITIES FOR INTEGRATION IN NEW TOWNS

Differing views have been expressed concerning the feasibility of utilizing the new town as a vehicle for racial and class integration. Some writers, such as Bernard Weissbourd, see the new town as offering opportunities for integration on a very large scale, with a consequent decrease in ghetto overcrowding and the opening-up of new educational and employment situations.[9] Others, such as Gans and Perloff, see more limited possibilities for integration in the new town and consider the new-town-intown as a more significant alternative, particularly in terms of equity for the urban poor.

In light of the burgeoning resistance to integration and the growth of separatist thinking among a number of racial and ethnic groups, it seems apparent there would be relatively little public support for the massive integration proposal of Weissbourd. Moreover a new-town policy that provided for racial integration even at such optimal current levels as in Columbia and Reston would have little significance for most black people.

Given the presently unrealistic goal of building 100 new towns of 100,000 persons each, plus an additional 10 cities of one million, and utilizing the highest current integration figure—the estimated 15-percent black population in Columbia[10]—only 3 million blacks would be provided for in new towns out of a total of 35-40 million anticipated by the year 2000. The reality of the situation is that such a policy would probably not facilitate the integration of more than the present 5 percent of blacks at Reston (down from an earlier 7 percent[11]), which, when applied in national terms, would bring only one million (or less) black persons into the proposed new towns.

New-towns-intown seem to be equally unrealistic as vehicles for significant racial integration. Millions of low-income blacks are locked into expanding urban ghettos, and the numbers of people and size of these areas are growing, as whites move to outlying places. It seems probable that differences in values and life style, combined with racial prejudice, and underscored by the fear of crime and violence, will not easily be overcome by improved physical environments, new geopolitical configurations, and even developmental processes geared to human needs.

Given the reality that present and projected integration strategies are unlikely to make much difference in light of the enormity of the problem, it may seem logical to suggest that efforts for integration be abandoned and that energies and resources be concentrated on the more pressing needs of the poor. This may be inherent in proposing the primacy of new-towns-intown, despite the suggestion that their catchment areas be enlarged to include diverse groups.

181

But while it is evident that the elimination of poverty must be the priority concern of all, it is also essential to find ways to improve interracial communication and contact everywhere. This applies equally to new towns, although at best they may primarily serve as models for integration, to show that the process can work given adequate support.

Some evidence concerning the integration of races and social classes is beginning to accumulate in Reston, Columbia, and other places where experiments in subsidized housing—e.g., 221(d) 3 and 236 projects—have brought together people of different backgrounds. One such place is the Copperstone project in Columbia, which is integrated both economically and racially. Some 108 families have come together voluntarily, knowing in advance they would be living with others of different races and incomes. The mix includes 40-percent blacks, families on welfare, families headed by females, the aged, the physically incapacitated, a substantial number of moderate-income people, and some families of higher incomes who are paying market-value rent.

As may be expected, the problems are very great, especially since public and private social services are not adequate to meet the need. One example is the grossly inadequate day-care facilities for working mothers whose children used to be cared for by grandmothers and extended families. Other difficulties are the limited accessibility of medical services for low-income families and the prohibitive costs of the otherwise excellent Columbia medical plan, which prices out even moderate-income families. This problem is being met in part by the new practice of accepting medical assistance cards at Columbia hospitals and clinics.

Differences in life style are also creating tensions among the Copperstone tenants. Chief among these is the problem of noise, as large families tramp across uninsulated floors and children play outdoors late at night, making it difficult for others with differing patterns to rest. Further there are some signs of racial antagonism, particularly in the schools.

One could well conclude from this that low- and moderate-income people should not be mixed. And yet the residents of Copperstone are making a valiant effort to work things out, aided by a well-motivated resident manager who acts as both landlord and social worker. A tenants' council has been formed to establish guidelines for children's play activities, residents assist each other by providing transportation, and some residents have been motivated to set up day-care facilities in their apartments for the children of working mothers.[12]

Things might have gone better if the manager and the residents had been adequately prepared for what was to take place. For those with special problems, a social worker might have been assigned to stay in touch with them before, during, and after the move—similar to what was reported in the New Haven relocation experience.[13] And, as suggested by the resident manager himself, how much more effective he could have been had he benefited from some training in social service and human relations before being exposed to such complex problems.

Under recent housing programs, similar experiments have taken place in various urban centers. Working with a consortium of religious groups, the American Jewish Committee was instrumental in creating a successful project, which is tied in with a comprehensive program of social services and is both racially and economically integrated, in the Hoover Urban Renewal Area at the University of Southern California.[14] In the Copperstone and Hoover projects, thousands of black and white low- and moderate-income applicants had to be turned away, indicating that under certain conditions (by providing amenities, services, and location, in addition to an attractive price), government-backed housing can have a great appeal for people of different classes and races.

This challenges the perception that such residents are merely captives in a seller's market, and suggests the feasibility of combining racial and class integration, given adequate economic and social help. It also supports the belief that in some areas where a heterogeneous population exists or can be attracted, racially and economically integrated new-towns-intown are possible.

While it is true that such efforts will not reduce the separation of the races on any meaningful scale, they can serve as symbolic reference points to show that intergroup living is possible and that diverse groups can relate in reasonable compatability and harmony. And despite the observation that the disadvantaged often get symbols and the advantaged get tangible benefits, these models do represent bridgeheads of integration, giving support and encouragement to those individuals and institutions, public and private, that continue to press for an open, integrated society.

As America becomes more upwardly mobile, more and more people may choose to integrate. Differences in life style and values will diminish, and class and racial integration will be more probable and acceptable. The process of preparing people to live together may be facilitated by the socializing mechanisms of society, including the media and their impact on mass culture. In time, and as a consequence of beefed-up human-resources programs provided through new-towns-intown and other urban programs, the cities may once again serve as "socialization centers" facilitating upward mobility for those who seek it, and lessening white resistance to integration.

AN INTEGRATION MODEL FOR NEW TOWNS

Notwithstanding such efforts, however, the fact is that most people, black and white, are not actively seeking integrated living. This is also true for many Mexican-Americans, Puerto Ricans, Asians, white ethnics, and others who choose to live among those like themselves.

In examining the opportunities for enclave-living in new towns, therefore, the feasibility of reserving housing entrances or blocks for individuals of different ethnic and racial backgrounds has been suggested. This concept could be expanded so that the prospective buyer or renter could be offered other choices, such as the following:

1. Reserved enclaves for particular ethnic and racial groups, or even extended families. This would be a form of macro-integration, providing both the advantages of primary-group contact on the block or neighborhood, and secondary-group contact in the service centers and town. Such areas could also be underwritten by racial, ethnic, or religious institutions, so that those who choose to relocate can do so in groups. In addition these places could be reserved by government to provide for group relocation of those such as the Urban Villagers and others displaced by urban renewal, new-towns-intown, and highways.[15] Such opportunities would in large measure help to overcome the sense of isolation and loneliness that individuals may otherwise feel as pioneers in a hostile environment.

2. Reserved areas for those who seek micro-integration. This would enable many socially motivated individuals of different backgrounds who wish to expose themselves and their children to an intercultural environment to live together on the block or in the neighborhood in appropriate proportions. Inducements of price and amenities could also be offered to stimulate others to select housing in these places.

3. Areas of random mix. These will probably be largely middle-class and white, although some middle-class blacks and others will be likely to choose this course as a means of validating their equality and mobility. These areas will also include some white ethnics who have abandoned the ecological enclaves, but who still maintain contact with fellow ethnics in psychological enclaves supported by new structures and forms of communication, and no longer constrained by the limits of neighborhood boundaries.[16]

4. New-towns-intown in white ethnic areas, which offer the prospect of helping to keep some of the younger generation more closely identified with their kinship group. It could also entail a larger catchment area, which would bring the core group into greater contact with others of diverse backgrounds. Opening up such developmental programs for working-class ethnics may well generate the

necessary political support by bringing them together with the disadvantaged in common, integrative programs.

All of the above options could allow for some socioeconomic differentiation, especially if jobs were made available for lower-income people. But if this is to be done successfully, it is essential to provide those social mechanisms that will help to deal with anticipated human-relations problems. It is here that intergroup-relations agencies and religious bodies can play a major role in ameliorating tensions and encouraging positive interpersonal contact. In addition more adequate support systems will have to be developed to facilitate access to employment, recreation, and urgently needed social services.

Various configurations could be developed in such experiments to see if they will work and to determine the best patterns. While their success would be somewhat speculative, these proposals could encourage new alternatives for integration by making available varied patterns of living. And even though they will not have a powerful quantitative impact on integration, they could be of considerable qualitative importance.

At the same time, racial and economic discrimination will have to be dealt with more effectively in all areas through the utilization of federal levers that compel cooperation. In this connection a Title VI-type program to assure equal access to all federally assisted housing could be of great significance.[17] Moreover improved enforcement efforts tied to programs of public education could sustain and nourish the notion of intergroup living as a seminal idea of a plural, democratic society.

In the unlikely conflict between the desire to maintain a separate area and the effort of someone to integrate it, the higher value will of course be freedom of mobility. Acceptance of this concept may help to overcome the resistance of those who will object to the use of group criteria in publicly assisted programs. The development of macro- and micro-integration models based on reserved areas and voluntary occupancy patterns could also be facilitated by a change in HUD guidelines, which currently stress the notion of random integration.

CONCLUSION

Despite the hope for a comprehensive approach to a more just society, it is apparent there are powerful obstacles to social progress. Current economic considerations suggest that serious constraints limit our potential for social investment, and political analysis underscores the heightened resistance to expenditures for human-resources development for the poor.

185

Moreover the burgeoning revolt against high taxes and government spending suggests that an approach geared largely to the core areas of the cities may not be acceptable to the majority of working-class persons, many of whom feel that they are the ones paying for progress for others. Large numbers of working-class people residing outside the central cities are themselves living a marginal existence, harried by inflation, rising taxes and technologically induced unemployment.

Faced with these seemingly insoluble difficulties, they have reacted more and more with a sense of alienation and outrage at what they perceive to be abuses perpetrated by a society that cares little about them. In this setting a strategy that commits most available resources to one area of need will probably meet with massive resistance and may be self-defeating. On the other hand the quest for low- and moderate-income housing in new towns as well as in the cities can serve the interests of both the increasingly mobile working-class whites and the disadvantaged minorities, thereby helping to bridge the gap between the competing interests and strengthening the possibility of common action.

This should be seen in the context of the present administration's efforts to shift certain aspects of decision-making from Washington to the states and local communities. The assumption behind this approach is that states and local communities are better able to determine some of their needs and priorities than is Washington. With the introduction and anticipated expansion of revenue sharing, local program direction is emerging, and this is backed by the financial and technical assistance of the federal government. (Hopefully, revenue sharing will not prove to be a euphemism for the avoidance of social responsibility.)

One consequence of this emphasis is the heightened need for a national urban policy which will serve to guide local, state, and regional programs, so that we can deal more effectively with the problems stemming from the chaotic and often destructive processes of unplanned urbanization. Despite the multiple and sometimes conflicting goals of the 1970 Housing Act and the ongoing struggle between the executive and legislative branches, many believe that such a policy, which incorporates rational developmental processes, can be created. This may lead to a conceptual framework through which new towns and new-towns-intown are viewed as important elements in a complex system for dealing with urban problems and developing optimal strategies for intervention. But, these approaches can be successful only if they are grounded in a profound respect for human and environmental values as much as a concern for market mechanisms.

Consequently it will be necessary to move beyond traditional cost-benefit analyses to include the social costs and benefits of policies that permit or encourage urban expansion. With respect to integration, this will require an examination of such matters as the alienation and loneliness stemming from living among hostile neighbors, the importance of family and friends, and the psychological and physical stresses resulting from mobility. At the same time the social costs of institutionalizing racial and class isolation will have to be considered and trade-offs will have to be made as plans are developed and programs implemented.

A basic underpinning of this effort would be the incorporation of a differential strategy that maximizes choices for individuals from diverse groups. This includes experimentation with new-town models of micro- and macro-integration, which serve to increase available options. However, it must also be related to the social, economic, and physical factors crucial to human growth and progress, such as income guarantees, universal health care, rent supplements, the restructuring of social services for improved delivery and assurance of employment for all.

But regardless of the rhetoric of social progress, little will be done, particularly with regard to low income housing and integration, unless there is some meaningful support from Washington. This will necessitate the continued and expanded pressures of individuals and institutions who seek to improve conditions for the disadvantaged and who value an open society with freedom of mobility for those desiring it.

Because of the present climate, successes will be limited and there will be many setbacks and failures. Hence, what has been proposed here represents a holding operation for a time—in the near future, one hopes—when conditions for integration may improve. It is self-evident that more comprehensive approaches are needed at all levels of government, but if we fail to take even these minimal actions, the adverse consequences may be irreversible and perhaps catastrophic to our concept of a democratic society.

NOTES

1. Robert S. Browne and Bayard Rustin, Separatism or Integration, Which Way for America? (New York: National Jewish Community Relations Advisory Council, 1968), pp. 7-15.

2. Marvin Wolfgang and Bernard Cohen, Crime and Race (New York: Institute of Human Relations Press, 1970).

3. See, for example, Stokely Carmichael and Charles V. Hamilton, Black Power: The Politics of Liberation in America (New York: Random House, 1967), Ch. II.

4. Bayard Rustin, "Black Power and Coalition Politics," Commentary XLII, #3 (September 1966), 35-40.

5. Horace M. Kallen, Culture and Democracy in the United States (New York: Boni and Liveright, 1924), p. 124; see also Milton M. Gordon, Assimilation in American Life (New York: Oxford University Press, 1964), pp. 132-59.

6. Nathan Glazer and Daniel P. Moynihan, Beyond the Melting Pot, rev. ed. (Cambridge: M.I.T. Press, 1970), Preface.

7. Neil C. Sandberg, "Design and Testing of a Group Cohesiveness Scale to Measure the Salience of Ethnic Identity Among Polish-Americans in the Los Angeles Metropolitan Area" (unpublished Ph.D. dissertation, University of Southern California, 1972).

8. Andrew M. Greeley, Why Can't They Be Like Us? (New York: Institute of Human Relations Press, 1969); see also Murray Friedman, Overcoming Middle Class Rage, (Philadelphia: The Westminster Press, 1971), pp. 15-49.

9. Bernard Weissbourd, "Satellite Communities," The Center Magazine, V, 1, (January/February 1972), 7-16.

10. Estimate of a Rouse Company executive, May 1972.

11. Estimate of a Gulf, Western Company executive, May 1972.

12. Interview with James A. Bohanon, resident manager of Copperstone, May 1972.

13. Katherine Feidelson, "A Total Approach to Family Relocatic Journal of Housing, 24, 3, (April 1967), 161-67.

14. Interview with Travis Kendall, Interfaith Housing Corporatic of Southern California, May 1972

15. Herbert J. Gans, The Urban Villagers (New York: The Free Press, 1962), p. 332.

16. Amitai Etzioni, "The Ghetto—A Re-evaluation," Social Forces, 37, 3, (March 1959), 255-62; Sandberg, op. cit.

17. HEW and Title VI, A Report on the Development of the Organization, Policies and Compliance Procedures of HEW (Washingtc D.C., Government Printing Office, 1970).

CHAPTER 12

VIEWS ON THE FEASIBILITY
OF INTEGRATION
J. Eugene Grigsby

Integration has often been posited as the means of increasing the well-being or quality of life of minority groups. My comments here focus on the potentials of integration as a means of improving the quality of life for racial and class minorities, and make use of the concepts of new towns versus new-towns-intown to provide the setting for examining this issue. Several conceptual points must be made in order to understand the use of the term "integration."

First, we must decide whether integration is to be viewed from a majority-normative perspective or a minority-normative perspective. The distinction is crucial in that the implications for policy will to a great extent depend upon which point of view is being reflected.

Second, we must understand the difference between integration and nonsegregation. Integration in the traditional sense implies the mixing of minorities with non-minorities (seldom if ever does it imply mixing non-minorities with minorities). Nonsegregation on the other hand implies both the right of people to remain indefinitely where they are, even if in ghetto areas, and the elimination of restrictions on their moving into other areas. Nonsegregation would provide for voluntary ghetto residence, while integration could result in involuntary non-ghetto residence.[1]

Let us examine the implications of the two possible points of view of integration in assessing its feasibility in new towns—from that of the majority (traditionally the white middle and upper-middle classes) as compared to the view of the minority (traditionally lower-class and nonwhite). Levittown, Columbia, and Reston would be the setting for integration from a majority view. Peach Tree and Soul City would involve integration from the minority point of view.

The majority-normative point of view is almost inevitably the way social scientists approach the question of integration. Gans, in setting the stage for his analysis of integration, elaborates the discussion of class and status by adding the variable of color, with light skin a significant indicator of acceptability. In this majority-normativ frame of reference, integration is feasible only to the extent that high-status people permit low-status people to live with them. While the terms "black" and "white" are not used, it seems apparent that the capacity for integration is defined as the extent to which whites allow blacks to live among them. From this point of view it is mandatory that blacks accommodate to whites if they are to be integrated. One of Gans' major arguments is that it is extremely difficult to mix different class groups irrespective of race. But by his own definition, class and race are virtually inseparable. And it is this distinction that makes nonviable the proposition that integration within new-towns development is the vehicle to raise the quality of life for minority peoples within the United States. The majority-normative orientation fails to account for the significance of culture, organizational structure, and power as critical variables affecting any improvement in the quality of life to be effected by integration. I am suggesting that these variables must be thoroughly understood before the implementation of effective policy on integration can bring about the desired result of improved quality of life for minority group

One of the myths of American social scientists is that there are basically no cultural differences between members of majority and minority groups.[2] But mounting evidence to the contrary is finally being recognized.[3] Subjects ranging from education and health care to entertainment, hair style, and dress have caused more than small amounts of stress between the two groups as to approach, style, and legitimacy.

From a majority perspective, Gans leads us to believe that much of the resistance to integration within new towns revolves aroun class differences. He hypothesizes that, if different racial groups were similar in class characteristics, then the probability of integrati would be enhanced, especially if incoming blacks were from the middl rather than lower classes.[4] It has been argued, however, that those fleeing from blacks have never taken the time to differentiate among those of the lower, middle, or upper classes. The fact that they were black and becoming more numerous was sufficient reason for getting away from these persons.[5] It may be a plain case of majority people trying to get away from culturally different neighbors.[6]

If we assume cultural differences, there should also be some logic to the argument that different cultures will support different types of institutions and/or organizational structures. Family structure would be a good example. I assume that the deviant families that Gans states should be screened out from potential new towns are the one-parent families that Moynihan says are the prime cause for the deterioration of the black family in American society.[7] Since a two-parent family is held as the norm (majority-oriented), then deviations from this norm are usually deemed undesirable. It is a fact that many black families have different family structures (one-third of the urban black families have female heads of household, according to 1970 census data). Consequently the roles of the various members of these families take on different functions. The extended family, for example, plays a supportive role within many black families,[8] a role not often recognized by the majority frame of reference. If new-town developments are conceived in such a manner that extended family contacts are discouraged, or at least not encouraged, then the possibility of providing an opportunity for supporting a structural relationship between members of black families diminishes. Sandberg has underscored this point in his new-towns integration model, which provides for those extended families and groups that need the social and psychological security deriving from living in close proximity to one another.

The significance of self-determination cannot be underestimated. One of the largest struggles taking place in American society today concerns the right of the have-nots to participate as well as to allocate when it comes to making decisions. As has been pointed out, developers usually maintain control of their developments at least until their profit has been realized. One of the unintended consequences of blacks occupying the central cities of the nation has been their increased political power, or perhaps more importantly, their new acquisition of information about the political process. These blacks have learned through some bitter lessons that they can alter the course of educational networks, that they can press city hall for increased services and that they can change the complexion of certain key decision-makers.[9] In fact, they have grasped the meaning of power and now have a short history in exercising it. Consequently those blacks moving into new towns are not about to forget this lesson, and will actively seek to exercise these new-found powers in order to influence events in their favor. Integration efforts will be perceived by them only as a means of diluting their numbers, with the expected consequence of depriving them of the potential for organizational strength. Gans' macro-integration (a small allocation of minorities scattered throughout the development) implies no real change. Every major American city has pockets of minorities, of poor people and of different class groups. Micro-integration (a street-by-street distribution of minorities), as laudable as it seems to be, requires that minorities, poor, or lower-class peoples dilute their numbers and submit themselves to a majority culture as a means of reaping rewards and benefits from this relationship. If new-town development does not afford them equal representation in decision-making, it is certain that they will make their presence known throughout the entire community.

Perloff has argued that new-town-intown should be the federal government's next major commitment to the welfare of the nation as a whole. He recognizes that, given the historical development of minorities within the United States, a positive self-image must be developed within a strong supportive environment. Blacks have stated they would like to forge such developmental programs out of a black identity and a black environment, without necessarily excluding nonblacks. The need for coordinating activities and securing enough financing from the federal government is a necessity within this scheme of things. For others, however, development of new towns is going to remain in the hands of profit-oriented private developers, who will always be at the mercy of the market. And as long as this is so, it will often be impossible for developers to let their efforts be representative of their constituencies' wishes, let alone responsive to their diverse needs. Even if these developers would want to be innovative and sensitive, they will always have to be responsive first to market demands and only second to resident needs.

To return to the concept of integration as a means of improving the quality of life for minorities, new-town developments are unlikely to have widespread national effects. With new-towns-intown, however where the largest numbers of minorities are concentrated, there lies some real hope of creating significant advances in living conditions through national policy and action. Advances to be made, though, are most likely through nonsegregation than through the more restrictive connotations of integration.

CONCLUSION

If the formulators of national policy are to embrace integration as a vehicle for improving the quality of life for a great number of individuals who have been excluded from mainstream America, then they will have to come to grips with some fundamental questions:

1. There is the basic issue of integration versus nonsegregation. The mixing of different groups does not necessarily increase quality of life. As currently used, the term "integration" is majority-normative, whereas "nonsegregation" encompasses the idea of opportunity to choose. There is little feasibility of nonsegregation in new towns, and new-towns-intowns have a greater potential for allowing freedom of choice.

2. Makers of national policy must come to grips with the majority-normative approach versus the minority-normative approach regarding the question of increasing the quality of life. This is by

far the most difficult of the questions to be broached. To come to some meaningful resolution of this matter will require a thorough examination of the very concept of quality of life. Who is to determine what exactly constitutes improved quality of life? If educational achievement is increased but the feeling of individual self-worth is decreased, has there in fact been an increase in the quality of life?

3. There is the question of participation. Who is to have a hand in the shaping of these policies? Is it to be the people who will be affected most by such policies, or will it continue to be the representatives from institutions that must finance any implementation of these policies? A key issue is to locate the source of political strength. For the minorities and the poor this is definitely in the cities. To assume that a wave of outlying new-town development will serve the cause of these urbanites is unrealistic. Gans has stated that the feasibility of integrating new towns depends on the minorities and the poor remaining in the minority. What then will the majority of this minority do?

NOTES

1. Robert E. Forman, Black Ghettos, White Ghettos, and Slums (Englewood Cliffs, N.J.: Prentice-Hall, 1971), p. 46.
2. N. Glazer and D. Moynihan, Beyond the Melting Pot (Cambridge, Mass.: M.I.T. Press, 1970).
3. Stephen S. Baratz and Joan C. Baratz, "Early Childhood Intervention: the Social Science Base of Institutional Racism," Harvard Educational Review, XL, 1, (Winter 1970), 29-50; Charles A. Valentine, "Deficit, Differences, and Bicultural Models of Afro-American Behavior," Harvard Educational Review, XLI, 2, (May 1971), pp. 137-57.
4. Herbert J. Gans, "The Possibilities of Class and Racial Integration in American New Towns," paper presented at the Conference on Human Factors in New Town Development, sponsored by the American Jewish Committee and held at the University of California, Los Angeles, June 22-23, 1972. A revised version of Gans' paper constitutes Chapter 9 of this book.
5. Edith Abbot, The Tenements of Chicago, 1908-1935 (Chicago: University of Chicago Press, 1936), p. 125; Forman, op. cit., p. 34; St. Clair Drake and Horace R. Cayton, Black Metropolis (New York: Harper and Row, 1945), p. 211.
6. Forman, op. cit., p. 49.
7. D. P. Moynihan, The Negro Family: The Course for National Action (Washington, D.C.: Government Printing Office, 1965).

8. Carol B. Stack, "The Kindred of Viola Jackson: Residence and Family Organization of an Urban Black American Family," in N. Whitten and G. Szwend, eds., Afro-American Anthropology: Contemporary Perspectives (New York: The Free Press, 1970); Valentine, op. cit., p. 149.

9. Mario Fantini and Marilyn Gittell, "The Ocean Hill-Brownsville Experiment," in Richard R. Heidenreich, ed., Urban Education (Arlington, Va.: College Readings, 1971). In 1971-72 in Los Angeles, two white school principals of predominately black schools were removed upon demand of the students' parents. Currently in Los Angeles a large section of the Mexican-American population is calling for redistricting of the city councilmen's areas in order that Mexican-Americans may be elected. (Currently there are no Mexican-American city councilmen serving predominately Mexican-American areas of the city.)

13

"COOKING SMELLS
AND LULLABIES
AND JOKES . . .":
SOME THOUGHTS ON NEW TOWNS
William R. Ellis, Jr.

Planning discussions tend to the categorical and to what may be termed a no-nonsense practicality. Mere possibility and humanistic speculations on life styles (like some discussions of "culture") appear evanescent and utopian by contrast.* But what renders the world human during and after planning and beyond abstracted considerations of class, race, and legislative probabilities is precisely the ordinary stuff of "cooking smells and lullabies and jokes," suggesting that effective planning not only can but must take place in light of these peculiarly human events.

Planners cannot be faulted for not spending their time on such issues. Most deeply problematical for those who do is the means by which a discussion of them becomes convincing, given the stark empirical realities of power, powerlessness, prejudice, status anxiety, and the like, which play such a basic deflecting role in the disposition of even the most practical of progressive plans.

It has been argued that the possibilities of integration and innovation constitute the central purposes of new towns, both of these being subservient to the greater aim of improving the quality of life in our urban areas. Clearly (but not exclusively) in the American context, age, racial, and ethnic integration is tantamount to innovation. But integration, particularly racial and class integration, has or should have two additional primary goals: (1) the equalization of choice, and (2) the equalization of access to "life chances." In this

---

*The fate of Max Weber's once efficient lebenstile probably revolves him in his grave. Such is the fate of concepts that strike the popular fancy and are removed for use from the scientific lexicon.

respect the new-town-intown seems to serve the goals of integration best; not the reduction of diversity to racial, ethnic, or stylistic homogeneity, but the arraying of human types in such a way that they confront equally the flow of advantage and disadvantage, privilege, power, and powerlessness. This underscores the futility of seeking broad new solutions to apparently insoluble old problems and suggests the need to take advantage of viable styles of existence that survive in our troubled cities.

Strategists for the poor know that the most important feature of integration is that "they"—those with power, privilege, and advantage— when integrated, are less able to secret away from their new neighbors their source of advantage. And there are some sources of advantage beyond being lighter skinned. But planners know there are certain class-, ethnic-, and race-based realities that stand as barrier to such integration, even when the motivation is less instrumental. Moreover, while integration may, as it often does, raise the market value of a middle-class white's house, the sight of a black face, the sound of the Spanish language, or the unfamiliar singsong lilt a child brings in his voice from the newly integrated school may symbolically lower the social value of an area.

Consequently I would argue that it is innovative simply to think in terms of saving a minority life style that may be anathema to the dominant culture but which is central to the culture, however evanescent, of the urban poor, the young, and the productively deviant. The setting for this is the new-town-intown, where we face in particular the problem of the "managed juxtaposition"[1] of widely divergent living styles, ethnicities, ages, style of space use, etc. Intown, then, we are dealing with the requirement of successfully juxtaposing what could be termed style centers, consciously mixed, adjacent to an agglomeration of such centers that has evolved through the less progressive de jure and de facto practices of the disadvantaged. We must think in terms of arraying people in such a way as to make available to them, relatively immediately, the jobs, cooking smells, lullabies, and jokes that already exist in the city onto which the new-town-intown is grafted.

While we still have a great deal to learn about the sociology of symbolically bounded space in complex urban areas,[2] we know from studies such as those of Kadushin, Orleans, and others, that the higher one's income the less traditional notions of territory are likely to circumscribe the area of one's friendships, associations, and work practices. The Flower Mound survey, which suggests that concern with territoriality varies inversely with income, is consonant with what we seem to be learning. We have now to learn how to arrange transportation, location, and other factors for the poor so that, as their incomes rise (as will surely be the case), they will be able to move on to interest-based, extraspatial communal ties that will still permit something precious from the past to survive.

Survival is at least about sniffing the air, pricking up your ears, opening your eyes, and recognizing yourself. As we grow as a nation and indeed as a world, this will happen less and less in simple territorial enclaves. New-towns-intown have the best possibility of becoming something other than that. They are the arena for the new conceptions of community.

NOTES

1. Harvey Molotch, Managed Integration: Dilemmas of Doing Good in the City (Berkeley: University of California Press, 1972).
2. Anselm Strauss, "Strategies for Discovering Urban Theory," in The American City: A Sourcebook of Urban Imagery (Chicago: Aldine Publishing Company, 1968), pp. 515-29 (especially pp. 521-22).
3. Charles Kadushin, "The Friends and Supporters of Psychotherapy: On Social Circles in Urban Life," American Sociological Review, XXXI, 6 (December 1966), 786-802; Peter Orleans, "On the Changing Conditions of Communal Life in the Contemporary City" (unpublished paper, School of Architecture and Urban Planning, University of California, Los Angeles, 1970).

14

NEW COMMUNITIES
OR COMPANY TOWNS?
AN ANALYSIS OF
RESIDENT PARTICIPATION
IN NEW TOWNS
David R. Godschalk

Since the closing of the American frontier, genuine opportunities to participate in the growth and development of a new town have been scarce. One of the exciting potentials of the fledgling U.S. new-town movement is the reappearance of community-development participation opportunities. Yet participation has been a neglected area of new-town policy, which has been informed neither by substantial analysis of firsthand participation experience nor by real alternatives to current practice.

Theoretically new towns could become "laboratories for democracy," in which new forms of local self-government are tested, and novel means of broadening resident participation in planning and governance are explored. These are the recommendations of a blue-ribbon task force on new-town governance, which held that "popular experience in the process of development is basic to creation of the public intelligence necessary to master the urban environment."[1] Many community activists seek out new-town living in order to test that premise for themselves.

As the activists have discovered, the reality of new-town participation does not yet approach this ideal.[2] Planning and decision-making have been deliberately prestructured by the developer to minimize citizen influence until the major building is completed. Participation has been subordinated to pay-back schedules of the massive development loans needed to build a complete new town. One observer of this expensive, complicated process has concluded that without public regulation we must accept a developmental period during which a "semi-democratic facade" prevails, since there may be no feasible way to combine development with meaningful resident participation.[3]

New towns have not been designed as laboratories for democracy, because it is generally assumed that their internal development must be centrally controlled in order to achieve planned objectives of growth, population composition, and cash flow. Behind the semi-democratic facade, the new-town development corporation seeks to control both the economics and politics of the development. This is a variant of the unitary power system that has characterized American company towns, where pluralistic democracy never got started because residents never could accumulate enough of a stake to get into the civic game. While the new-town developer does not directly control most residents' jobs as in a company town, it could be argued that influence over the economics of new-town development takes on a similar importance in shaping the educational, recreational, cultural, and civic activities of the family. To protect the investment of the new-town developer and his financial backers, including the federal government in some cases, the balance usually gets tipped toward unitary corporate power and away from active citizen participation.

At issue are the basic objectives of new-town policy and how they are to be achieved. Present federal government policy appears to side with those "pragmatists" who believe that central control is necessary to achieve "orderly development of well-planned, diversified and economically sound new communities"—the goal of the Urban Growth and New Community Development Act of 1970. The extreme version of this view holds that new-town residents are not competent to participate in development decisions, since they will selfishly misunderstand the public interest aspects of the plan, try to exclude new residents who differ by class or race, and seek economically unsound amounts of low-density housing and open space. Supporters of central control identify participation with protest.

My own view is that, if we are to go beyond construction of physically new towns to build new social communities, where institutions are designed to assist people in developing collective competence and trust, then we must look beyond the simplistic confines of unitary power and of participation as protest. My analysis proceeds in three steps:

1. Some insights into a broader type of new-community development are derived from comparisons of experience with first-generation participation at Reston, Virginia, and Columbia, Maryland, both started in the 1960s. These analyses are based on a field study during the summer of 1970. Since new communities are constantly changing, any cross-sectional study is liable to be outdated within a relatively short time. My findings are intended to illustrate two general alternatives, rather than to describe completely, or to criticize, either community.

199

2. An analysis of proposed second-generation participation arrangements in the present federally guaranteed new towns demonstrates some problems inherent in current federal participation policy.

3. A new model of community development partnership, based on resident-developer collaboration, is proposed.

CURRENT PARTICIPATION IN AMERICAN NEW TOWNS

Planning and governance in U.S. new towns are characterized by two American inventions designed to cope with private market forces. These additions to new-town development technology are (1) governance by a private association, dating from Radburn in the 1920s; and (2) systems-oriented planning based on a detailed economic model, dating from Columbia in the 1960s. Both devices influence citizen participation in planning and decision-making.

Economic Models

Central to the planning of any contemporary American new town is the preparation of an economic model for fiscal programming. No new community project will be attempted unless, in the beginning, the model can be made to show that the large initial investments in land, facilities, and services will eventually return a reasonable profit. For example, after a sizable investment in planning and feasibility studies, the General Electric Corporation took the advice of its computerized economic model and abandoned its ambitious plans for a series of new-community development projects. When a project is undertaken as development proceeds, no major changes in the initial plan will be approved unless the economic model indicates that their impact can be accommodated without rocking the fiscal boat. Finally, substantial participation in planning and decision-making is not opened to the new-community residents until repayment of the massive development loans is assured, which may be into the second decade of the community's life.

Economic models come in varying degrees of complexity and sophistication. At heart, however, all of them are simply accounting procedures for projecting and keeping track of cash flow.[5] Revenues and expenditures are compared over the span of the development period for both capital and operating budgets. Separate accounts may be set up for the development corporation to balance costs of converting raw land to an urban systems-framework against revenues from prepared land sales and, for the homes association, to balance costs of providing recreational and other services against revenues from dues and other sources.

By themselves economic models are neutral planning and scheduling tools. Used by the developer to manage complex problems of public-service delivery, facility construction, and financial scheduling, the models are sometimes seen by citizens as restrictive corporate control devices for limiting the amount of resident participation in planning. To date, economic models have been tools of the developer, but there is no reason why they could not become tools of the community as well. The development schedule—what is to be built, when, at what cost—contained in the economic model provides the real discipline of current new-community planning.

The discipline of a cash-flow model designed to achieve the goals of developer and investor leads naturally to market-oriented planning. From there it is an easy step to the assumption that corporate control is absolutely necessary in order to carry out the marketing plan. The developer takes the role of producer. Residents are then cast as consumers, who vote with their dollars for a particular plan when they buy a house in a new community. If they wish to go beyond consumerism to active participation in planning, citizens must understand the cash-flow basis of planning decisions.

Private Governments

Next to the economic model in terms of its significance for new-community planning and governance is the homes association—the typical device for handling the producer-consumer contract. Homes associations were originally designed to provide maintenance and services to planned unit developments—special subdivisions with common facilities—rather than to socially and economically complex new communities.[6] The homes association, an incorporated, non-profit organization, operates under recorded land agreements to maintain private and common property and to provide services for which residents pay annual dues.

Decision-making control within the homes association is retained by the new-community developer during the early years, and is then gradually transferred to the residents. Established as part of the predevelopment process before residents arrive, the homes association has its policy set by officers and a board of directors, who are initially appointed by the developer. Over time, and in accordance with a pre-set schedule derived from the economic model, the developer's men are replaced by residents. Significant participation by residents on the board does not occur before the project's cash flow has "turned positive"; that is, until the developer's revenue has begun to exceed his costs. Typically this is projected to take place between seven and twelve years from the start of the project. This timetable for the withering away of developer control over the homes association is drawn up by the developer before construction starts, and not unexpectedly it tends toward the conservative side.

The homes associations at Reston and Columbia, two precedent-setting, first-generation American new towns, have been criticized on the grounds that the "one unit—one vote" rule does not satisfy equal voting rights under the Fourteenth Amendment to the U.S. Constitution. Young adults living with parents, older people, renters, and possibly even spouses with differing views, may be disenfranchised from voting on important matters of community governance. This appears to be a legal technicality, which could be remedied by tinkering with the voting rules. It is not nearly as fundamental an issue as the question of separation of political and economic power in the new town's organization for decision-making.

Community Resource Exchange

One way of abstracting and understanding the complex dynamics of participation in planning and decision-making is through analysis of community resources and the way they are exchanged. Differences between Reston and Columbia begin to show up clearly when these resource-exchange dynamics are assessed as transactions among various institutional actors, each seeking to profit.

The social-profit concept of exchange theory was first used in analyzing interpersonal behavior in small groups.[7] It since has been applied to an exchange model of politics in which governments exchange public goods and services with citizens for support, compliance, and resources. Terry N. Clark holds interchange between groups to be an important mechanism for community integration. The Clark model centers on the imbalance of power created when one actor is able to offer to others some commodity that places them in his debt. Uncollected debts become a form of social surplus, generating social capital in the form of power and status.

A general proposition from exchange theory holds that the greater the quantity and exchange value of resources available to a particular sector in a community, the more actors from that sector are likely to become involved in decision-making, and the more decisional outcomes are likely to reflect their values and interests. Thus the more valuable the resources held by new-community residents, the more they should be able to participate and the greater their influence over development decisions.

What resources can be traded for influence in development decision-making? Obviously control of community organizations, knowledge and technical skills, money and credit, legal authority, budget-making power, jobs, plan-approval capacity, information, and political support are valuable resources. More subtle, but equally important for citizens, are group solidarity, cooperation and problem-solving aid, political protest, and threats to the market image of the developer.

In a pluralistic decision-making system citizens would be expected to control enough resources so that development plans would have to be made with them. In a unitary system the developer would be freer to make these decisions for the residents, since he would control both the economics and the politics of development. As Schattschneider has observed, "The function of democracy has been to provide the public with a second power system, an alternative power system, which can be used to counter-balance the economic power."[8] Reston and Columbia illustrate the alternatives.

Plural Participation At Reston

Reston, an unincorporated development in urban Fairfax County, was not originally designed as a pluralistic system. It has a standard homeowners association. All property owners automatically become dues-paying members through deed covenants running with the land. The homeowners board of directors is elected by members, who have one vote for each housing unit owned, and by the developer, who has a vote for each unit he owns and for each unsold platted lot. The developer will control at least one-third of the directors until 1985. Renters cannot vote for board members. Nine directors, including three residents, are elected for three-year terms to govern the association. In addition, all townhouse owners automatically belong to a cluster association, which maintains common property within the cluster.

Following some community conflict over the role and structure of the homeowners association, an interim superstructure of organizations advisory to the homeowners association was created at Reston in 1970. These included two "village councils," each with five members elected by all residents over sixteen years of age (including renters), and a "town council" made up of the chairmen of the two village councils, plus the three resident members of the homeowners association board. This semi-democratic advisory structure did not change the final decision-making power of the developer-controlled board of directors.

In 1967 financial problems had led to the forced departure of Reston's first developer, Robert E. Simon, and set the stage for the mobilization of a citizens organization independent of the homeowners association. The activist founders of the Reston Community Association (RCA) saw it as a countervailing force, out from under the new developer's control and thus able to represent the citizens directly. RCA took advantage of the crisis of uncertainty over the future of Reston's innovative master plan under Gulf Reston, Inc., the new developer, to build resident solidarity. As RCA matured and gained legitimacy as the residents' representative with the Fairfax County Board of Supervisors, it became a third force in a pluralistic community organizational equation—alongside the developer and homeowners association.

Dissatisfaction with this organizational mix has since led to a recommendation for a new arrangement. In their report, the citizens Study Team on RHOA Role and Structure concluded that the advisory town council and village councils, and the Reston Community Association should be replaced with a nine-member independent Reston Council. The council should consist of registered voters elected by county voting precincts within Reston. It would derive its authority both from the community and the Fairfax County Board of Supervisors. Finding that the homeowners association structure was designed for control of common land and not community participation, the report recommended that the homeowners association be restricted to fulfilling its corporate obligations, and that it drop its "surrogate government" functions. The study team's report thus formalizes a classic dual power system in which political and economic power are separate. The recommended Reston Council would provide an independent power system and public forum in which conflicts can be politicized, while the homeowners association would provide an economic power system in which corporate control can be exercised and decisions can be taken in the privacy of the boardroom.

The Reston system could be described as a form of limited pluralism, which achieved a rough balance of power by limiting to two organizations citizen participation in major development decision making. Simple pluralism, while a necessary condition for effective participation, is not a sufficient condition.[10] Four major actors control the bulk of the community development resources at Reston; their exchange system as of 1970 is diagrammed in Figure 14.1.*

---

*This picture is oversimplified in that it omits the other outside "governments," such as the county educational agency, whose decisions are important to the community. However the general pattern of interaction tends to be similar, the citizens having an influence with these agencies as well as with the board of supervisors.

204

FIGURE 14.1

Exchange among Planning Actors at Reston,
1970

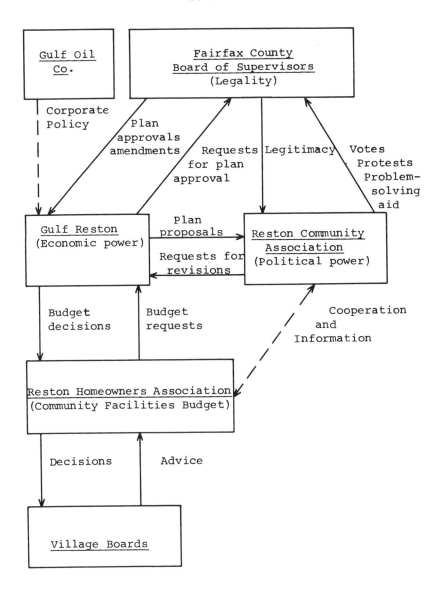

Reston residents created their own community political resource when they organized the independent Reston Community Association and established its legitimacy with the Fairfax County Board of Supervisors. RCA's prime resource became its solidarity, which enabled it to claim before the supervisors that it represented the citizens of Reston and had their commitments. Such commitments supposedly could be equated with votes in county elections. Another important resource was the knowledge and technical skill of the many professional Reston residents who were active RCA members. In its exchanges, RCA made use of both a cooperative style (volunteering its professional skill to assist in problem-solving) and a protest style (attacking the plans and behavior of the developer directly and also indirectly through third parties). In this respect RCA had broader strategy choices than the low-income inner-city groups described by Lipsky and Peattie—groups that were limited to activating influential third parties through dramatic public protests.[11]

The developer, Gulf Reston, controlled the economics of development, including financing, planning, and scheduling. They also controlled the Reston Homeowners Association through its board of directors. Through its staff and consultants, Gulf Reston had access to plentiful planning knowledge and skills. However its autonomy was limited by its parent organization, Gulf Oil Company, and by the Fairfax County supervisors, who had to approve the plan for each new section of Reston before it could be opened. Gulf Reston generally maintained cooperative relationships with the county and the citizen organizations. However, during the conflict over consolidation of the two associations, it had threatened to limit the facilities and services of the members of the dissident second homeowners association, and, as a last resort, it was in a position to threaten the future of the Reston concept itself by selling off its Reston holdings to less sympathetic or less progressive developers.

The Reston Homeowners Association controlled the revenues from property owners' annual dues through the annual operating budget for community facilities. In turn the association was itself controlled by the developer, despite the existence of two elected village boards and a town council, three resident members of the nine-member homeowners association's board of directors, and a fledgling annual programming and budgeting process with widespread participation. The homeowners association's manager felt that he had to serve two masters, the residents and the board of directors, who often disagreed. Most of the homeowners' exchanges consisted of cooperation with other Reston organizations; their formal exchange with the county board had been preempted by RCA and the developer.

The main resource of the Fairfax County Board of Supervisors, as the legitimate governing body, was legality. This gave the supervisors the power to confer legitimacy on RCA in its conflicts with Gulf Reston, as well as to regulate the developer's plans. Also controlled by the board were public funds and services, such as police protection, that were important to Reston. Supervisors were elected by districts, and the supervisor whose district included Reston had developed a close working relationship with leaders of RCA. Rather than simply accepting Gulf Reston's plans for each new section of the community, the county board listened to the protests of RCA as well, and then required that conflicts over plans be negotiated. Through RCA, Reston citizens had access to county political power, counterbalancing the economic power of Gulf Reston and the home-owners association.

Unitary Planning at Columbia

By contrast, Columbia's development decision-making system has not evolved away from its designed merger of political and eco-nomic power within a unitary corporate-style system under firm professional control. The Columbia Park and Recreation Association has been called a private government because of its broadened financial base (which includes assessment of business as well as residential property) and its wide-ranging power to provide all municipal services not offered by the county, including roads, walk-ways, parks, libraries, community service facilities, mass trans-portation, and energy distribution systems.[12]

No independent residents' organization has been mobilized at Columbia. Instead an elaborate hierarchy of citizen-developer organizations is built into the Columbia association's operation. This federal-type system starts at the village level, where the property owner or tenant is automatically a member of a community associ-ation with an elected board of directors. Each resident has the right to vote for a village representative to the Columbia Council, a form of "electoral college" whose members nominate candidates to the board of directors of the central Columbia association.

Control of the Columbia association will be transferred from the developer to the residents as the community grows. All the members of the original board were developer appointees. For each 4,000 units of occupied housing, one Columbia resident is added to the board. Between 1976 and 1980, the developer appointees' terms will all expire, leaving the residents with 100-percent control of the board in 1980.

Provision for a uniquely high level of amenities is the charge of the Columbia association. James Rouse, the developer, has argued that separating this function from the "coercive" powers of local government will encourage people to participate and to use the Columbia association for community purposes. Still there is evidence that at least the activist residents of Columbia would prefer a more political form of governance. Seeking a community-wide forum for representation of residents' views, as opposed to the developer-resident homogeneity of the Columbia association structure, the three existing village boards have taken it upon themselves to meet and speak out on issues as a tri-board.

Exchange at Columbia has tended to follow the corporately designed channels of the unitary private government, as shown in Figure 14.2. My impression is that this was due to the developer's effective management, which prevented crises of the type that mobilized Reston, and to his monopoly over community resources, which enabled him to acquire a large fund of reciprocal obligations and to coopt potential dissidents from the resident ranks. The prevailing atmosphere in 1970 was one of benign paternalism, with professionals providing a wealth of community services and a few frustrated resident activists seeking a way around the system.

The developer provided every resource the citizens had, usually through the Columbia association. Local homes associations, through their elected village boards, were designed to advise the Columbia association concerning territorially based citizen interests. They were provided with meager staff resources, in the form of one part-time village manager per village. They controlled almost no financial resources; even their dues were voluntary. Their access to the decision-making power of the Columbia association was filtered through the electoral college of the Columbia Council. Forced to rely on their own civic skills, which were not inconsiderable, on volunteer labor, and on largely symbolic rewards, the activists on the village boards were frustrated by their lack of political power.

Attempting to overcome the weakness of their separatism, the individual boards began to meet together as an ad hoc tri-board. Seeking to establish itself as a legitimate political actor, the tri-board opposed the developer and the Columbia association on several relatively minor issues. But it had not built a broad base of citizen support nor had it brought any outside influence to bear. Unlike the Reston Community Association, the Columbia tri-board did not seek legitimacy with county politicians but confined its protests to internal community issues.

The development company, Howard Research and Development, actually drew on the staff resources of several interdependent corporations with interlocking directorates, including the Rouse Company, American City Corporation, and the Columbia association. Both the politics and the economics of development tended to be monopolized by the developer. James Rouse had become a nationally known and

208

FIGURE 14.2

Exchange among Planning Actors at Columbia,
1970

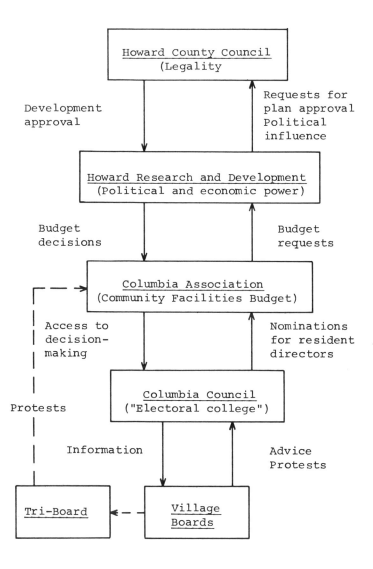

respected figure as a result of Columbia's success, which had been used as a model in drawing up the federal new-community program. His high social status and personal popularity, combined with the money and credit, knowledge and technical skills, and manpower and organizational control at his disposal, enabled him to influence the rural Howard County government, as well as the Columbia citizens. Part of his power derived from his ability to reduce the complex business of building a new community to a controlled economic model.

Yet this near-monopoly over resources, very effective in regulating the physical and economic growth of Columbia, became something of an embarrassment in promoting social development. Citizens who accepted the developer's role as an environmental designer tended to rebel at his social-engineering attempts. For example, an early attempt by the developer to convene a human-resources council was thwarted by the village boards, which misconstrued the motives behind the planned council.[13] Still even the activist citizens have worked within the bounds of the developer-controlled governance system. This is probably due to the Rouse style of promoting consensus, as well as to his abundant resources. Potential issues are defused by prompt action, rather than being allowed to grow into full-scale community conflicts.

The Columbia association, as the community's private government, held financial and budgetary power over the assessment revenues. A sizable professional staff was at the command of their developer-controlled board of directors, including a Department of Community Services that combined the role of community organizer and ombudsman. Not only did the Columbia association make decisions about community-facility location, design, and operation, it also was responsible for the organized citizen participation structure through the village boards. The association's board was buffered from the citizens by the Columbia Council, but its staff worked with the residents on a direct basis. In 1970, in an effort to improve its municipal service operations, the Columbia association brought in a manager with municipal government experience to replace its manager whose experience had been in the corporate business world.

The Howard County Council governed a rural county of less than 50,000 population at the time Columbia's development began. Since then Howard County has changed its governmental system, adopted a home-rule charter, and instituted a modern county management system. Through its new-town district zoning provisions, largely composed by Howard Research and Development staff, the county legally must approve the new-town plan and any changes to it. Interaction between the county government and the developer has been cooperative in spirit. In 1971, however, the Columbia Commission—a group of Howard County citizens appointed by the county council—reported that "some members of the Commission have expressed concern at what they consider to be an erosion of the 'great American dream' philosophy under which the NT [new town] concept was developed, 'sold' to the county, and, at least in its early stages, became a partial reality."[14]

In retrospect even Columbia development company executives who I interviewed felt that the need for unitary control had been initially overemphasized. Their resources overwhelmed the residents, and made later attempts at pluralism very difficult. These executives would be favorably inclined to a system in which residents had a more active part in planning and governance. Planning at Columbia has been gradually opening up to citizen participation. The Columbia association's budget process now involves residents, and in 1972 the board of directors' meetings were opened as a result of recommendations by the Columbia Conference on Community Governance.

No comparison between Reston and Columbia can conclude without reference to the undisputed market and economic successes of the Columbia project. Reston may have a more pluralistic and accessible decision-making system, but it has less of the amenities— in the form of community facilities and services—than Columbia. Since these facilities will eventually be controlled by residents, it could be argued that Columbia citizens will have more resources at their disposal in the long term. At a 1970 symposium on new-community management, a Reston resident declared that "some large percentage of the so-called problems of Reston citizen unrest . . . can be eventually boiled down to the fact that we lack money to provide the kinds of facilities and services that many of us assumed were going to be here when we chose Reston."[15] My own interviews of activists in the two communities suggest that this "consumer" explanation of citizen dissatisfaction is greatly oversimplified, and certainly does not explain the attitudes of the active participants. For my respondents, the "opportunity to participate" was second only to the "community concept" among most often-mentioned reasons for moving to a new community.*

---

*In my sample of 18 selected activists, "community concept" (plan, philosophy) had ten mentions, "opportunity to participate" had nine, "attractive physical environment," had five, "location of job," had three, "recreation opportunities" had two, and "alternative to central city or suburbia" had two. Some respondents mentioned more than one reason for choosing a new community. These findings differ from those of Lansing et al., whose randomly selected respondents did not mention participation as a reason for moving to Columbia or

In any event the difference between the numbers of community centers, pools, and recreation programs has resulted from differences in the financing mechanisms for the two communities, rather than from differences in the participation structures. Reston's original facilities were paid for by the developer, who added their costs to his land sales prices, and deeded them debt-free to the homeowners association. Residents' dues of $50 per year pay for maintenance. Columbia's facilities were programmed into the economic model and paid for by the Columbia association, with a loan from the developer. Dues from residents, businesses and industries, along with user fees, pay for debt service and maintenance. Maximum annual dues are $0.75 per $100 of assessed value. Thus, by going into debt and broadening its financial base, the Columbia association could do extensive pre-servicing—putting community facilities and services in place before residents moved in.

Of course the financial plan is not completely separable from the total concept. Columbia's more farsighted fiscal program depended on staffing the Columbia association with many professionals to handle the multi-million dollar budget and program. Management of the Reston Homeowners Association, with its program limited to maintenance activities, could be done with a much smaller staff. Both the number of professionals and their organizational loyalties are important variables influencing citizen participation.

Without clearly specified citizen roles and citizen-oriented staff support, more professionalism tends to result in less significant participation in the planning process. Activists at Columbia were frustrated in the early years because there was little for them to do. The professionals took care of everything important, and then worried about being too paternalistic. Activists at Reston, on the other hand, have had leading roles in planning the community bus system,[17] the health system, and the reorganization of governance, and they have therefore been much more a part of the scheme of things.

FEDERAL PARTICIPATION POLICY

A second generation of American new towns is now under way with federal assistance under the Urban Growth and New Community Development Act of 1970 (Title VII of the Housing and Urban Development Act of 1970). In exchange for meeting specific HUD requirement

---

Reston, although it could be argued that their top ranking reason (liking for the new town's concept) carried an implicit promise of opportunities for participation.[16]

an approved new community receives a federal guarantee of its development obligations. But does federal new-community policy incorporate the participation lessons learned in the first-generation new towns of Reston and Columbia?

Nowhere in the 1970 act itself is there mention of citizen participation. The federal law emphasizes the role of the developer, the governmental aid program, and the uses of new communities in implementing national urban-growth policy. In the regulations issued by HUD's Office of New Community Development to carry out the law's provisions, however, four basic participation provisions may be found.

Under the eligibility criteria for community services and government, a full range of public services are required. When a new-community developer or developer-controlled organization is to perform general governmental functions during development, then provision must be made for an orderly transfer of these functions to an appropriate government unit at the earliest appropriate time. Under the criteria for social elements, new-community development programs must "reflect or incorporate"

1. use of citizen advisory groups, opinion surveys, or other methods of improving communications and developing a design and structure for the new community that will be responsive to the needs of residents, both at the beginning and, through continuing evaluation, at later stages of development; adequacy of provision for public hearings and opportunity for comment by local residents affected by the project;

2. location and distribution of housing types and price ranges so as to prevent segregation and afford full access to facilities, and participation in activities, of the community and neighborhood by groups, families and individuals of different economic, social, and racial backgrounds;

3. a program of citizen participation in project activities, including use of home associations and civic organizations . . . to supplement . . . opportunities offered by governmental or public institutions, and to provide for full opportunity for participation by renters and low income residents.[18]

In general either Columbia or Reston would be able to qualify under these guidelines, which do not explicitly recognize the difference between a unitary system of political and economic power and a pluralistic system. The HUD regulations point out the need for a planned transfer of governmental functions from the developer, use of citizen advisory groups and public hearings, participation by all class and racial groups, and participation in project activities (including homes associations). They do not require that resources be made available to citizen groups in order to ensure that such groups will be able to take part in exchanges with the developer on some reasonable basis of power parity. In reading the regulations, the image of a producer-consumer relationship comes through, rather than one of a citizen-developer partnership in community development.

None of the twelve new communities approved by HUD through June 1972 has yet had significant experience, but examination of the participation statements in their official plans turns up mostly high-sounding, but rather nonspecific, rhetoric. Governmental organizations shall be established "to enhance the free expression of views and participation in community decision-making for all residents." At Park Forest South, para-governmental entities will "give an adequate voice and appropriate level of control to the residents." At Jonathan, the "Developer shall at least once each year offer a briefing to residents . . . concerning general development plans and shall take cognizance of their comments and suggestions." The phrases are almost identical, no matter what the community. Citizens may well ask what is the intended meaning of "enhance," "adequate," "appropriate," and "take cognizance."

Statements on community governance and resident involvement in the official plans mix political participation and social interaction. Identical phrases in many plans say that the developer's role, as designer of the "social architecture" of institutions, is one of "fostering interaction and participation" among residents. Site planning, open-space systems, and location of community facilities are to increase interaction. Several plans propose to establish a "social development team, with citizen representation, which will have responsibility for locating and evaluating social innovations from other localities." One developer commissioned a citizens survey by a research organization and considered the results in planning. Maumelle is considering appointing a "community animator," who is skilled in establishing and working with citizen groups and anticipating their needs. At St. Charles Communities, the developer will have the unlikely role of "advocate for citizen and tenant associations." The most unusual participation scheme is the Riverton's "systems barter," a program under which "people may perform services in exchange for credits that may be used to pay fees associated with activities and the use of community facilities." Shades of Walden Two!

More specific evidence as to the effects of HUD policy on participation can be deduced from the governance arrangements in the twelve approved new communities, all of which are satellites except for one freestanding new town (Soul City) and one new-town-intown (Cedar-Riverside). As shown in Table 14.1, eight of these new towns potentially have some form of homes association as well as a municipal government. Admittedly, many of the existing local governments involved are small and "under-developed," and their present constituencies will be totally overshadowed by the future growth of their attached new communities. Also, the developer is bound to be a major influence on their decisions. But they do provide a political power system independent of the developer-controlled homes association.

A report on planning for Jonathan states that its arranged marriage with an existing municipality was consciously weighed: "The developers of Jonathan had two choices in creating a means for participation by residents and for decisions about development and services—a homeowner's association, or an existing local government structure. . . . They reasoned that the homeowner's association had too many limitations. . . . The developers concluded that in providing for their residents, an existing local government was a better choice, it provided more benefits."[19] The decision also involved the developer in another aspect of new-community participation, the issue of incorporating the preferences of the "old timers" who lived in Chaska. The Jonathan developer felt his plan was strong enough to weather this scrutiny.

In practice, therefore, most of the federally approved new communities have committed themselves to pluralistic governance, despite the absence of a clear-cut federal policy statement on this issue. Perhaps this ambiguous state of affairs should be expected, given the confusion abroad about what an appropriate level of influence for residents should be, and given the "banker-client" relationship between HUD and the new-community developers. Much of the national concern to date has focused on whether the new-community developer is strong enough to make a go of it and not leave the federal tax-payers holding the bag. Under these circumstances HUD has been understandably cautious about adding any unreasonable participation regulations that may reduce the developer's stock of resources or build up resident political power. On the other hand there have been few real alternatives proposed, particularly alternatives that make use of systems tools to promote democratic participation in planning.

A COMMUNITY DEVELOPMENT PARTNERSHIP MODEL

Rather than pitting residents against developer in an adversary relationship or treating residents simply as consumers, the idea of

TABLE 14.1

Governance Arrangements in Federally Approved New Communities,
as of June 30, 1972

Community	Local Government	Citizens Association
Jonathan, Minn.	Annexed by City of Chaska*	Homeowners and tenants association
Park Forest South, Ill.	Annexed by Village of Park Forest South*	Homeowners and renters association
Flower Mound, Tex.	Within Town of Flower Mound*	Homeowners and renters association
Cedar-Riverside, Minn.	Within City of Minneapolis*	Residents association and urban renewal project area committee
Riverton, N.Y.	Within townships of Henrietta and Wheatland	Community association
San Antonio Ranch, Tex.	To be annexed by City of San Antonio in 3 years; now under Bexar County*	Citizens association
Gananda, N.Y.	New community district set up by townships of Macedon and Walworth, Wayne County	Community association
Woodlands, Tex.	Montgomery County; within City of Houston's extraterritorial jurisdiction, and may be annexed*	Community residents association
St. Charles Communities, Md.	Charles County	Community Service Corporation
Maumelle, Ark.	Pulaski County; may incorporate later*	Homeowners association
Soul City, N.C.	Warren County; may incorporate later*	Civic association
Lysander, N.Y.	Township of Lysander	Community association

*Existing or potential municipal government.

Source: Compiled from HUD project agreements, environmental impact statements, and interviews.

216

a community development partnership suggests that both citizens and developer work together to produce the community. This implies that the new-town building process need not be a win-or-lose contest, but instead could result in a social profit for all concerned. It goes beyond pluralism to active collaboration, incorporating four key elements: (1) a dual power system, (2) agreement on planning domains, (3) open planning, and (4) community-action capacity.

Pluralism is a necessary but not sufficient element in a community development partnership. Thus a first requirement is a dual power system that ensures that citizens have access to sufficient political resources to balance the developer's economic resources. Without a reasonable balance of power there can be no reciprocal exchange and hence no partnership. This suggests a form of limited pluralism, in which citizen resources for development planning are concentrated in a town-wide organization, rather than dispersed in many ineffectual interest groups. For example Reston's proposal to focus citizen participation in a community council, leaving the homes association to operate in non-democratic corporate style, should facilitate a partnership. The new communities with both municipal governments and homes associations may also become partnerships, depending on the extent to which the residents mobilize political power.

A second necessary element is agreement between partners concerning each other's planning domain. This agreement should be spelled out in a formal document, perhaps in the form of a community constitution that details overall participation rights and responsibilities. This constitution would be subject to amendment, and would also be amplified in specific situations by project-planning contracts, which would allow for participation by spontaneous organizations—or coalitions of organizations—interested in a particular project. In this way obligations would be clearly understood. For example, the developer could be given domain over the master plan, but be required to open all project plans to interested citizen organizations on a performance contract basis giving responsibilities as well as rights to the citizens. The community council or citizens association could be given domain over social and institutional planning, with the advice and consent of the developer. The homes association could have domain over all common lands and facilities, but be obligated to submit its budget for review to the community council. Finally, conflicts over those matters of joint development that inextricably mix social, physical, and economic issues so that domain boundaries are confused, could be required to be mediated by a higher authority, such as a county or regional body.

A third important element is open planning. This would require that economic models, development schedules, and master plans be highly visible parts of the civic culture, available as community learning tools to school children as well as adults. Citizen participants need to be aware of the developer's cash-flow burdens as well as the timing of construction. A resident activist at Columbia told me that, although the economic model was often invoked as a reason for a particular decision, it was never seen by citizens. With the computerization of these models, they could be available in simplified form as continuously updated public documents. Computerization should also make these models more flexible—and hence adaptable to plans developed after residents have begun to settle in the new towns. All planning decisions cannot be made irrevocably by the developer before the arrival of residents. HUD guarantees require annual updating of short- and long-term development plans. This ongoing planning should be open to participation, using project contracts, Charrettes—i.e., intense planning periods during which citizens and professionals collaborate to resolve controversial planning issues[20]—and even two-way electronic communications. Both Reston and Columbia opened the planning of their latest village centers to resident participation after completing the previous centers that had been planned prior to development.

A final element that appears to be necessary is a capability for community action. This could take the form of a nonprofit community institute which would monitor the development process. It would not be an arm of the developer, but would be an advocate for the community itself. There is a wealth of citizen energy and skills in a new-community population, but without a crisis such as occurred at Reston on the departure of Robert Simon it is difficult to mobilize the citizens. One early role for the community institute could be helping set up the governance system. Then it could sponsor joint project-planning efforts by citizens and development staff members. Its overall aim would be to increase citizen competence in community affairs, recognizing that citizen involvement tends to be cyclical. Many activists at Reston and Columbia have begun to suffer from "participation fatigue." Without some continuing staff support, volunteer participation will be too short-lived to be effective. Support for the community institute could come from grants or from income from community activities or capital resources. For example the proceeds from the leases on certain lands could be dedicated to the community to support its citizen participation.

Building new towns with community development partnerships between residents and developers should result in communities that are adapted to the people living there. As one citizen at Columbia said, "I don't think planners know better than people what people want. They can guide them . . . they can present alternatives, but dammit, the people have got to make the decisions. . . . The greater the participation, the more successful the planners are going to be." Such partnerships should also build citizen competence to take part in planning and governance. A senior planner at Columbia told me that "the failing is not in structure. . . . The failing is in the overall lack of . . . sophistication on the part of American people to be good citizens. . . . The role of active participant in a positive, creative, continuing partnership between people who have a development responsibility and citizens who have a user responsibility is a role that very few citizens are able to play, or even are interested in playing."

Participation is a two-edged sword. Planners must be open to working with citizens, and citizens must be active and competent in planning. The concept of a community development partnership based on collaborative exchange between residents and developer offers a feasible alternative to present confused participation schemes. Such alternatives are necessary if American new towns are to become authentic new social communities.

NOTES

1. Twentieth Century Fund Task Force on Governance of New Towns, New Towns: Laboratories for Democracy (New York: The Twentieth Century Fund, 1971) p. 56.
2. Richard Brooks, "New Towns and Citizen Participation: A Policy Analysis," Journal of the Community Development Society, Vol II, No. 2 (Fall 1971).
3. Albert A. Foer, "Democracy in the New Towns: The Limits of Private Government," University of Chicago Law Review, XXXVI (Winter), p. 394.
4. David R. Godschalk, "Participation, Planning, and Exchange in Old and New Communities: a Collaborative Paradigm" (unpublished Ph.D. dissertation, University of North Carolina, 1971).
5. Mahlon Apgar IV, "Managing Community Development: The Systems Approach in Columbia, Maryland" (New York: McKinsey & Company, 1971).
6. Urban Land Institute, The Homes Association Handbook (Washington, D.C.: The Institute, 1964).
7. George C. Homans, Social Behavior: Its Elementary Forms (New York: Harcourt, Brace & World, 1961); William C. Mitchell, "The Shape of Political Theory to Come: From Political Sociology to Political Economy," American Behavioral Scientist, II, 2 (November-December 1967), 8-37; Terry N. Clark, "Community Structure Power, and Decision-Making," in Terry N. Clark, ed., Community Structure and Decision-Making: Comparative Analyses (San Francisco: Chandler Publishing Company, 1968).

8. E. E. Schattschneider, The Semisovereign People: A Realistic View of Democracy in America (New York: Holt, Rinehart and Winston, 1960), p. 121.

9. Study Team on RHO Role and Structure, "Toward New Town Governance," A Report to the Reston Homeowners Association (Reston, Va., 1972).

10. See Gans account of the planning and governance of the new town of Levittown for an instance where pluralism did not suffice to generate effective resident participation. Herbert J. Gans, The Levittowners: Ways of Life and Politics in a New Suburban Community (New York: Pantheon Books, 1969).

11. Michael Lipsky, "Protest as a Political Resource," The American Political Science Review (December 1968), pp. 1144-1158; Lisa R. Peattie, "Drama and Advocacy Planning," Journal of the American Institute of Planners, XXXVI, 6 (November 1970), 405-10.

12. Royce Hanson, "Managing Services for New Communities," in A Report on the Symposium on the Management of New Communities (Washington, D.C.: Washington Center for Metropolitan Studies, 1972).

13. Richard Brooks, "Social Planning in Columbia," Journal of the American Institute of Planners, XXXVII, 6 (November 1971), pp. 373-79.

14. Columbia Commission, "Impact of New Town Zoning in Howard County, Maryland," in Report to County Executive and County Council (Ellicott City, Md.: The Commission, 1971), p. 17.

15. Hanson, op. cit., p. 8.

16. John B. Lansing et al., Planned Residential Environments (Ann Arbor: Survey Research Center, Institute for Social Research, University of Michigan, 1970).

17. Henry Bain, The Reston Express Bus: A Case History of Citizen Action to Improve Urban Transportation (Washington, D.C.: Washington Center for Metropolitan Studies, 1969).

18. Draft Regulations: Urban Growth and New Community Development Act of 1970, U.S. Department of Housing and Urban Development (Washington, D.C., 1971), Section 32.7 (h).

19. Robert C. Einsweiler and Julius C. Smith, "New Town Locates in a Municipality: Jonathan Saves Money and Chaska Increases Tax Base," Planners Notebook, I, 3-4 (June-July 1971), 6.

20. Peter Batchelor, "Citizen Participation in Design/Shaw Southside Charrette," North Carolina Architect (May-June 1970), pp. 12-33.

IV

VARIOUS POSSIBLE KINDS OF NEW TOWNS IN NATIONAL URBAN-GROWTH POLICY

15

NEW-ON-OLD TOWNS
IN THE SYSTEM OF CITIES:
A NATIONAL PERSPECTIVE
Wilbur R. Thompson

The central question posed in this study is: what does the nation
need in the way of new urban places that can be most effectively or
most expeditiously filled by new towns? Where are the critical gaps,
if any, in the national system of cities?

The nation may be "seen" in maps or on machine print-outs or
in the mind's eye in three overlays:

1. a frequency distribution of urban places by populations size—
a profile of the relative number of hamlets, villages, towns, small
cities, and great cities;

2. a functional hierarchy of "little economies" among which
the industries of the nation are distributed—complementary bundles
of industries ranging from trade and service centers to tightly knit
manufacturing complexes to regional capitals that replicate the national industrial profile; and

3. a spatial distribution of population and economic activity—a
geographical pattern of orderly spaced places, curvilinear strips of
cities and remote places.

The free-market mechanism may or may not steer the national
system of cities into a near-optimum number of urban places of each
size, based on reasonably satisfactory industry-mixes and located in
appropriate relationship to each other. If the free market is at all
inefficient—sometimes moving in the "wrong" direction and often
acting only after unnecessarily long and costly delays—there will be
"gaps" in the system of cities that need filling. Gaps are also opportunities: where do new towns fit in?

ON CITY SIZE

The pursuit of the optimum city size typically ends ingloriously
in a full retreat into pluralism: let many flowers (or towns) bloom.

But it is not enough to agree that the optimum we seek is a wide varie of city sizes for the fullest choice in life styles. Variety alone is not an inventory policy; we need to move toward stocking the nation with the appropriate number of each of the many city sizes. Even if we can agree that there should be some small towns available to those with very strong preferences for that special habitat, we may now have too many of them. Even if "great cities" are indispensable com ponents of an urban hierarchy, we may be overproducing (very) ordina "big cities." Even if middle-sized cities are growing in number, we may need more of them—and sooner than they are scheduled for delivery.

Shying away from any dubious adventures into the mysteries of optimum city size, the relative rate of growth of each population-size class of urban places will be taken as a rough measure of the relative consumer preference for that city size. In Figure 15.1, the percentag change in population is related to the total population of the local econ omy (local labor market), in general schematic form, based on the experience of the U.S. system of cities over the past three decades. The rate of population growth varies widely among smaller urban places and narrows sharply with greater city size. Within these uppe and lower limits (dotted lines), the average performance (solid line) first rises sharply to a flat peak around one-half million population and then falls slowly and moderately with passage into the multi-million population class. There is some reason to believe that the very largest metropolitan areas are increasingly underbounded, and

FIGURE 15.1

General Relationship between City Size
and Rate of Growth

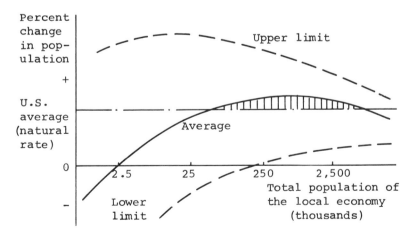

therefore that their current populations (and their recent rates of growth) are understated. Setting this uncertainty aside for the moment, the solid line of average performance is tentatively interpreted as the "revealed preference" of the national population for various size cities as places of residence, all things considered. To the extent that birth and death rates are similar in small, middle-sized, and large places, the local rate of population growth expresses the balance of in- and out-migration for that locality. Where the population growth curve lies above the national (that is, natural) rate of population change (shaded area) more people are moving into cities of that size than are moving out of them. Let us take one more logical step and argue that the demand for cities of this fast-growing size class is greater than the supply of such cities—that is to say, do we need more of them?

The fact that middle-sized cities are growing faster than average and are attracting net in-migration does not necessarily imply that we should create more of them. The same number of such cities— the current set—could continue to absorb a heavy net in-migration, in addition to their natural increase, by growing very rapidly. But if the relationship between the local rate of growth in population and "well-being" (however measured) is as suggested in Figure 15.2, local and national welfare will be appreciably higher if the market success of middle-sized cities leads to more such places rather than faster rates of growth of the existing set.

The logic of an inverted U-shaped curve in which well-being peaks at a growth rate somewhere near the natural (that is, national) rate of population increase is that both heavy net in-migration and out-migration impose significant strains on the local economy. Briefly, to grow slower (in job formation) than the natural rate of increase (in

FIGURE 15.2

Growth and "Well-being"

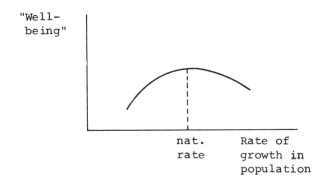

225

the local labor force) is to sustain either chronic unemployment (and underemployment) or to suffer the natural market "corrective"—depopulation that takes the debilitating form of a youth-and-brain-drain. To grow much faster than the natural rate of population increase is to invite acute shortages and congestion, especially in the critical public sector where entrepreneurship and management are hobbled by sluggish political processes—schools on half-day sessions, traffic jams on narrow "mile roads," and flooding for lack of storm drains. If we cannot prove rigorously that local growth at or near the natural rate of population increase is optimal, we can at least argue persuasively that it is relatively easy to accommodate. And this tentative position is further strengthened by the corollary that for any place to grow faster than average, some other place must grow slower than average; one locality's burdens of rapid growth become another's burdens of sluggish growth if not contraction.

FIGURE 15.3

City Size and "Well-being"

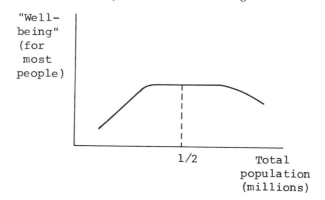

If we can infer from faster-than-average growth a net preference of consumers (householders) for such places, perhaps we can further infer that since middle-sized places (one-half million population or so) exhibit the fastest growth of all, they are, to most people, the best size of all, as depicted in Figure 15.3. If so, we should not hurry urban places through the population range from, say, one-quarter million to one million, where most of the deficiencies of small size have been left behind and many of the problems of great size have not yet been encountered in a major way. Thus faster-than-average growth in middle-sized places cuts twice: (1) directly through the strains imposed by rapid growth, and (2) indirectly through a too-quick passage through their "golden age." There is, therefore, a

226

strong case to be made for promoting new middle-sized cities.

ON THE RATE OF GROWTH

Our next round of new middle-sized cities would be new towns—all new—or they could be "new-on-old towns;" that is small cities of, say, 20,000-30,000 population inundated with new growth that carries them to three or four times their initial size in a decade or two. Urban places between 10,000 and 50,000 population generally tend to be too small to be healthy but are much too large to die; bled of the young and the talented, they tend to suffer a mild form of anemia. New towns could be superimposed on top of such places.

If there would be extra costs and complications arising out of mixing the new and the old (e.g., interfacing dual utility systems to incorporate new technologies, as in old aboveground and new underground pipes and wires), so too there would be extra benefits. Some of the gains are obvious, such as the saving grace of having even old and obsolete facilities during the difficult pioneering period. Old-fashioned sidewalks that cross streets in unprotected ways may be inferior to the separated grade crossings to come, but they are superior to the mud ruts that must be "temporarily" endured. And the old homely strip commercial facilities can be endured a little longer—better than a ten-mile drive for an odd item of food or hardware.

Less obvious and closely related to the preceding discussion of growth rate and well-being is the fact that new-on-old towns have the considerable virtue of slowing the very rapid rate of growth endemic to new towns. As illustrated in Figure 15.4, a new town that is scheduled to attain a certain size—say, 128,000 population (32,000 dwellings)—in 20 years, must sustain a rapid acceleration in the rate of residential construction up to a little over the 20-year average rate of 1,600 houses per year. This would be followed immediately by a sudden and sharp drop in residential building, because, with the full housing stock new or almost new, nothing needs to be replaced. Even allowing for continuing growth at a natural rate of increase of 1.5 percent per year, following the initial surge, local residential construction would amount to only 480 units per year, down by two-thirds from the peak level.

In striking contrast, a new-on-old town in which the same total population was attained in the same time period by adding 24,000 new dwellings on to a base of 8,000 old dwellings (a quadrupling of population from 32,000 to 128,000), exhibits only a fraction of the instability of the new town started from scratch. The local construction industry would take off from a base of perhaps 200 dwelling units per year (covering normal replacement and slow growth) and rise, on the average, to only 1,200 units per year over the next two decades—only three-quarters of the all-new new-town rate. But much more telling, after 20 years of building the new part of town, the local construction industry can then turn to the work of renewing the old part of town. If the "old town" is fully rebuilt over the next 20 years, this will provide a replacement demand of 400 houses per year (8,000 original units prorated over 20 years) to be added to the 480 units needed to accommodate the assumed 1.5 percent natural increase in population. This combined production of 880 dwellings per year is only a little over a one-quarter cutback from the peak rate of 1,200 units. Moreover, combining new town and old town in proportions of 2:1 instead of 3:1 would have supported local residential construction at 95 percent of the peak rate. We should not leave this illustration of local stability without recalling that fluctuations in construction employment would have a local multiplier effect that would create a roughly equivalent fluctuation in local trade and service employment, doubling its social impact.

One can easily foresee other important social by-products that would come out of slowing growth by building new towns on top of old towns, in proportions of two or three or four to one. One way to ensure that good intentions to include the poor in planned new communities will be honored is to ensure that the completed town will include some old houses inhabited by poor people who need only resist eviction (much easier than gaining admission). To the physical planner who would argue that superimposing a new town on an old place will mean that the new community will begin life with some nearly obsolete

FIGURE 15.4

Relative Fluctuations in Construction Activity in
a New Town and a New-on-Old Town Programmed to Attain
a Total Population of 128,000 in 20 Years

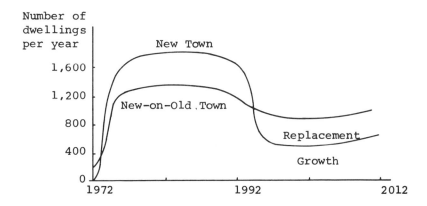

facilities, the answer of the social planner would be that therein lies its strength. Finally, to be all new at one point in time is to become someday massively old and shabby, and almost invariably depressed. Margaret Mead has pointed out that even the simpler cultures of the Pacific region appreciated that a village built all at once will fall down all at once. Does not the all-new new town forebode a "great gray area" to come?

A second clear social advantage of building from a preexisting base is that the very great instability of local construction activity in the new town started from scratch leads to the creation of an unusually large number of migrant construction workers, with all that portends for family stability, the education of the children, and local citizenship. If the numerical example developed above has any appreciable validity, new-on-old towns would offer permanent residency to perhaps three-quarters or so of the construction workers, as many as would probably choose to stay and probably as many as society has a critical interest in "demobilizing" (families with school-age children).

To impart some air of realism to these numbers, it may be noted that the new town of Milton Keynes in Great Britain is being built on an old town base of 50,000 population (Bletchley) and is scheduled to attain some 250,000 people in the 1990s; Ciudad Guayana, in Venezuela, rose from a 1960 base of 40,000 residents to 122,000 in 1968. The proportions of new-to-old residents in these two places fall on either side of those used in the illustration above.

This has, of course, been only one part of only one side of the story: there are arguments favoring rapid growth in new towns. One in particular deserves mention here because it is not necessarily at variance with the above logic. Bureaucratic processes and reasoning may require accelerated spending to convince legislators and other doubters that the relevant agency is doing its job. But this criterion would seem to apply to the overall program, not to any particular project. Clearly two projects going at half speed have the same budgetary effect as one going at full speed.

The concept of the new-on-old-town is clearly an intermediate position between the traditional new town, at one end of the spectrum, and the growth center, at the other end. This compromise strategy would slow the explosive growth of the new town but it would still force growth to a rate well above that typical of the growth center. Again, while the new town would begin life with virtually all of its capital stock nearly new, and the growth center would have a more normal age-distribution of capital, the new-on-old-town would lie between the two, much more new than old. Less certain but still likely, this compromise form would tend to gather a population more biased toward affluent, young families than the growth center, but not quite so much so as the new town. In location, the growth center must build on a potentially strong base and a new town must seek a remote, or at least open, space (a "no place"), while the new-on-old-town looks more to a small, weak place. All in all, the new-on-old-town may be best described as a "mixed strategy."

ON THE RATE OF
NATURAL INCREASE IN POPULATION

The natural rate of increase in population would seem to be a most important determinant of the kind of new town that would best fit our needs. If we expect the aggregate national population to increase significantly and steadily to a level of 300 million by the year 2000 or soon thereafter, then "controlling" (managing better if not tightly containing) the population growth and size of our largest metropolitan areas suggests a larger role for "dispersal" new towns. The strategy could be either to drain off population into nearby satellite new towns or to build them as interceptors somewhere between the origin of the in-migrants and the city to be contained.

But if instead our currently declining rate of population growth should move us steadily toward zero population growth (ZPG), perhaps as soon as the year 2000, containment of great city size would almost certainly fade away as a critical national problem. This would be especially true if our farm areas are emptied out to a point of population stability and if we are forming as many small towns for new purposes (e.g., recreation, retreat, and retirement) as we are eliminating old obsolete ones (e.g., rural service centers), and if middle-sized places continue to more than hold their own in the competition for migrants. With little or no natural increase and little or no net in-migration, the population of our great cities would stabilize.

But the normal aging of the housing stock, typically from the center outward, is even now beginning to open up sizable vacant areas in the inner cities of our central cities—holes in the doughnut. Throughout the postwar period and until very recently, the heavy natural increase in local population plus the heavy in-migration from rural areas and small towns have combined to produce serious housing shortages in most of our largest metropolitan areas and to maintain inner-city populations. Thus the early postwar urban-renewal approach that reduced the supply of low-income housing in the process of cleaning up the central business district was in large measure a program ahead of its time. Similarly, Perloff's first advocacy of new-towns-intown, over a decade ago, was an idea ahead of its time, remembering the scale at which it would have to take place to hold out reasonable promise of success.

230

But the forces of depopulation—the inexorable aging of the inner-city housing stock and the almost undeniable American quest for space—have been gaining strength while the forces of repopulation (declining birth rates and slowing in-migration) have been losing strength, to the point where virtually all of the central cities of the largest Eastern and Midwestern metropolitan areas have experienced absolute loss of population for the past two decades. (Boston, Buffalo, Cleveland, Detroit, Pittsburgh, and St. Louis each lost between 20 and 30 percent of their population between 1950 and 1970.)

Thus our central cities have been emptying out well ahead of ZPG, suggesting that further declines in the natural rate of increase over the next decade would probably not be fully offset by spot urban renewal and a return to the central city under even the most optimistic expectations. One is led almost inexorably to the conclusion that, if current population trends continue, the opening up of the inner city will almost certainly greatly enhance the stature and prospects for new-towns-intown. One of the principal physical planning problems of the next decade may well be to restrain central-city officials from becoming over-anxious, and prematurely stuffing odds-and-ends into every vacant lot in town. Inner cities would benefit in many if not most cases from a cathartic depopulation that lays the base—that is, provides the necessary elbow room—for a healthy repopulation. Not only do the potential intown new-town sites become larger and more flexible as the oldest dwellings in the inner city are abandoned, but also, as the most impoverished and embittered residents drift outward into the next lowest grade of housing, these sites become less burdened by nearby squalor and more insulated by distance from violence. Perloff's new towns-intown may well derive their moral force from egalitarian principles, but their implementation may derive more from current population trends and enlarging vacant areas in conspicuous places.

ON INDUSTRIAL STRUCTURE

New-town planners should not only have some general notion about the appropriate niche in the spectrum of city size for their creations in the larger system of cities; they should also anticipate the industrial role that the town will play in the national economy. The cliché in local industrial planning is that the objective is to achieve industrial diversification. Unfortunately this is more a pious hope than a realistic expectation, because a balanced industry mix is hard to find, short of a half-million population or so. Still, one of the most attractive features of new towns is the challenge they offer to plan industrial diversification at a significantly smaller scale than that at which it occurs naturally; that is, via free market processes.

231

A balanced local economy would offer (1) steady growth at or near the national average rate, (2) a local business cycle not appreciably worse than the national performance, (3) a "normal" (nationlike) distribution of income, and (4) a reasonably rich mix of occupations in the local labor market. Occupational balance has become the cause of some concern because low-skill work has been conspicuously absent in virtually all the new-town ventures to date. To the extent that low-skill work is associated with the older, slower-growing industries, new towns are at a very great disadvantage in adding these jobs to its skill mix. Old industries, saddled with excess capacity, are not for the most part adding new plants in significant numbers. New-on-old towns, however, could draw strength from their weakness. Beginning "burdened" with a legacy of old industries (old plants) and overrepresented in low skills, they are destined to move toward labor market balance with rapid growth, as they add the newer industries with higher skills and higher levels of formal education.

What can a new town expect with reference to the level and distribution of income? Empirical work has firmly established that median family income (or income per capita) rises with increased city size. This general tendency does not of course preclude selected middle-sized cities from exhibiting higher levels of income than the average for large cities, nor selected small cities from exceeding the middle-sized city average. (The scatter diagram of city size and median family income resembles the city size/growth rate relationship of Figure 15.1, with a narrowing variation in median income with greater city size; it differs, however, in that the regression line—the centerline—drifts upward as it moves to the right.) To the extent that this pattern from the past (still as strong as ever in the 1970 census data) carries over into the future, we can make some educated guesses about the likely course of new-town income levels.

New towns begin life with bright all-new plants, presumably embodying the latest technology and generating the highest labor productivity. Further it is highly likely that these local economies will be based on relatively new industries, with a relatively high-skill job mix. Lacking the nonworking poor and underrepresented in the (low-skill) working poor, new towns would seem to be off to a good start, with an above-average income for cities of their size. But new plants age and lose their technological edge, and even new industries age as once-innovative processes become rationalized and routinized with time and, under the pressure of competition, settle for lesser skilled, lower-wage labor. Thus one very real possibility for those new towns that are based on a very few manufacturing activities—a couple of large plants—is that they will, over the course of two or three decades, slide steadily down from above-average to below-average in labor skills and wage rates. New towns may age with their industries.

Another possible outcome is that the new town will not stand pat with its original industry mix but will instead spin-off work, as it becomes simpler, to other places of lesser industrial sophistication, continually renewing its own economic base by reaching out aggressively for higher-skill work that has recently become marginal for the most sophisticated industrial centers. Instead of passively filtering down through the industrial hierarchy with a fixed set of industries, the new town may run hard to stand still (retain its rank order position) by becoming a conduit for a succession of industries—an intermediate stage in the development of each. But attaining the capability to evolve steadily and surely from, say, textiles to apparel to synthetic fibers to apparel machinery and beyond, must be firmly grounded in a large and growing urban infrastructure (e.g., universities and technical schools, research parks and engineering facilities, varied and flexible transportation systems and so forth). The larger the city, the brighter the prospects of attaining a state of continuing industrial renewal—of finding the way to the industrial fountain of youth.

It is relevant here to point up Lichfield's observation, in connection with the early concern that children of the first (blue-collar) in-migrants may not find suitable (white-collar) employment, that "factories of the first wave of incoming firms . . . have been followed by enough office-centered concerns to prevent this exodus." But only the early returns are in.

The early literature of regional economics stressed manufacturing as the principal export base of local economies, although some attention was paid, largely implicitly, to export services in the discussions of central place theory. It became quite natural, therefore, to "think manufacturing" in new-town planning and to place a high if not first priority on arranging binding agreements with a couple of large manufacturing firms in order that they locate branch plants in the new community. Current discussions of the export base of new towns have become much more appreciative of the income-generating power of retail trade and, even more, professional and personal services rendered to the population residing in the hinterland. The economic planning of new towns is now much more sensitive to the size of the potential trade area or market shed of the town.

Central place theory arose out of a need to explain the complementarity—the economic symbiosis—of farms, hamlets, villages, towns, and cities in nested hierarchy. What is too rarely appreciated, even to this day, is that a hierarchy of trade areas and range of functions tends to generate a corresponding hierarchy of occupations, skills and education, wage rates, and income. Central place theory is a basic if largely unappreciated component of regional income theory. As we ascend in city size, we progress in socioeconomic status from justices of the peace and gas station proprietors to

233

district court judges and automobile advertising account executives. If then we rationalize as natural and logical the linked progression of occupations and population clusters that we know as central place theory, do we not also have to expect and accept substantial income differentials between the ranks?

Roughly one-half of the population of the United States lives in metropolitan areas (local economies) of one-half million population or more, which suggests that the median-income city occurs at about that population size. Can we plan new towns of significantly smaller size, remote from larger places, that will develop local economies capable of generating parity incomes, decade after decade?

The two separate lines of argument developed above tend to reinforce each other. Small urban places typically lack the infrastructure necessary to generate, spin-off, and regenerate manufacturing industries in a strategic way. They tend, therefore, to end up with the dregs of that sector, and/or to be assigned only the lower-skill service functions because of their small trade areas. After the temporary advantages of all-new capital and the initial absence of the poor have been eroded by time and the tides of change, will the remote small town become, more often than not. just another small town?*

ON LOCATION

A priori the location of new towns would seem to be important. Where in space should they be placed to fit best into the national system of cities? But most discussions of new towns seem to be much less concerned with the issue of "where" than with "how big" or "how soon" or "of what mix?" Even those discussions that are apparently addressed to location—satellite new towns to drain growth away from very large central cities—usually prove to be only nominally concerned with the specifics of location. How far away from the parent body should the satellite be in order to drain off more congestion than it adds (e.g., in the movement of commuters), while still drawing strength from the parent?

To lead from strength, location is not only an important dimension of new-town strategy, it dominates the urbanization decision

---

*These remarks are directed to new towns that have a high degree of economic closure—for the most part those that are beyond commuting range of larger places. New towns of modest size that are designed as (or just become) satellites of large metropolitan areas will, of course, reflect the economic fortunes of the parent body.

in the case of the exploitation of new natural resources that come to light in remote places. We would be surprised if, in general, the best sites had not been preempted by existing cities and towns (e.g., the best harbors and the most fertile soils), leaving the lesser sites for new communities. But with new power sites and new ore deposits will come new towns and could come new towns. Some of the most glaring gaps—best opportunities—in the national spatial pattern of cities would then be based on natural resources. (Lichfield's example from the past of Kitimat could be joined by western Colorado oil-shale new towns in the near future.)

Again, existing cities and towns have largely preempted the best locations with reference to sunk capital. They have become the nodes of the existing road network, the electric power grids, and other utility systems. But the overall pattern does change appreciably and many of the subsystems seem almost volatile at times. The National Interstate Highway System has created some almost vacant intersections—potential transportation hubs in cornfields. An Oak Ridge National Laboratory research group, sponsored by the U.S. Department of Housing and Urban Development, has proposed a new community at the intersection of I-40 and I-81, near the village of Dandridge, Tennessee.

Again, to the extent that central place theory is an accurate description of the distribution of population in space, there are very few openings for new higher-order centers—gaps at the top of the heap. In general, county seats could be built-up to larger size and greater stature with less social and political "displacement"—less disruption and resistance. But once more this may be too static a view of the urbanization process. The steady drift in population out of agriculture and other extractive industries into manufacturing and services has left some thinly populated regions with widely scattered small places that need a new center about which to regroup for new functions. There may be a number of places in which a new system of cities would be formed if a new center of gravity were to arise. A new town could, from an amorphous mass, crystallize what is now only a potential constellation of urban places. Airports and major branches of large state universities have been located in open spots between established towns, in part to draw on the combined markets and in part to resolve local jealousies. New towns could become national instruments for promoting new urban systems.

New technology creates new locations for cities. Probably more than any other single factor, the development of low-cost air conditioning for homes is the basis for the rapid growth of Phoenix, Arizona, to a metropolitan area of one million inhabitants. And rising productivity, expressed in higher incomes, shorter hours, and earlier retirement, is creating whole new sets of towns and small cities oriented toward recreation, retreat, and retirement. The existing cities and towns—a legacy from the age of agriculture and manufacturing—have not preempted many of the best sites of the post-industrial age, such as remote and rocky places in Arizona, Colorado, and Oregon.

Out of all of this one gains the strong first impression that the case for new towns gains considerably from external circumstances— discoveries of new deposits of natural resources, technological change in transportation and climate control, and new patterns of consumer preference. Perhaps the principal conclusion of this study is that new towns are most convincing when applied as instruments of national policy. When contemplating federal subsidies, new-town planners should ask not what their country can do for them but rather what new towns can do for their country.

16

NEEDED AND
SPONTANEOUS
NEW TOWNS
William Alonso

I believe that a major new-towns policy for the United States today would be at best irrelevant and more probably counter-productive in terms of our needs, our problems, and the limits of our political energy and our willingness to commit resources to these problems. Even if new towns were delightful places, this would still be so. I have published elsewhere and will not repeat here the arguments for arriving at these conclusions.[1] This is not to say that new towns and cities are not indicated in the United States in some cases today and in other countries at various times. But the justification must be concrete in time, circumstances, and purposes; the new town must be needed as an instrument for some purpose rather than a romantic expression of voluntarism.

The purposes of needed new towns are and have been extremely varied. For the sake of brevity the following list is highly simplified:

1. the acculturation and absorbtion of migrants, as in Israel and Australia;

2. the development of frontier regions, ranging from tiny ones (Holland, Israel) to vast ones (the nineteenth-century American West, Siberia, and the center of South American today);

3. the exploitation of concentrated resources (Ciudad Guayana and Kitimat) and of extensive ones (central place systems such as the nineteenth-century American Midwest);

4. defense and related structuring of territorial possession (Israel, India and West Germany with respect to their borders; Louis XIV's creation of a capital and a military perimeter for his nation-state);

5. accommodation of social, political and technological change in rural areas (Cuba);

6. symbolism and politics (Washington, Brasilia, and Soul City);

7. separation for the protection of social experiments (many utopias, including Salt Lake City and today's communes);

8. isolation of certain functions (penal and exile settlements, atomic think-towns, and retirement towns);

9. showcase for certain innovations (Ebenezer Howard's towns and, to some extent, Reston and Columbia).

This last point, the use of new towns as showcases to generate and accelerate the diffusion of innovations, is frequently cited in the United States today, and there is some validity to it. But some notes of caution must be sounded. First, that the necessary small scale of new towns (at least when they are new) precludes certain significant technoeconomic experiments, such as new transportation modes applicable to metropolitan dimensions. Second, that American new towns have attracted an egghead population and that this, together with the Hawthorn effect, voids generalization from their social experiments. And lastly, that a review of the literature reveals few if any concrete ideas for such experiments.

Many American new-town advocates, when pressed, admit with surprising candor that the label of new town is being used for salesmanship. It is in such good odor that they try to associate it with such diverse matters as the achievement of scale economies in the construction of suburbs and the redevelopment of central cities. My own preference is to avoid such a wide range of language.

However, if salesmanship is the game, I have other candidates for the "new town" label. I would like to have accepted the concept of a pluralistic new town. The conventional concept of a new town assumes monopoly control over development by a public or private corporation. But whereas such new towns are very hard to bring about in significant numbers, we are awash in spontaneous new towns where decisions are made by the many. Such new towns (mostly suburban or satellite) are now absorbing the greater share of growth of our population and jobs. They have, I believe, most of the attributes associated with new towns (size, growth, evolving social structure, etc.) except for monopoly control over development. Many or most are developing along social, economic, functional, and aesthetic lines in ways that are not satisfactory. Yet here is where the action is, these are the new towns. Can we not find ways in our democracy to harness the energies of their pluralism toward better outcomes? They are molding most of the shape of our future environment. I think we should take up the challenge and opportunity they present rather than escape to those rare instances of monopoly control.

At a larger scale, one must contrast proposed new cities of about one million population to the real phenomenon of new cities, of spontaneous growth centers.[2] These are the rapidly growing metropolitan areas that are absorbing most of the nation's population growth. They have been doing so at least since the turn of the century, and the trend is for a declining share of our urban areas to absorb an increasing share of our national growth. Yet most of these spontaneous growth centers are small and medium-sized urban areas, not giant ones, and they have shown surprising constancy in the momentum of their growth. If our concern is with national population distribution and the size of urban areas, we should be concentrating on understanding the dynamics and consequences of these forces, and finding ways to guide them along national purposes. It is idle to dream of the voluntaristic creation of brand-new cities of a million when we do not understand or control (or indeed, hardly perceive) the dozens of instances in which the dynamics of our society are creating de facto new cities.

The traditional perception of new towns has stressed their creation by an act of will, their development under the single direction of a development corporation, and their following faithfully a master plan in form and timing. But all of these factors change if we substitute the concept of pluralistic new towns for this traditional view. In the first instance, the problem of their creation disappears since they are so prevalent. Second, the will and control by the single developer gives way to the interaction of a wide diversity of individuals, groups, and institutions. Third, instead of the master plan, alternative forms must be found to give coherence to the development.

It is this last that is most difficult. A master plan is as complete a specification as possible of a future environment, the coherence of which derives from the technical competence and systematic beliefs of the makers of the plan. But a main problem of master plans is that they are poorly equipped to deal with uncertainty and changing realities. The rigidity of its completeness makes it unbending. Another great difficulty of master plans—and a related one—is that once the plan is formulated, continued adherence to it precludes participation in important decisions by the people who live in the town. And in the traditional new town the plans must be thoroughly formulated before there is anyone living there.

In a pluralistic new town, alternative ways of achieving order and harmony must be found. Instead of the master plan's firm specification of the physical form of the future, these alternative ways must stress the processes by which decisions are made, and how past decisions may be reviewed and if necessary changed. It will be helpful to have as clear a sense as possible of general purposes and objectives, in the light of which particular choices may be evaluated as they come up. Standards of social and environmental performance should in many cases be used for design criteria. Most importantly, legal, institutional, and political procedures must be found to arrive at negotiated or consensual agreements, preferably in ways that ensure implementation based on adherence and legitimacy rather than on enforcement from outside. Goals, standards, and procedures become the pluralistic town's alternative to the master plan.

One cannot specify fully the range and limits of these processes. There will be occasions, to be sure, where command rather than negotiation and consensus is the only alternative to chaos. After all, the issue of planning arises in large measure because of the failure of the free market to take account of externalities; the processes suggested, which are intended to correct some of the causes and consequences of market failure, will run into many situations with which they cannot deal. Nonetheless it is quite clear that concrete steps can be taken with respect to aesthetic and other physical design standards, to the provision and pricing of public services, to the social and economic composition of the town, and a number of other matters. The key point again is that, since the results of the unconstrained market are unsatisfactory, there is much to be gained from group and community definition of problems, purposes, and objectives, from the establishment of functional standards in some areas, and from the development of institutional bases and forms for discussion, negotiation, and joint decision—instead of central control and master plan.

In brief, as far as virginally new towns are concerned, I think that the laboring mountains will produce few mice. Yet we have dozens and hundreds of slightly less virginal new cities and towns that spring from the realities of our social system and will in turn give it much of its shape. They are too complex, recalcitrant, and vigorous to come under a single will. But we cannot escape them, even if we ignore them for more tractable puzzles. We must work at finding better ways for their physical, social, economic, and political organization and development. This will be challenge enough for our limited resources, intelligence, and will.

NOTES

1. These were presented in two similar papers, "What Are New Towns For?" Urban Studies (February 1970), and "The Mirage of New Towns, "The Public Interest (Spring 1970).

2. See W. Alonso and E. Medrich, "Spontaneous Growth Centers in Twentieth Century American Urbanization," in Niles Hansen, ed., Growth Centers in Regional Economic Development (New York: The Free Press, 1972).

William L. C. Wheaton

Practical utopias have always served an important role in
stimulating innovative thinking about society, life styles, alternative
possibilities, and the like. The attention paid in their day to Le
Corbusier's and Wright's images of the high- and the low-density city,
and the astonishing attention being directed toward Soleri's notions
currently, are evidence of a continuing inventive function.

During the nineteenth century hundreds of utopias were invented
and many were tried. The twentieth century has been less fruitful.
Indeed its social utopias have tended to be pessimistic ones; contrast,
looking backward for tomorrow; that brave new world and animal
farm. Only Goodman in the twentieth century is widely recognized
as an optimistic utopian.

Model utopian communities provide an opportunity to test many
ideas that otherwise may not be tested, either as new technologies or
for market expansion. Worlds fairs and airports have proven the
market acceptability of technologies that could be adopted much more
widely. However the urban fabric is resistant to experimentation.
With some types of technologies it is impossible to install a fully
automated transit system in an existing city whose form and behavior
were designed with other modes of transportation in mind. While it
may be possible to experiment with a neighborhood in novel forms of
housing, one neighborhood will not prove market acceptability over
a wide range of locations and family types. Similarly we can experiment with novel school or tax systems for a neighborhood or other
special areas, but unless the experiments are very wide in nature,
we are left in the dark about their applicability to communities.

These and other concerns about our failure to mount city-wide
experiments led to the formation of the Minnesota Experimental City
Corporation (MXC). The sponsors sought to incorporate the widest

possible range of innovations, including physical innovations, technological innovations, social service innovations and, indeed, population composition innovations. While they have failed to secure the massive federal support that an experimental city could justify, they have attracted substantial interest closer to home.

MXC has not to date sought to reconcile its many and varied proposals in a single plan or plans. It has enunciated ideals in a variety of fields without testing whether they are reconcilable; i.e., is it possible to have an air-conditioned city and at the same time have quick access to nature? Is it possible to have a fully automated, and presumably publicly owned, transit system serving all internal needs, and still provide the opportunities for travel outside the community, which, in the United States, must depend upon individual automobiles?

The proposals, even in their present "unreconciled" state are interesting enough to deserve detailed attention.

The Minnesota Experimental City is a proposal for a large-scale, freestanding new city whose primary purpose is to be the application to a whole community of novel and experimental technologies and social arrangements, aiming at the creation of what is frankly described as "a practical utopia." In the words of the Minnesota State Legislature when it authorized the formation of the Minnesota Experimental City Authority:

> It is the objective of MXC to create benefits extending
> throughout the state, and particularly in undeveloped
> regions as a regional focus for public and private invest-
> ment, by providing greater direct employment and train-
> ing opportunities for unemployed or underemployed
> citizens, increasing the general level of economic activity,
> and reducing outmigration; to improve the quality of life
> of all persons; to test and demonstrate an alternative to
> increasing densities and megalopolitan growth, and new
> approaches to pollution control and the protection of the
> total environment, and new methods of land use and develop-
> ment, construction techniques, and ordering community
> life and residence that will be available and useful in
> developing solutions to problems of existing cities and
> metropolitan areas; and to serve as a model for the
> solution of the social problems of urban life in a demo-
> cratic society. The achievement of this objective is
> determined to be necessary in the public interest and to be
> a proper public purpose for which governmental powers
> can and should be exercised in the manner and to the
> extent provided in this chapter.

The idea of such a city originated more than four years ago with a small group of business and civic leaders, scientists, and university professors. They originally envisaged a community of a half-million people that would be sufficiently far removed from existing centers so that it would not be dependent upon them for employment or intrusion by them in institutions or life styles. The original interests of the group were chiefly directed toward urban technologies—a fully automated transportation system for a whole city, the city-wide use of utility corridors, the conservation of energy through linking utility systems, the city-wide application of two-way cable television, the creation of a fully climate-controlled city, the adoption of the most modern construction methods, and the attempt to build a city with minimum intrusion into a maximum preservation of the surrounding natural environment.

To these original technological purposes there were quickly added goals to ensure a representative population, an educational system employing the best available knowledge, a community-wide health system, full employment and, indeed, the use of the entire city as a means of education and popular enlightenment. These goals, both technological and social, were later spelled out in four volumes of studies prepared for the MXC Corporation by a University of Minnesota group and others. These reports stress that an experimental city could clearly demonstrate that modern technology and social organization were capable of providing an ideal environment that would be immensely productive without generating the technical and social problems commonly associated with urban growth.

The influence and perceptiveness of this private group were demonstrated during the next two years. The committee attracted an advisory board that included leaders from a wide variety of fields of technology, the social sciences, and the humanities, not the least of whom was Buckminister Fuller, whose design of future cities has always excited wide attention. Further the group secured informal commitments from Minnesota-based industry, which seemed to ensure that if the project were to be launched there would be no difficulty in attracting to it the economic base necessary to sustain the resident population. This did not necessarily mean manufacturing employment alone, since it was recognized that services now constitute the largest single component of urban economies, and that they, particularly education, would tend to dominate any such community.

The influence and persuasiveness of the committee were further demonstrated when the Minnesota State Legislature approved the establishment of a public agency, the MXC Authority, with responsibility for preparing additional plans and cost estimates, for selecting a site and suspending public construction on the designated site. The legislature itself would then review the site and the plans; thus considerable power is conferred upon the MXC Authority without at the same time giving it the resources necessary to proceed.

The site selection is, itself, a difficult and controversial matter. Some members of the authority are eager to choose a site north or west of Minneapolis-St. Paul, on the grounds that this is a less developed part of the state, and on the further grounds that, since much of this area is under public ownership, site acquisition will involve a minimum of local controversy and cost. On the advice of economic consultants, others on the authority judge that the project could in the long run have greater chances of success if it were located in the southern and eastern portion of the state, between the Twin Cities and Milwaukee. There a site would be more diffficult and expensive to acquire and may arouse some local opposition, but this would follow conventional economic wisdom and be in a path of economic development that would more naturally attract activity. The judgment of local observers is that the former line of reasoning will prevail in the authority and with the legislature. If the authority and the legislature do agree upon a site, the formidable problems of financing such an experiment will then arise. In a rational society the expenditure of $5 billion per year for getting a man on the moon may have been preceded by an expenditure of at least $1 billion per year for a five-year period in building a novel urban environment, which may reduce the incidence of human discontents. Yet we have not only failed in any such experiment, we have even shamefully neglected urban housing, municipal services, and urban technology, devoting far less of our national resources to these important fields than to more esoteric subjects.

A new city of the type proposed would probably cost in the range of $3-5 billion. While a considerable portion of these funds could ultimately prove to be private (to the extent that the site involved novel location or unusual design features), there would most assuredly have to be public guarantees and direct investments. Thus the MXC Authority would face the dilemma of trying to find hard-to-get money for novelty and experimentation, while possibly turning away readily available funding for a more conventional development.

Other questions arise with equal force. By any logical definition such a proposal cannot be an "experiment." An experiment should have one independent variable. Instead, what is proposed is to have almost every variable new. This would surely result in the attraction of a population different from the national profile and willing to accept novelty. It could, therefore, tell us little about the acceptability of novel technologies in the population at large. It would strain existing polling techniques to ascertain which features were attractive and which were not. On the other hand, if the experiment is to attempt to apply all possible new technologies in some internally constant way, then surely such a city would be among the most dramatic and exciting of man's efforts to find a better environment. It would reach far beyond the limited experiments employed in such British new towns as Cumbernauld, Runcorn, and Thamesmeade, where density or the city center or the transportation system have been the chief novel features. One of the most interesting experimental features proposed by the MXC is that it should also experiment with a single urban government, getting away from the superimposed layering of municipality, special district, school district, and county that is universal in American society. Upon the presumption that the site will be one in a relatively isolated and unpopulated area, and that the state legislature will ultimately agree to this feature, after some transition period this could be an interesting experiment in local government of the type that is rare in our national history.

On economic-locational grounds alone, Minnesota would seem to be an inauspicious place to attempt to build an experimental city. On the other hand it has many advantages. Most importantly a very influential group of business leaders has become seriously interested in the project and is prepared to commit considerable resources and influence to its execution. The state is one of extraordinarily attractive scenic and recreational resources, which would surely be enhanced by the concentration of population growth in a compact new city that would attract many would-be residents. Equally important, the geographic location and climate of Minnesota provide an opportunity for a fully climate-controlled city, which might have a considerable import for the rest of this overcrowded planet as space for urban development gets more constricted, and locations in less inhospitable climates become relatively more attractive and presumably more numerous. For these reasons MXC may have a considerably larger impact upon future urban development than would appear at first.

245

HARVEY S. PERLOFF is Dean of the School of Architecture and Urban Planning at the University of California at Los Angeles. He is an economist-planner whose specialty is the interrelation of behavioral, physical, economic, and social factors in urban and regional development. He helped create and develop—and during the years 1950-55 he headed—the Program of Education and Research in Planning at the University of Chicago, which, by shifting the focus of attention from a narrow physical base to a broad social science base, has had a profound influence on planning education.

While at the University of Chicago, he developed the new-town-intown concept, which was incorporated as a major provision of the U.S. Housing and Urban Development Act of 1970.

Dean Perloff has served as consultant to the U.S. Department of State; the U.S. Department of Commerce; the U.S. Department of Housing and Urban Development; the U.S. Department of Health, Education, and Welfare; the Tennessee Valley Authority; and the United Nations.

He was formerly director of the program of urban and regional studies of Resources for the Future, Inc.; member of the Committee of Nine, Alliance for Progress; and member of the Environmental Studies Board, National Academy of Science-National Academy of Engineering. He is currently a member of the Commission on the Year 2000, American Academy of Arts and Sciences; fellow of the American Academy of Arts and Sciences; and member of the Advisory Committee Research Applied to National Needs, National Science Foundation.

Dean Perloff is widely published. Among his books are How a Region Grows; The Future of the U.S. Government: Toward the Year 2000 (editor and author of lead paper); The Quality of the Urban Environment (editor and author of lead paper).

Dean Perloff was educated at the University of Pennsylvania, the London School of Economics, and Harvard University (Ph.D. in Political Economy).

NEIL C. SANDBERG is Adjunct Professor of Sociology at Loyola University in Los Angeles. He has been a practitioner in the field of human relations for more than twenty years, lecturing and writing extensively on intergroup problems in a plural society. As Western Regional Director of the American Jewish Committee, he is an advisor on community relations to a number of government, private, and religious institutions.

Dr. Sandberg is a consultant to the City of Los Angeles on problems of urban redevelopment and government efficiency. Recently he served as chairman of the California Service Alliance, a committee convened by the governor to coordinate the programs of voluntary organizations. He was also a member of the attorney general's commission studying police-community relations in California.

Dr. Sandberg holds a B.A. from Columbia University and a M.Pl. and Ph.D. from the University of Southern California. His doctoral dissertation on the salience of ethnic identity has received the annual award of the Kosciuszko Foundation and will be published in 1974 by Twayne Publishers, New York.

IRA M. ROBINSON is Professor of Urban and Regional Planning at the University of Southern California and was formerly director of its Graduate Planning Program. He is the author of New Industrial Towns on Canada's Resource Frontier. His most recent publication is a reader for Sage Publications, Inc., entitled Decision-Making in Urban Planning: An Introduction to New Methodologies. During the 1971/72 academic year, Dr. Robinson was on sabbatical leave, during which time he lectured, conducted research, and consulted in Israel and several European countries.

ARIE S. SHACHAR is Professor of Urban Geography at the Hebrew University of Jerusalem, and the director of the Institute of Urban and Regional Studies. He is a member of the board of governors of the Israel Association of Environmental Planning and the Council of the Israel Institute of Professional Geographers. Dr. Shachar has served as consultant to numerous planning agencies in Israel and has worked with A.I.D. in Latin America in urban-development programs. He is directing several research projects on development policies and national urbanization policies, the major one being in the North-east of Brazil.

NATHANIEL LICHFIELD is Professor of the Economics of Environmental Planning at the University of London. He specializes in the economic aspects of town and regional planning, development, and renewal. In 1962 he founded the firm of Nathaniel Lichfield and Associates, which advises on various aspects of planning at the national, regional, and local level both in the British Isles and over-seas. Dr. Lichfield is presently working on several major aspects of planning in Israel.

HUGH MIELDS JR. is a senior associate and vice president of the Washington (D.C.) consulting firm of Linton, Mields and Coston, Inc. He is currently serving as a consultant on urban programs to a number of major cities throughout the country. He is a senior consulting associate on a governance study of federally assisted new communities for the U.S. Department of Housing and Urban Development. He is editor of New Towns: A Handbook on Title VII Federal New Communities Program for the Urban Land Institute. He formerly served as associate director of the U.S. Conference of Mayors.

FRANCINE F. RABINOVITZ is Associate Professor of Political Science at the University of California at Los Angeles. Her most recent book, On the City's Rim: Politics and Policy in Suburbia (1972), focuses on the national political process as it affects policies for suburban communities.

HELENE V. SMOOKLER is currently Research Associate at the Center for Urban and Regional Studies of the University of North Carolina, Chapel Hill. She is working on a two-year evaluation of new-community characteristics that contribute most to residents' quality of life. At the time her chapter in this book was written, she was a Ph.D. candidate at the University of California at Los Angeles.

MARGARET MEAD is Curator Emeritus of Ethnology at the American Museum of Natural History and Adjunct Professor of Anthropology at Columbia University. She spent many years studying various cultures and the development of cultural theories of human behavior. Dr. Mead has lived with a number of South Seas peoples and has written extensively on primitive and contemporary cultures.

MARSHALL KAPLAN is a principal in the firm of Kaplan, Gans, and Kahn in San Francisco. He has directed a number of nation-wide studies concerning urban development for, among others, the U.S. Department of Housing and Urban Development; the U.S. Department of Health, Education, and Welfare; and Model Cities. A member of several Presidential commissions concerned with urban growth problems, he has served as consultant to the National Academy of Sciences and numerous new communities around the country. His most recent book is entitled The Irrelevance of the City Planner in the Sixties.

HERBERT J. GANS is Professor of Sociology at Columbia University and a senior research associate at the Center for Policy Research. He is both a sociologist and planner who has studied new towns (particularly Park Forest, Illinois, and Willingboro, New Jersey) and helped to plan them (Lake Superior mining towns and Columbia, Maryland). Dr. Gans is the author of The Urban Villagers, The

Levittowners, and People and Plans, and of nearly 100 articles in academic, professional, and popular magazines.

J. EUGENE GRIGSBY is Assistant Professor in the School of Architecture and Urban Planning at the University of California at Los Angeles. His extensive experience includes research and programming on health attitudes and delivery, urban life styles, social indicators, transportation, and community control. Among Dr. Grigsby's publications are "Races and Cities: An Interpretive Analysis of Recent Work," in Urban Affairs and Annual Review, "Race and Urban Society" (Beverly Hills: Sage Publications, 1971) and "Stratification in American Society: A Case for Re-appraisal," Journal of Black Studies (Beverly Hills: Sage Publications, December 1971).

WILLIAM R. ELLIS JR. is Assistant Professor of Behavioral Sciences in Architecture at the University of California at Berkeley. Dr. Ellis is currently conducting urban anthropological studies of time and space scheduling in educational environments and in the environments of the black urban poor, with particular emphasis on the relationship of the factors to the envelope of the built environment. He is co-editor with Peter Orleans of Race, Change and Urban Society.

DAVID R. GODSCHALK is Associate Professor of City and Regional Planning at the University of North Carolina, Chapel Hill. He is also secretary of the board of directors of the Warren Regional Planning Corporation, the planning organization for the new community of Soul City, North Carolina. He has been a city planning director and a planning consultant. From 1968 to 1971 he was editor of the Journal of the American Institute of Planners.

WILBUR R. THOMPSON founded the doctoral program in urban economics at Wayne State University. He is involved in urban affairs programs at Northwestern University and in the Urban Policy Conferences of the Brookings Institution, and he is a consultant to various governments. A former research associate at Resources for the Future, Inc., Dr. Thompson is author of A Preface to Urban Economics and numerous articles on urban development and public policy.

WILLIAM ALONSO is Professor of Regional Planning at the University of California at Berkeley, and a member of the Institute of Urban and Regional Development. He is the author of a number of books and articles on urban and regional topics, and is an international consultant. Dr. Alonso is also a consultant to the Rand Corporation and a member of the National Academy of Science Advisory Committee to the U.S. Department of Housing and Urban Development.

WILLIAM L. C. WHEATON is Dean of the College of Environmental Design at the University of California at Berkeley. He is widely known as a consulting city planner, author, and educator. Dr. Wheaton has served as U.S. representative to the U.N. Committee on Housing, Building and Planning, and as an official of the Housing and Home Finance Agency. He has been president of the National Housing Conference and of the Regional Science Association.

HOME OWNERSHIP FOR THE POOR
A Program for Philadelphia

Charles Abrams
with the assistance of Robert Kolodny

INNER-CITY HOUSING AND PRIVATE ENTERPRISE
Based on Studies in Nine Cities

Edited by Frederick E. Case

INDUSTRIALIZATION: A NEW CONCEPT FOR HOUSING

C. A. Grubb and M. I. Phares

LOW AND MODERATE INCOME HOUSING IN THE SUBURBS
An Analysis for the Dayton, Ohio, Region

Nina Jaffe Gruen and Claude Gruen

FINANCIAL ANALYSIS AND THE NEW
COMMUNITY DEVELOPMENT PROCESS

Richard L. Heroux and William A. Wallace

COOPERATIVE HOUSING AND COMMUNITY
DEVELOPMENT
A Comparative Evaluation of Three Housing Projects
in East Harlem

Donald G. Sullivan